Methodism in the American Forest

Methodism in the American Forest

RUSSELL E. RICHEY

OXFORD
UNIVERSITY PRESS

OXFORD
UNIVERSITY PRESS

Oxford University Press is a department of the
University of Oxford. It furthers the University's objective
of excellence in research, scholarship, and education
by publishing worldwide.

Oxford   New York

Auckland   Cape Town   Dar es Salaam   Hong Kong   Karachi
Kuala Lumpur   Madrid   Melbourne   Mexico City   Nairobi
New Delhi   Shanghai   Taipei   Toronto

With offices in

Argentina   Austria   Brazil   Chile   Czech Republic   France   Greece
Guatemala   Hungary   Italy   Japan   Poland   Portugal   Singapore
South Korea   Switzerland   Thailand   Turkey   Ukraine   Vietnam

Oxford is a registered trade mark of Oxford University Press
in the UK and certain other countries.

Published in the United States of America by
Oxford University Press
198 Madison Avenue, New York, NY 10016

Library of Congress Cataloging-in-Publication Data
Richey, Russell E.
Methodism in the American forest / Russell E. Richey.
pages   cm
Includes index.
ISBN 978-0-19-935962-2 (cloth : alk. paper)
1. Methodist Church—United States—History.
2. Methodist preaching—United States—History.
3. Camp meetings—United States—History.
4. Forests and forestry—Religious aspects—Methodist Church.   I. Title.
BX8235.R527   2015
287.0973—dc23   2014026495

1 3 5 7 9 8 6 4 2

Printed in the United States of America
on acid-free paper

Contents

Methodism in the American Forest

Introduction

METHODISM AND THE AMERICAN WOODLAND

As we drew near the shore, the pleasing view of the green trees, and many of them towering high above the rest, made the prospect delightful. . . . The prospect was charming and delightfully pleasant on both sides of the river. The spreading trees, and the great variety of shades, heightened the scene; with the addition now and then of a plantation, with large orchards of peach and apple trees, as also large fields of Indian corn. Indeed, I never beheld such a lovely prospect in any part of my life before.

Annamessex-Chapel, Somerset, Monday 22. I preached to a tolerable congregation in a forest. It is quite romantic to see such numbers of horses fastened to the trees. Being engaged in the most solemn exercises of religion for three or four hours every day, and that in the middle of the day, I hardly know the day of the week: every one appearing to me like the Lord's-Day.*

SO JOURNALED THOMAS Rankin and Thomas Coke, two English Methodists, about the American woodland.[1] Commissioned and dispatched across the Atlantic roughly a decade apart by John Wesley to give leadership to new world Methodism, each needed the superlative to describe the American forest. Rankin did so as he sailed around Cape May in 1773, headed up the Delaware, and first sighted land. On his first preaching tour in the new

---

* P. P. Sandford, *Memoirs of Mr. Wesley's Missionaries to America. Complied from Authentic Sources* (New York: G. Lane & P. P. Sandford, for the Methodist Episcopal Church, 1843), 219, for June 1, 1773. Thomas Coke, *Extracts of the Journals of the Rev. Dr. Coke's Five visits to America* (London, Printed by G. Paramore; and sold by G. Whitfield, 1793), 17.

nation (1784–85), Coke detailed, as would countless other Methodists before and afterward, the experience of preaching and worshiping in the woods. For Methodists, the outdoors was a second home or perhaps better, a second church. Accustomed to reaching crowds by preaching in fields, on greens, and in public squares, British Methodist missionaries to the new world found that very different settings—in the woods, under spreading oaks, in shady groves—would congregate Americans. So began the saga of Methodism in the American woodland.

Theme

Methodism—the Pietist,[2] revivalistic, evangelistic renewal movement, led by John and Charles Wesley in Britain, by George Whitefield on both sides of the Atlantic, and later by Francis Asbury in the colonies and new nation—prospered in the open air. In Great Britain, first Whitefield and then the Wesleys discovered that they could best reach the poor, the unchurched, the neglected, and the religiously indifferent if they resorted to unconventional, nonecclesiastical, relatively public space and preached in market squares, on commons, outside mines, in graveyards, and in the fields. Theatrically gifted Whitefield drew huge crowds as he itinerated over the American colonies and across Britain.[3] The Wesleys, initially reluctant, eventually turned Whitefield's "act" into a program, an important tactic in their endeavor to reform the Church of England.[4] They not only emulated Whitefield themselves but also raised up other preachers, primarily young men, religiously motivated but without Oxbridge credentials. They (and primarily John) put these unordained or lay Methodist preachers under mandate to preach in the fields; "field preaching" becoming a shorthand for any such outside-of-church-building speaking.

Soon John Wesley and his nascent Methodist movement found such "natural" venues a necessary recourse. Angered over his untrained interlopers, their intrusion into the parishes, and their emotion-eliciting preaching, Anglican clergy increasingly barred Wesley and his preachers from their churches and made field preaching an evangelical necessity. Wesley turned vicissitude into strategy. In his journal for Sunday the 23rd of September, 1759, Wesley, after preaching to a "vast multitude of the immense congregation in Moorfields" and noting the "expediency of *field preaching*," commented: "By repeated observations I find I can command thrice the number in the open air [that] I can under a roof. And who can say the time for field preaching is over while (1) greater numbers than ever attend, (2) the converting as well as convincing power of God is eminently present with them?"[5]

The preachers commissioned by Wesley to take his movement to the new world doubtless came intent on honoring his field-preaching imperative. They soon discovered that only a fool would stand in a field under the blistering American summer sun or expect a congregation to endure such folly. Instead, when crowds exceeded the capacity of a home or small chapel, the preachers gathered congregations in the shade of a stately forest or under an oak's spreading branches. (Wesley had, to be sure, occasionally made his own sylvan retreat from the heat.[6]) Relishing these natural forest cathedrals, the American preachers also found the woods a place for solitude, prayer, and devotions. And as they took Methodism into sparsely settled areas and particularly as they followed the frontier west, they found forests to be wilderness, full of dangers, some life-threatening, a challenge.

All three experiences of the American woodland—in a shady preaching spot, in the woods for prayer, in a forest challenging to itinerant preachers, OR, as experienced, as natural cathedral, as devotional retreat, as wilderness challenge—proved important, as we shall see. For illustrative purposes, who better might evidence American Methodism's threefold relation to the American forest than its first great leader and second bishop, Francis Asbury. In July 1776, traveling in present-day West Virginia, Asbury spoke of the twofold character of the forest—confessional and challenge: "*Wednesday, 31. Spent some time in the **woods** alone with God, and found it a peculiar time of love and joy. O delightful employment! All my soul was centred in God!*" In June 1781, itinerating in Berkeley County, also in West Virginia, Asbury again spoke of wilderness as a challenge but also as a place to find God: "*Tuesday, 5. Had a rough ride over hills and dales to Guests. Here brother Pigman met me, and gave an agreeable account of the work on the south branch of Potomac. I am kept in peace; and greatly pleased I am to get into the **woods**, where, although alone, I have blessed company, and sometimes think, Who so happy as myself?*"[7]

In June 1787, while in New Jersey, Asbury recorded one of many instances of cathedral-like preaching in the woods, following that report with spiritual ruminations that might well have taken him to the woods to pray:

> *Sunday, 24.* I preached in the **woods** to nearly a thousand people. I was much oppressed by a cold, and felt very heavy in body and soul. Like Jonah, I went and sat down alone. I had some gracious feelings in the sacrament—others also felt the quickening power of God. I baptized a number of infants and adults, by sprinkling and

by immersion. I felt my body quite weary in, but my spirit not of, the work of God.

Successive entries for August 1787, in present-day West Virginia again, reference the importance of the woods for communion with God, one of many such as we shall see:

> *Friday* 10. I feel calm within, and the want of more life, and more love to God, and more patience with sinners. I read my Testament. O! what a weariness would life be without God, and love, and labour!…My soul has been under great trials, at times, but hitherto the Lord has helped. *Tuesday,* 21. O, how sweet will labour, and Christian society, and the solitary **woods** be to me.[8]

Asbury's sylvan ruminations were echoed again and again by the preachers he deployed across the countryside and into wilderness areas.

Woodland preaching was hardly the Methodist norm. Preachers commonly held forth in homes, in chapels when and where erected, and in any buildings that could be borrowed. Nor probably did they retreat routinely to the woods for prayer, meditation, or study. And wilderness retreated as Americans moved west and as Methodists succeeded in planting their classes and societies. But when the preachers' religious duties took them to forest and woods, they dwelt on that experience in their journals, reminiscences, and autobiographies. They deemed the woods or forest to be religiously special, significant, and noteworthy.

Since the forests constitute the centerpiece of and provide the evidence for this study, the reader will find many, often extensive, quotations exhibiting Methodist efforts toward and reflection on woodland worship. The richness of the movement's sylvan religiosity becomes more accessible today thanks to the digitizing of the array of Methodistica by United Methodist libraries and librarians. (See below for a word of appreciation to schools and libraries.)

Contents

Chapter 1 takes further note of the importance of field preaching in the British phase of the Wesleyan movement, acknowledging its occasional resort to shady trees and groves (see Appendix). It then documents at some length the more complex, several-fold Methodist experience of the

American woods. Methodists sacralized American woodlands, we suggest, as cathedral, as confessional, as challenge—as shady grove (nature's cathedral), as garden (a Gethsemane where temptations might be fought and spiritual solace sought), and as wilderness (a challenge through and into which the Methodist "gospel" must be taken).

All three of these spiritualizations of the woodland would eventually come together in the dramas known as camp meetings, staged revivals that became a Methodist signature, if not a Methodist creation. Camp meetings appealed to Methodists and became a programmatic feature of Methodists' outreach, in no small part, because they had for three decades gathered large crowds, often outdoors and under the trees, for their quarterly conferences or quarterly meetings. To the transition from quarterly to camp meeting and to the evolution of the camp meeting, chapter 2 is devoted. It concludes by treating Methodism's racial wilderness and camp meeting's dramatization of the movement's equivocal engagement with African Americans.[9]

Chapter 3, in something of a constructive theological move, revisits the images, emotionally laden terms, and metaphors with which Methodists wrote of their sylvan experiences. Readers not versed or interested in doctrinal treatment of forest and camp meetings or eager for more descriptive account of camp meetings can readily jump straight to the fourth chapter. Chapter 3 does endeavor to read the woodland accounts for their theological premises, understandings, and import. The chapter takes note of John Wesley's considerable attention to doctrines of creation and new creation to suggest that the Americans had foundations on which to build had they been inclined and ready to work explicitly and theologically on their woodland experience. Had they been equipped intellectually and theologically to range more deeply or broadly, the circuit riders might have drawn on the Christian tradition's reflections in nature and natural revelation or the rich, biblically informed meditations on garden and wilderness.[10] European settlers from the very beginning, after all, had experienced America as wilderness and fought to subdue fearful forest into garden.[11] And contemporaries would reflect on the American environment drawing on Puritan typology and Romantic nature ideals.[12] However, Methodist reflections are largely brief and occasional, an aside here and there in their journals. The absence of sustained or wilderness meditation perhaps explains why Methodists do not figure in literary treatments of the theme.[13] That means that elaborating American Methodist theological self-understanding involves teasing out implicit or implied meanings or even the doctrinal potential in early American Methodism's engagement with the forest. And when so extrapolated or extracted, it turns out that the preachers' engagement with the woods yielded not doctrines of creation, world, or nature but something of a practiced or enacted soteriology (doctrines of God, Christ, Spirit). On the latter, the Holy Spirit, the chapter concludes to wonder whether Methodism had in that doctrine and in Native American belief in the Great Spirit, the social-intellectual grounds for a more constructive evangelistic engagement.

A fourth chapter tracks later sylvan program and policy as Methodists moved across the continent and moved as well into increasingly middle-class denominational patterns.[14] In some regions and especially as it marched into frontiers, Methodism continued to call rustic camp meetings. In the east, Methodism moved as well but made camp meetings into family leisure villages. At places, assembly grounds served various reform causes. And camps proved to be ideal settings for holiness campaigns.

Across rural America, Methodists replicated and even institutionalized primitive sylvan patterns. Meanwhile, Methodism filled up small towns with churches, settled itinerants into parsonages, evolved into a middle-class denomination, and domesticated the camp meeting. It also mythologized its encounter with the frontier wilderness, an informal theologizing that produced several somewhat one-dimensional takes on the encounter with the American woodland.[15] Indeed, as the century wore on, camp meetings and their adherents sorted themselves drawing on but reinventing the evangelical, Wesleyan, episcopal, and republican ecclesial patterns that Methodism had owned in the late eighteenth century.[16] That fourfold pattern of self-imaging to that extent gave shape to the several camp meeting configurations, their differing practices, and their distinctive place in the church's life.

A short concluding chapter compares these four somewhat spontaneous responses to the retreating of true American wilderness and Methodism's several-fold institutionalization of forest religiosity (of chapter 4) with a fifth. Or might one say two versions of a fifth or two-fifths? Late nineteenth-century Methodism reimagined and reinvented its wildernesses in a two-fold manner—by Chautauqua's and Methodism's extensive, national Sunday school training and programming on the one hand, and on the other, by transforming the informal holiness camping (treated in chapter 4) into a nationally orchestrated and carefully planned campaign for denominational renewal. So groves and gardens came to map on the American landscape Methodism's tensions between its emergent liberal and evangelical wings. One wonders whether more cooperative and sustained reflection by

Methodism's parties might have equipped the church for ongoing American leadership on environmental and ecological matters. One might imagine that the Methodist movement's constitutive forest commitments and program might have yielded the church's significant guidance to state and federal caring engagement with the American woodland.

An appendix exhibits John Wesley's resort to preaching under trees and in groves so that the reader can see that the Americans sustained and complexified a Wesleyan pattern.

Practices and Theology

This will be my seventh book rethinking Methodist history, attending in passing or in conclusion to theological implications of findings, and drawing on Methodist practices, emphases, and institutions for their constructive import for the church today. Here, as in each of the following earlier efforts, I strive to undertake responsible historical reconstruction before turning to theology and examining my findings theologically. The titles of these books suggest something of the effort to understand church and ministry historically and theologically:

Episcopacy in the Methodist Tradition: Perspectives and Proposals, with Thomas Edward Frank, 2004;

Marks of Methodism: Practices of Ecclesiology, 2005;

Mr. Wesleys True Heirs: Extension Ministers, 2008;

Doctrine in Experience: A Methodist Theology of Church and Ministry, 2009;

Methodist Connectionalism: Historical Perspectives, 2010;

Denominationalism Illustrated and Explained, 2013; and

Formation for Ministry in American Methodism: Twenty-first Century Challenges and Two Centuries of Problem-Solving.[17]

I have mined history in a theological fashion on the premise that early American Methodists proved better at enacting, practicing, and programming their beliefs, hopes, and commitments than in giving them doctrinal expression. So I have teased out theological implications of the distinguishing Methodist practices, as, for instance, itinerancy and connectionalism.

This little volume operates on the same presumption, namely that the Methodist encounter with the American woodland, recorded in the journals of the preachers, might have dramatized notions or feelings about nature, ministry, and the church that deserve further exploration and exposition. It does represent a departure from my earlier efforts to read Methodist practices theologically in that prior enquiries explicated denominational features inherited from Wesley— discipline, for instance.[18] Preaching and worship in the forest, by contrast, seems to be a venture on which the American Methodists did a little exploration and clearing on their own.

Focus

A thematically focused study does not attempt to cover the entire American Methodist story and exhibit all of its many ecclesial peculiarities. I believe that my presentation offers sufficient explanation of key Methodist events, developments, and individuals for readers new to this denomination's history to make sense of the sylvan experiences and development. Persons puzzled by one or another feature of Methodist life will find further exposition in *The Oxford Handbook of Methodist Studies*, the *T & T Clark Companion to Methodism*, *The Cambridge Companion to American Methodism*, the *Timetables of History for Students of Methodism*, the *Historical Atlas of the Methodist Movement*, *The Ashgate Research Companion to World Methodism*, and the *Historical Dictionary of Methodism*, as well as the older *Encyclopedia of World Methodism*.[19] For narrative rather than topical or thematic treatment, readers are invited to three volumes in which I have had a hand as coauthor: *The Methodists* (1996/1998); *The Methodist Experience in America: A History* (2010); and *American Methodism: A Compact History* (2012).[20]

Not only does this study focus on Methodism and the American woodland; it also features the sylvan experience of preachers (rather than Methodist laymen and laywomen). Deployed across the American landscape, appointed to frontier circuits, obliged to itinerate through and evangelize in the wilderness, the preachers exhibited in journals and diaries the threefold encounter with and experience of forest. By featuring and reflecting on preachers-in-woodland, this book then offers yet another look at Methodist ministry, its hallmark pattern of itinerancy, and ministerial dimensions of ecclesiology. Relying on the American preachers' journals means taking seriously their self-presentation, vocational self-understanding, and myth making. They knew that John Wesley had published his journal, had encouraged his preachers to keep diaries and journals, and had facilitated their publication in his *Arminian Magazine*. And Wesley had several times importuned one of their own, Freeborn Garrettson, already a leader of colonial Methodism (and to be a greater one), to publish his journal.

> Some time ago I was solicited by Mr. Wesley, to send him an account of my experience and travels.... After I began to write, I found some scruples in my mind which I communicated to him. But some time after, I received a second, and then a third letter, in which he intreated me to lay aside my scruples and comply with his request.

Garrettson, to become one of American Methodism's great leaders, complied and shipped it. The manuscript apparently was lost at sea. Garrettson prepared another version and published his *Experience and Travels* in Philadelphia in 1791. He had been partly motivated to reproduce the effort, as he explained, by news of Wesley's death.[21] To his important account we return in the following chapters as we examine Methodist preachers' journals and their experience of the American forests.

Point of View

As the reader might have surmised by this point, I write as an insider. A cradle Methodist, an ordained United Methodist minister and son of the same, I taught ministers-to-be for four decades in three UMC seminaries. That privilege led me, along the way, to make Methodist studies a specialty, earned me a spot on various denominational initiatives and committees, and led to being coeditor of the online *Methodist Review*. To this work I have contributed by looking to history to provide insight on the presenting tasks, issues, and dilemmas. At some point in these historical enquiries, I discovered that what I was about belonged at the very heart of Methodism's identity and that almost from its founding American Methodism has rendered its self-understanding in historical terms.[22] Particularly in regard to ecclesiology, the doctrine of the church, Methodists have resorted to history for emphases that other communions have typically theologized more conventionally in systematic or scriptural terms. Also, as noted already, Methodists have dramatized their ecclesial convictions in practice, event, program, and institution. By realizing that the church has enacted ecclesiology, theologized history, and narrated its theology, I have been further encouraged to look to history for perspective on the church today, in this case to its stance on matters ecological and environmental, and to explore their theological import.

Acknowledgments

This volume is simply studied with quotation after quotation and citation after citation covering items from the theological collections from Asbury Duke, and Emory and from the items that they, along with other libraries have lodged on the World Wide Web in the American Methodism Collection. My thanks go to the heads and staff of these three libraries and schools for the special courtesies extended to me for access and support, now nearing a half century. Thanks as well and especially to three colleagues who have read and critiqued the final draft, Jennifer Woodruff Tait, Randy Maddox, and Charles Lippy. Tait, managing editor of *Christian History Magazine* and of Patheos Faith and Work Channel, is author of *The Poisoned Chalice: Eucharistic Grape Juice and Common-Sense Realism in Victorian Methodism* (Tuscaloosa: University of Alabama Press, 2011), and a contributor to *American Denominational History: Perspectives on the Past, Prospects for the Future* (Tuscaloosa: University of Alabama Press, 2008).Lippy, recently author of *Introducing American Religion* (New York: Routledge, 2009) and coeditor of the four-volume *Encyclopedia of Religion in America* (Washington, DC: CQ Press) is the LeRoy A. Martin Distinguished Professor of Religious Studies Emeritus, University of Tennessee Chattanooga and recent past-president of the American Society of Church History. Maddox is author of or contributor to various recent works on John Wesley, associate general editor of *The Bicentennial Edition of the Works of John Wesley*, and editor of the recent three-volume set in that series subtitled *Doctrinal and Controversial Treatises* (Nashville: Abingdon Press, 2012).He is the William Kellon Quick Professor of Wesleyan and Methodist Studies at Duke Divinity School.

Wilderness, Shady Grove, and Garden

I preached on the quay, at Kingswood, and near Kingswood
Square. To this day, field-preaching is a cross to me. But I
know my commission and see no other way of "preaching
*the gospel to every creature."**

"What can shake Satan's kingdom like field preaching!"

In 1739, George Whitefield invited John Wesley to Bristol so that he (George) might move on to evangelize Wales. Wesley discovered that Whitefield had been drawing huge crowds by preaching outdoors and witnessed a Whitefield gathering of something like thirty thousand. Though reluctant, Wesley gave in and began preaching in and around Bristol, taking advantage of any space made available—parish churches, the few buildings that Methodists had acquired, and various outdoor sites. He also experimented with outside or field preaching around London. Wesley did not draw quite the numbers of the flamboyant Whitefield, but claimed crowds of ten and fifteen thousand. Evangelistic success with this adopted practice, in Wesley's understanding, stamped field preaching as "providential." He deemed it so divinely commissioned because by field preaching he reached populations of laborers or the poor not always well served by existing Anglican parishes.[1]

In similar pragmatic or "providential" fashion, Wesley came to an equally offensive practice, deploying some of his converts who had the gifts and grace to provide leadership to small groups, to guide others in their Christian walk, and to exercise other clergylike roles. When one of his lay leaders took it upon himself to begin preaching and experienced success in so doing, Wesley was led, with some coaching from his mother, to authorize the practice, eventually to extend the prerogative to others, and so to find this breach

---

* Wesley, *Works 22, Journals and Diaries*, V (1765–1775), 348, for Sunday, September 6, 1772.

of ecclesial protocol also providential.[2] Calling them "sons in the gospel," Wesley came to appoint them to circuits and so expect them to itinerate between and among the places that Methodism had experienced success. Wesley and Whitefield's practice of field preaching became thereby a movement signature and effective modes of outreach and of care of those reached.

In his various publications—another of his successful stratagems to advance the Methodist renewal cause—Wesley explained that he had resorted to programmatic field preaching when frustrated in efforts to preach in church settings.[3] In *A Short History of the People Called Methodists* (1781), Wesley insisted that he preached in the open air "which I did at first, not out of choice, but necessity" because blocked from many churches by their clergy and because he remained committed to reaching the people.[4] "On Monday and Tuesday evening, I preached abroad near the Keelmen's Hospital to twice the people we should have had at the house. What marvel the devil does not love field preaching? Neither do I—I love a commodious room, a soft cushion, and handsome pulpit. But where is my zeal if I do not trample all these under foot, in order to save one more soul?"[5] Wesley drove himself to this practice, expected field preaching from his preachers as well, and came to see inattention to it as a source of weakness in the movement. So, he remarked in journal entries:

> Believing one hindrance of the work of God in York was the neglect of field preaching, I preached this morning at eight in an open place near the city walls. Abundance of people ran together, most of whom were deeply attentive. One or two only were angry and threw stones, but it was labour lost, for none regarded them.[6]

> About seven, I preached at the Gins, and the people flocked together from all quarters. The want of field preaching has been one cause of deadness here. I do not find any great increase of the work of God without it. If ever this is laid aside, I expect the whole work will gradually die away."[7]

Noting a large congregation at Cork, Wesley observed, "I had often been grieved at the smallness of the congregation here, and it could be not other while we cooped ourselves up in the house. But now the alarm is sounded abroad, people flock from all quarters. So plain it is that field-preaching is the most effectual way of overturning Satan's kingdom."[8] He sounded the same theme two years later:

I preached to a large and very serious congregation on Redcliff Hill. This is the way to overturn Satan's kingdom. In field-preaching, more than any other means, God is found of them that sought him not. By this, death, heaven, and hell, come to the ears, if not the hearts, of them that "care for none of these things."[9]

Field preaching came then to be part of a complex of practices, gatherings, beliefs, and structures by which the Wesleys, led by John, sought to renew and revitalize the Church of England. Indeed, the Methodist purpose statement, enunciated in conferences of preachers whom Wesley called together, insisted that the movement belonged within and oriented its reformist work toward the Church. The *Minutes* of Wesley's conferences, from 1744 onward, consolidated into "Large" *Minutes* in 1763, conceived of Methodism as a renewal effort within the Church:

> *Quest.* 4. What may we reasonably believe to be God's Design, in raising up the Preachers called *Methodists*?
>
> *Answ.* To reform the Nation, particularly the Church; and to spread scripture holiness over the land.[10]

Consistent with this ambitious church- and nation-reforming mission, Wesley incorporated his mandate for and strategy of field preaching into the movement—defining and directing "Large" *Minutes.*

Dutifully, the American Methodists carried that exhortation over into their first *Discipline,* crafted from the *Minutes* at the denomination-organizing 1784 Christmas Conference (see below). Both *Minutes* and first *Discipline* queried:

> Q. 6. Where should we endeavour to preach most?
>
> A. 1. Where there is the greatest number of quiet and willing hearers: 2. Where there is most fruit.
>
> Q. 7. Is field-preaching unlawful?
>
> A. We conceive not. We do not know that it is contrary to any law either of God or man.
>
> Q. 8. Have we not used it too sparingly?
>
> A. It seems we have: 1. Because our Call is, to save that which is lost. Now we cannot expect them to seek *us.* Therefore we should go and

seek *them*. 2. Because we are particularly called, by *going into the highways and hedges,* (which none else will do,) *to compel them to come in*. 3. Because that reason against it is not good, "The house will hold all that come." The house may hold all that *come* to the house; but not all that would *come* to the field.[11]

The pretense that the Methodists happily observed their reforming efforts within the Church of England and were not separatists became less and less plausible as the Wesleys generated quite an array of renewal features, field preaching among them. And Methodism's circuits, classes, and religious practices sufficiently engaged the populace and paralleled comparable elements of the Church of England as to constitute what looked to critics like another ecclesial body altogether. Nevertheless, despite building up church infrastructure, including their own buildings, regularized times of worship, ethical guidelines for daily living, and structures for order and discipline, the Wesleys insisted that they were not separating from the Church. That commitment or pretense extended to Anglicanism in the New World insofar as the Wesleys could direct Methodist efforts there.

"I...trust you...will not forget the church in this wilderness"[12]

The Wesleyan movement in the colonies did not grow out of the disastrous sojourn of the two Wesleys in Georgia in the 1730s or from the seven dramatically popular preaching tours of Whitefield up and down the coast over the next three decades. Nor did John Wesley launch Methodism by deputizing preachers to come over. Instead, Methodists who had migrated on their own—Robert and Elizabeth Strawbridge in Maryland and Barbara Heck, Philip Embury, and Thomas Webb in New York—took the initiative to start classes and organize societies (the local structures of Wesleyanism) and to begin the missionary itinerating that spread the movement.

Members of the infant Methodist societies in North America, while appreciative of the beginning efforts, wrote Wesley pleading for stronger leadership. A letter from Thomas Taylor, which provides the header for this section, described those then working in New York and recalled earlier efforts by Whitefield. He concluded:

We want an able, experienced preacher—one who has both gifts and graces necessary for the work. God has not despised the day of small things. There is a real work in many hearts by the preaching of Mr. Webb and Mr. Embury, but although they are both useful, and their hearts in the work, they want many qualifications necessary for such an undertaking, where they have none to direct them. And the progress of the Gospel here depends much on the qualifications of the preachers.

...[W]e must have a man of wisdom, of sound faith, and a good disciplinarian, one whose heart and soul are in the work, and I doubt not but by the goodness of God such a flame would be soon kindled as would never stop until it reached the great South Sea.[13]

In response, John Wesley sent over successive pairs of itinerants. Richard Boardman and Joseph Pilmore came in 1769. Francis Asbury and Richard Wright followed in 1771, Thomas Rankin and George Shadford in 1773, and James Dempster and Martin Rodda in 1774. Several preachers came to the colonies on their own, including John King, Joseph Yearbry, and William Glendenning. Those whom Wesley sent came with orders.

Pilmore and Boardman and successors knew themselves to be under explicit directives about implementing the Wesley system—open-air preaching, itineration on a planned basis, making and meeting appointments, inviting into connection all of any confession who would "flee the wrath to come," admitting the same as probationers, organizing classes, holding love feasts, maintaining the society's boundaries, establishing circuits, and cultivating good relations with the churches and their clergy. Implementing the Wesleyan system meant also discerning those who could serve in key leadership posts—steward, class leader, exhorter, local preacher—and appointing them to these key local posts.

"I was glad to stand up in the Wood & the people were finely sheltered from the extreme heat of the sun by the spreading branches of the Trees"[14]

The manifold efforts that Pilmore and successors made in bringing colonial Methodist initiatives into conformity with the Wesleyan system lie beyond the purview of this book.[15] From the start, Americans and those laboring for the Methodist cause in North America had their own ideas about how best to adapt Wesleyanism to a new society. Whether and how much to itinerate would become one area of struggle, and Pilmore was among those with their own ideas about this Wesleyan mandate. But Pilmore started out itinerating widely and provided one of the few instances of actually preaching in a field. In and around New York in June 1771, he recorded "preaching to a vast multitude of people in the Fields near the City." And again a year later in early July in and around Baltimore, Pilmore reported that after "an abundance of rain" had "refreshed the ground and cooled the air," he preached "on the Green in the Evening where a large congregation attended."[16]

More typically, Pilmore took to the woods. In mid-September 1771, he encountered "a vast congregation assembled at Chestnut-hill (a place about ten miles from Philadelphia) so I began immediately, and discoursed to them on the words of the Baptist *Flee from the Wrath to come* (Matt. 3:7). The fine spreading Oaks formed a noble Canopy over us, and we were as happy in the Grove as if we had been in the most pompous Temple." A month later, on October 12, Pilmore headed again toward Chestnut-hill, the "new Chapel would not near contain the congregation," so he preached in the Wood. "The stately trees extended their branches and afforded us a fine refreshing shade, while I called upon the listening multitude to look unto the Lord, whose wings are ever stretched out to cover and defend the upright in heart." The next day, at Chestnut-hill, he again drew upon a biblical image apt for the wood. He "found a vast concource [sic] of people assembled in the Grove where I preached before, I began immediately and was greatly assisted from above while I explained the Parable of the fruitless figg tree. It was one of the most solemn seasons I ever knew in preaching abrode (abroad) and had great reason to beli(e)ve the word of the Lord was made the savour of life to many of the people." A month later, on November 17, back again at Chestnut-hill and again finding "a vast concourse of people gathered from all quarters," he reported "I took my old stand in the wood, and explained the Parable of the tares of the field."[17] The next summer found Pilmore again going sylvan. For Sunday June 21, 1772, he noted going to "Baltimore Forrest where I found about five hundred people assembled in the Wood, so I immediately took my stand under a shady Tree, and had great liberty to explain the parable of the Wheat and the Tares." A week later, near Deer-Creek he intended to preach in the "new Chapel" but "found four times as many people as it would contain, so they made me a place in the Wood, and stood beneath the spreading branches of a stately Oak." When the people would not go away, he promised to preach again and so returned to that Wood. And on the 30th, he "found a noble congregation" at the Forks off

Gunpowder and as "no house…would near contain them, I was glad to stand up in the Wood & the people were finely sheltered from the extreme heat of the sun by the spreading branches of the Trees."[18]

Englishmen, unaccustomed to the intensity of the American summer, understandably would retreat to shade. Wesley and his preachers sometimes did the same in England (see appendix). For June 6, 1753, Wesley reported, "It being still sultry hot, I preached under a shady tree at Barley Hall; and in an open place at Rotherham in the evening." And for September 12, 1784, Wesley alluded to his own experience with an American summer.

> *Sun.* 12.—Dr. Coke read prayers, and I preached, in the new room. Afterward I hastened to Kingswood, and preached under the shade of that double row of trees which I planted about forty years ago. How little did any one then think that they would answer such an intention! The sun shone as hot as it used to do even in Georgia; but his rays could not pierce our canopy; and our Lord, meantime, shone upon many souls, and refreshed them that were weary.[19]

Wesley's English missionaries to America were not, however, the only Methodists to forget "fields" and seek shade. Indeed, for decades until they began to build cathedral-style churches that would accommodate and shelter crowds, Methodists—Americans and Brits—reflexively took to the woods. So American-born Freeborn Garrettson, one of the movement's most important leaders, an almost-bishop, recorded in late 1775 "preaching under the trees"—in September 1778 under "a large spreading tree," and in October 1778 "in a forest, to hundreds who gathered, both morning and afternoon, to hear the new doctrine." In late spring 1779, he spoke "to a thousand, or fifteen hundred souls assembled under the trees." For a Sunday in June, Garrettson, who lived spiritually with vivid dreams and dramatic visions, imagined Jesus both inspiring his preaching and being present with him in the woods:

> At twelve about 1500 gathered, and the Lord made bare his arm under the spreading trees. After a short intermission, I preached another sermon: and it seemed as if the whole country would turn to the Lord. While preaching I was so wonderfully drawn out, that it appeared to me as though I saw our blessed Saviour working prosperously through the Assembly. Weeping was on every side.

And on July 6 1779, he remarked on "a listening multitude under the trees in Mother Kill."[20] Other sylvan worship services did not make it into Garrettson's published journal—June 19, 1779; September 4, 1780; April 17, 1783; May 18, 1783; August 18, 1783; September 8, 1784; January 5, 1790.[21]

Quite a few of the resorts to the woods, reported by Garrettson and others, occurred in the quarterly meetings or quarterly conferences when the crowds gathered exceeded the capacity of a house or small chapel. Those constituted the first level of the Wesleyan governance system and very early came to be two-day affairs in the American colonies. We treat quarterly conferences in the next chapter but illustrative is this account from Jesse Lee, Methodism's first historian, looking back from 1810. He recalled a 1776 quarterly conference that required outdoor accommodations:

> On Tuesday and Wednesday, the 30th and 31st day of July, quarterly meeting was held at Mabur's dwelling house in Brunswick (now Greenville) county. No meeting house in Virginia could have held the people. We had a large arbour in the yard, which would shade from the sun, two or three thousand people. The first day was a blessed season; but the second day was a day never to be forgotten. We held the love feast under the arbour in the open air; the members of society took their seats, and other people stood all around them by hundreds. The place was truly awful, by reason of the presence of the Lord. Many of the members spake; and while some declared how the Lord had justified them freely, others declared how, and when the blood of Jesus had cleansed them from all sin. So clear, so full, and so strong was their testimony, that while some were speaking their experience, hundreds were in tears, and others vehemently crying to God, for pardon or holiness.
>
> Such a work of God as that was, I had never seen, or heard of before. It continued to spread through the south parts of Virginia, and the adjacent parts of North Carolina, all that summer and autumn.[22]

Four years later, American Methodism regularized the two-day quarterly conference, preferably as a Saturday-Sunday affair, and so "institutionalized" its crowd-gathering function and tendency to require a sylvan setting.[23]

To be sure, like their English counterparts, American Methodists used whatever space they could commandeer—chapels, homes, churches belonging to other denominations, public buildings, and barns as well as forests, shady groves, and spreading oaks. So another itinerant, John Kobler, sent out from a conference in "Petersburgh," spent three weeks reaching his mountain appointment, the Bedford Circuit. He reported for May, 15 [1791]: "Sund. 15. I preached for the first time to a crowded company in a barn. I never shall forget what a weeping there was. Poor old greyheaded sinners was bathed in sweat and tears." A little later he noted, "one Sunday, the congregation exceeded the capacity of house so went to the woods where I stood upon a table and preached..." And again "Sunday, June 12 preached at...to a large company in a barn...At night I gave an exhortation at the same place to a stout company of whites and blacks."[24]

Preachers and those who gathered to hear them chose the most suitable and comfortable venues available. And eventually, as already noted, Methodists would build to specification and head indoors for worship. But sylvan settings seemed to elicit emotionally charged treatment in Methodist journals, diaries, and autobiographies, those of the preachers especially. So David Lewis noted for the Brandon Circuit (New York) in 1812: "We labored under great disadvantage through want of meeting-houses. We had but one on this large circuit, and that was built on a cheap plan, and quite small. Our preaching was in schoolhouses, dwellinghouses, barns, shops and in God's own temple, the leafy grove."[25]

Because they itinerated, because they must honor an appointment and travel there, because a horse and strong lungs constituted requisites for ministry, because their circuits could be four or six weeks around, because they were sent out in exploratory assignments to evangelize and convert, the preachers experienced the American landscape in remarkably distinctive if not unique fashion. They filled their journals with geographical adversities—getting lost, falling into rivers, weathering snowstorms, worrying about Indian attack, losing their mounts, begging accommodations. So Seymour Landon recalled as he regaled the New York East Conference over his fifty years in itinerancy: "I encountered in my early ministry some of those things that are accounted, now-a-days, great trials; such as swimming rivers, floundering through swamps, losing my way in dense forests, getting struck in the mud, or in snow-drifts; and hair-breadth escapes from death on treacherous ice, or more treacherous waters lashed into foaming waves or mountain billows."[26] The land, the forest, the continent came to have special meaning for American Methodism.

"God's Design, in raising up the Preachers called Methodists? To reform the Continent"

"As our *American* Brethren are now totally disentangled both from the State, and from the *English* Hierarchy," explained John Wesley, "we dare not intangle them again, either with the one or the other: They are now at full liberty, simply to follow the Scriptures and the Primitive Church. And we judge it best that they should stand fast in that Liberty, wherewith God has so strangely made them free."[27] Along with this 1784 guidance, John Wesley made church-establishing provisions for his offspring. In so doing, he conferred his blessing on the translation of the movement, till then ostensibly a renewal effort within colonial Anglicanism, into a church for the new nation. Aspirations for full ecclesial status, ordination, and authority to administer the sacraments had increased during the Revolution as Anglican clergy fled home or to Canada. The pretense that Methodism functioned within the colonial Church of England became less and less plausible. American Methodism had experienced its first schism when the regularly convened 1779 conference, meeting in Fluvanna, Virginia, determined to effect its own independence. The conference "elevated" itself into a church with self-administered ordinations, creating something of a hybrid, Presbyterian structurally, Episcopal sacramentally (and highly unlikely to be recognized by either denomination). A branch of the movement, gathered by and around Francis Asbury, resisted the break, read the Fluvanna adherents out of Methodism, sought a solution from Wesley, and eventually elicited capitulation and compliance from their independence-bent colleagues.

Having failed to persuade the Bishop of London to ordain Methodists for America, Wesley determined to establish a church on his own authority. He did so with fellow Anglican clergy Thomas Coke's counsel, whom Wesley then ordained a superintendent for the American movement and sent over to implement the transition of reform movement into church.

By his several acts and literary conveyances, Wesley created, in effect, a new "Methodist" Anglicanism for the new nation:[28]

- ordaining fellow priest the Rev. Thomas Coke a superintendent (bishop) and directing that Francis Asbury be also so ordained;
- providing a revised *Book of Common Prayer* (BCP), including services
  - for the ordination of deacons and elders and consecration of bishops;
  - for the Lord's Supper, baptism, marriage, Communion of the sick and burial;

- and for Sunday morning and evening (the volume being curiously titled *The Sunday Service of the Methodist in North America. With Other Occasional Services*);[29]
- reducing the Anglican "Articles of Religion" to suit the American scene and presuming on reliance on his *Explanatory Notes Upon the New Testament* for scriptural guidance;
- providing a hymnal filled with his brother Charles's verse;
- sending what had become the quasi-constitution of the Wesleyan movement, the "Large" Minutes, to be further revised by the Americans to constitute a Discipline for the new church; and
- expecting the Americans to rely on his "Sermons" as the Church of England did the *Homilies*.

Wesley's provisions on paper perhaps looked Anglican—a church led by superintendents (soon renamed bishops), with a threefold order of ministry (deacons and elders as well) and with liturgies, which in places followed the BCP word for word. Fittingly, the Americans in their organizing "Christmas Conference" of 1784 chose to give themselves an Anglican name, the Methodist Episcopal Church (MEC).[30]

If to superficial appearances and on paper the new church looked Anglican, in substance, style, form, and purpose it remained what it had been—Wesleyan through and through, albeit nuanced for a new world. So, in its *Discipline*, the MEC Americanized Wesley's purpose statement:

> *Quest.* 3. What may we reasonably believe to be God's Design, in raising up the Preachers called Methodists?

> *Answ.* To reform the Continent, and spread scripture Holiness over these Lands. As a Proof hereof, we have seen in the Course of fifteen Years a great a glorious Work of God, from New-York through the Jersies, Pennsylvania, Maryland, Virginia, North and South Carolina, even to Georgia.[31]

The query remained that of British Methodism. The answer mentioned reform but reform of the continent, not of the nation or church. And the statement pluralized land to lands. This change was one of quite a number, several significant, that the Americans wrought on Wesley's plans. For instance, they insisted on calling the conference of preachers, the organizing "Christmas Conference," rather than simply letting Wesley's documents, designs, and appointments stand without some American acts of reception. The conference worked the "Large" *Minutes* into a *Discipline*, continuing emendations that Coke, Asbury, and others had done in preparation. They chose the name for the church. And most important, with Asbury's urging, they insisted on electing both Coke and Asbury as superintendents (the name soon changed to bishops), rather than acceding to Wesley's designation of Coke and nomination of Asbury to that office.[32]

But the mission statement that would take them to the woods—"To reform the Continent, and spread scripture Holiness over these Lands"— what could it have meant? Foreseeing Methodism's spread across the continent and growth to become the country's largest denomination was quite beyond the imagination or aspiration of the roomful of young preachers who finalized the editing of Wesley's "Large" *Minutes* into a *Discipline*. Rather, the linguistic changes adjusted purpose to the amorphous 1784 political and social realities of revolutionary America. But roaming the continent or at least the seaboard portions under colonial settlement for two decades? The preachers had done that! Seeking to convert, renew, and reform those who would hear them? Done that also! And surveying the American landscape mile after mile on horseback? Absolutely! "To reform the Continent" described and prescribed. To "spread scripture Holiness over these Lands," the preachers would continue to wander through the American forests and to gather people in its shady groves (except in winter).

And it was to the woods rather than to the fields that they must go. The first *Discipline* had, as we noted above, carried over Wesley's injunctions about field preaching from the "Large" *Minutes*. In 1787, the Americans revised the curious order of Wesley's *Minutes*, explaining that it was "Arranged under proper Heads, and Methodized in a more acceptable and easy Manner." They sustained the mandate to evangelize. Gone were the words that recalled the bucolic, pastoral English countryside—fields, hedges, and highways.[33] Goodbye Britain's ordered landscape. Hello wilderness. The Americans had dropped "field preaching" from the Methodist lexicon. Or perhaps they had substituted "continent" for "field." In either case, it was the forest they faced.

How could an itinerant ministry be preserved through this extensive continent…?

The preachers experienced land and continent together as Francis Asbury's own commitment to itinerate and his journal dramatically attests. That others would live into his resolve had everything to do with his exercise of the authority to appoint preachers to their circuits and his deeply held conviction that changing appointments served the mission of spreading scripture Holiness over the continent and through its woodlands. He and colleague Bishop Coke explain (below) that missional philosophy and the above heading. This account from late 1792 into early 1793 by Freeborn Garrettson illustrates something of the traveling regimen:

Thursday 27—After an agreeable time with Brother and Sister M_____Y The young preacher rode with me to Sharon (Conn.)...

Saturday 28 and Sunday 29—was our Quarterly Meeting in Pittsfield (Mass.)...

Monday, December 31—was a remarkably stormy day. I rode in a sleigh accompanied by three preachers and others, to Lanes-Borough...

Tuesday evening, January 1, 1793—We rode to Adams, (Mass.)...

Wednesday 2—In Williamstown (Mass.) the room was crowded....

Thursday 3—Brother (D. or B.) and I continued together....

Friday 4—We went on to Ashgrove (N.Y.)...

Saturday 5—Quarterly meeting began. Five preachers were present....

Sunday 6—Our love feast began a little after sunrise...

Monday 7—We rode 15 miles and there were four preachers with me....The following day we had a solemn sacramental occasion at B_____d's, Esq. As the preachers continued with me, I again gave up the evening meeting to them. I suppose 200 were present, we had two sermons, and an exhortation....

Wednesday 9—This morning I parted with three of the brethren, and Brother Dillon and I set out for Albany....

Monday 14—Two of the preachers left me....

Tuesday 15—We rode to Johnstown and I preached....

Wednesday 16—I was accompanied in a sleigh by two preachers, and one young convert 30 miles to Springfield....

Thursday 17—We are now five in number, four in the sleigh and one on horseback. We traveled through a severe snow storm about 11 miles....

Friday 18—We still pursue our journey to the west....

Saturday 19—We still pursue our journey to the west, our number has increased to seven...

Tuesday 22—...At present we are only four in company....

Thursday 24—I have only one preacher with me, and we turned our faces toward the Delaware...

Friday 25—Nine of us set out for Quarterly Meeting....[34]

Garrettson's journaling would prove prototypical. Methodism was clearly living into its mission to "reform the Continent." Clearly, it also sensed the enormity and importance of that task, an appreciation indicated by Bishops Thomas Coke and Francis Asbury when they got around to annotating the 1796 *Discipline*. They defended the appointive authority and power of the episcopal office in terms of its capacity to deploy Methodist preachers across the continent:

May we not add a few observations concerning the high expediency, if not necessity, of the present plan. How could an itinerant ministry be preserved through this extensive continent, if the yearly conferences were to station the preachers? They would, of course, be taken up with the *sole* consideration of the spiritual and temporal interests of *that part* of the connection, the direction of which was intrusted to them. The necessary consequence of this mode of proceeding would probably, in less than an age, be *the division of the body* and *the independence* of each yearly conference. The conferences would be more and more estranged from each other for want of a mutual exchange of preachers: and *that grand spring, the union of the body at large*, by which, under divine grace, the work is more and more extended through this vast country, would be gradually weakened, till at last it might be entirely destroyed. The connection would no more be enabled to send missionaries to the western states and territories, in proportion to their rapid population. The grand circulation of ministers would be at an end, and a mortal stab given to the itinerant plan. The surplus of preachers in one conference could not be drawn out to supply the deficiencies of others, through declensions, locations, deaths, &c. and the revivals in one part of the continent could not be rendered beneficial to the others. *Our grand plan*, in all its parts, leads to an *itinerant* ministry. Our bishops are *travelling* bishops. All the different orders which compose our conferences are employed in the *travelling line*; and our local preachers are, *in some degree*, travelling preachers. Everything is kept moving as far as possible; and we will be bold to say, that, next to the grace of God, there is nothing *like this* for keeping the whole body alive from the centre to the circumference, and for the continual extension of that circumference on every hand.[35]

Methodists indeed traversed the American landscape, tracked the moving frontier, and experienced the forest wildernesses, feats that they insisted on glamorizing and dramatizing when narrating it later. The Methodist itinerant—so it went, so it goes—showed up at cabins in the wilderness before settlers had finished building. Accordingly, James B. Finley began the first chapter, "Introduction of Methodism into the West," of *Sketches of Western Methodism*:

> Many years ago, during the Revolutionary struggle, and before the bloody scenes of Lexington or Bunker Hill were enacted; before these states were declared independent, and before there was a President in the chair of the Union; when all the western country was a waste, howling wilderness, untenanted except by the savage who roamed over its broad prairies, or through its dense forests, or sped his light canoe over the surface of its mighty rivers, the pioneer Methodist preacher might have been seen urging his way along the war-path of the Indian, the trail of the hunter, or the blazed track of the backwoodsman, seeking the lost sheep of the house of Israel in these far-off, distant wilds. Before the sun of civilization shone upon these mountains or in these vales, or over these prairies, or on these rivers, the herald of the cross, with his messages of mercy, was seen wending his way to the desolate haunts of savage man.[36]

The wilderness of the old northwest was Finley's theme. He used the word eighty-five times and described the ordeal of itinerant preachers braving the wilderness when not actually invoking the term. Recounting his own struggle with call to ministry, Finley remembered it as a wilderness encounter:

It seemed as though my happiness depended upon a life in the woods — "the grand old woods," where Nature had erected her throne, and where she swayed her scepter.

Alone in the deep solitude of the wilderness man can commune with himself and Nature and her God, and realize emotions and thoughts that the crowded city never can produce.[37]

Wilderness, Shady Grove, and Garden

Doubtless when imaging and communicating their experiences in the American woods and forests, the preachers, members, and onlookers sought to communicate a range of visions, feelings, impressions, and concerns. Certainly, the Methodists employed various terms and images to convey their experiences. Nevertheless, much of that richness, we suggest, is captured by the three terms of the chapter's and this short section's title—wilderness, shady grove, and garden. The experience of wilderness, of forested landscape, of the American woodland, of the challenges of hostile environments—as ordeal, as challenge, as expectation, or as "charge" as Methodists came to name "appointments"—underlay the Methodist preachers taming of it into cathedral (shady grove) and resorting to it for confession (garden).

Each of these dimensions of encounter with the landscape offered spiritual and potentially theological experiences, as well as emotional/personal aspects. Methodism's engagement with woodland America might have yielded a full-fledged, biblically imaged denominational self-understanding, ecclesiology, and corporate vision. Methodists might have tracked Israel out of the wilderness into Canaan. Or, they might have imagined themselves enduring an American version of the temptations of Jesus in the wilderness, or being sent out like he sent his disciples onto this continent's (shady) landscape, or with him retreating to a garden for prayer. Hints of such an ecclesiology and biblical self-understanding in itinerants' journals we will note and underscore. Indeed, collecting and ordering such theologically potent images of Methodism is one of the purposes of this book. For the American version of Wesleyanism acted out a richer, more dynamic, more promising ecclesiology than it has ever been able to cash out textually or descriptively. Such a theologically informed and fully articulated vision early Methodists lacked both the theological training and the leisure to undertake. Excuses for later Methodism are harder to imagine. (Two personal investments in such a concern I should note. First, I have in several other books, including particularly *Marks of Methodism*, sought to tease out a denominational ecclesiology. Second, I am a member of United Methodism's Committee on Faith and Order, a body established in 2008 to deal explicitly with the church's self-understanding.)

As Gregory Schneider has shown, Methodists made foundational to their religiosity the spatial and the narrative—the "sacred place set over against a threatening environment" and "the narrative pattern [as] the way of the cross."[38] By contrast to Schneider's treatment, which accents the experience of Methodist laity, this exploration focuses on the preachers. With them, the threefold relation to the American woodland rested on the Wesleyan imperative to honor an appointment, to go where sent, even if sent into the challenge of the frontier, and to adapt spiritually and evangelistically to that setting. The following three sections deal successively with these three Methodist ministerial experiences of the American landscape—as wilderness, shady grove, and garden.[39] Then follows a concluding, late Revolutionary War vision by Asbury of a new America, a vision for which the Asbury-led Methodists would indeed strive.

"We followed you to the wilderness"

That Methodism lived by the imperative to deploy its ministry west, tracking the population, was the focus of Bishop Francis Asbury's reminder to a western gathering (old northwestern):

> "We followed you to the wilderness," said he, "when the earth was our only resting place, and the sky our canopy; when your own subsistence depended on the precarious success of the chase, and consequently you had little to bestow on us. We sought not yours but you. And now show us the people who have no preacher, and whose language we understand, and we will send them one; yet, we will send them one: for the Methodist preachers are not militia, who will not cross the lines; they are regulars, and they must go."[40]

Asbury's own journal evidences that engagement with the wilderness on page after page. Here, for instance, he described traveling on what is now the Virginia-West Virginia border in July of 1781:

Monday, 16. We set out through the mountains for quarterly meeting. It was a very warm day, and part of our company stopped after thirty miles' travelling; brother William Partridge and myself kept on until night overtook us in the mountain, among rocks, and woods, and dangers on all sides surrounding us: we concluded it most safe to secure our horses and quietly await the return of day; so we lay down and slept among the rocks, although much annoyed by the gnats. Next day I met with several preachers, with whom I spent some time in conversation about the work of God. At twelve o'clock the people at Perrill's met, and we all exhorted.

Friday, 20. I had some liberty on 2 Cor. vi, 2. I have been obliged to sleep on the floor every night since I slept in the mountains. Yesterday I rode twenty-seven miles, and to-day thirty.[*]

In resolutely braving the wilderness, Asbury typified and modeled Methodism's response to the challenge of a spreading American society. In April 1779, working the Delmarva, Garrettson, whose woodland preaching we have already noted, reported being "led still farther in the wilderness to enlarge the circuit." Some days later, he detailed something of the ordeal that such resoluteness entailed: "One day I was wandering thought the wilderness in search of poor lost sheep, and called at several houses; but they did not want me. At length night came on; and I had been all day,

---

[*] Asbury, *Journal* 1: 429; cf. JLFA 408–09. His entries on the challenge of the wilderness are too numerous to reproduce but here is another sample, from the same area the following year:

"We crossed the mountain at the Gap, near my bed where I slept last summer, and riding up the North River made our journey near twenty miles: when we came there, we found that the people had gone to bury our old friend S, so that we had seven miles farther to go: arriving, we found them handing about their stink-pots of mulled whisky. We have, not unfrequently, to lodge in the same room with the family, the houses having but the one room, so that necessity compels us to seek retirement in the woods; this, with the nightly disagreeables of bugs to annoy us, shows the necessity of crying to the Lord for patience: in the midst of all, I thank God, I enjoy peace of mind. O how many thousands of poor souls have we to seek out in the wilds of America, who are but one remove from the Indians in the comforts of civilized society, and considering that they have the Bible in their hands, comparatively worse in their morals than the savages themselves: the want of religion among them, arises, I apprehend, from the badness of their own hearts, and from their hearing corrupt doctrines."

Asbury, *Journal* 1:448; cf. JLFA 1:427.

at least from the morning, without any refreshment for myself or horse; and I got lost withal in thick wilderness, called the Cyprus Swamp. The night was dark and rainy...." Garrettson finally found a house that would accept them, in the morning elicited their spiritual struggles, gained a guide from the husband, and visited them on another round of his circuit. Then, doubtless as he prepared his journal for publication, Garrettson glossed his wilderness efforts and needed image and language from Scripture to celebrate:

> Glory to God! I preached in a variety of places all through the wilderness; and many were convinced and brought to the knowledge of the truth. They built a church, and the Lord raised up several able speakers among them. There was an amazing change both in the disposition and manners of the people. The wilderness and the solitary paces began to bud, and blossom as the rose; and many hearts did leap for joy. Hundreds who were asleep in the arms of the wicked one, awoke and were enquiring the way to Zion with their faces thitherward.[41]

So Garrettson, in his 1791 *Experience and Travels*, established engagement with wilderness as a Methodist religious commitment, spiritual challenge, and evangelistic accomplishment. He may be the first to enunciate this Methodist myth. Celebration of Methodism's taming, civilizing, and Christianizing the wilderness would become a central theme in Methodist historiography. And the horseback circuit rider became iconic and remains a stratagem for understanding Methodist ministry. A successor bishop to Asbury, Thomas Morris, described this first experience of the woodland, its challenge as wilderness, as evidencing "the spirit of enterprise":

> [W]e were continually on the lookout for chances to enlarge our work. If we heard of any neighborhood that was destitute of the Gospel, we went directly to it and talked with the people; and, if one man in the settlement would open his house for preaching, we made it an appointment, and the next time we came around we were there. When we had an appointment we filled it; not if it was convenient, or if the weather was pleasant, and we could do it without sacrifice, but always, unless providential circumstances, over which we had no control, prevented us. If we wanted to gather a congregation, we had to be punctual; and if we wanted to hold a congregation, we could not

disappoint them. When the streams were swollen, we sometimes found great difficulty in crossing them. If we could find a bridge or a boat, it was well; but if we could not, we committed ourselves to Providence, and, plunging in with our horse, forded or swam the stream. This is what we mean by the spirit of enterprise.[42]

Illustrating such enterprise and its challenges, James Quinn headed alone in 1801 to establish an Erie circuit with the three books itinerants needed:

[H]e went forth with his Bible, Hymn-Book, and Discipline, visiting the various settlements, and, from cabin to cabin, preaching Christ and him crucified, and praying most fervently for the salvation of the people. His labors were greatly blessed of God, and he finally succeeded in permanently forming a circuit between three and four hundred miles round, embracing about twenty preaching-places, and eight or ten small classes.[43]

Following settlers to the wilderness had meant entrusting huge areas (charges) to the two circuit preachers and even larger assignments to the presiding elders who oversaw several such teams (yokefellows they called themselves). So when Quinn assumed the role of presiding elder of Muskingum (Ohio) district, comprising seven charges in 1808, his biographer noted the progress: "For many years the whole of Ohio formed but one district, and for the three preceding years John Sale, as presiding elder, had charge of all the circuits in Ohio, and two in Virginia."[44] No one faced the challenges of the American landscape more consistently and heroically than Francis Asbury, who as bishop drove himself relentlessly across the entire expanse of Methodist outreach, yearly going south to north, east to west, to attend the annual conferences, successively staged to that he could personally assign the preachers to their circuits. His biographer, John Wigger, estimates Asbury's circling covered some 130,000 miles and took him across the Alleghenies sixty times.* Asbury lived the wilderness commitment.

---

* John Wigger, *American Saint: Francis Asbury and the Methodists* (Oxford and New York: Oxford University Press, 2009), 3. Here is Asbury's account for July 1810, the Genesee Conference, and traveling from New York into Pennsylvania:

Sabbath, 22. Preached at the encampment. Wednesday. Conference ended—great order and despatch in business—stationed sixty-three preachers. Came away to Geneva. Thursday. Went round Seneca Lake. Friday. Bread and water. Came to Newton, and stopped at the widow Dunn's a few minutes for prayer, and continued

"[A]bout 1500 gathered and the Lord made bare his arm under the spreading trees"

American Methodists did not typically name sylvan preaching as cathedral-like or employ Pilmore's pejorative image of "the most pompous Temple." None of them, save for the few English preachers that Wesley had sent over (and almost all of whom returned home during the Revolution), had entered a cathedral or a temple or perhaps even seen either depicted. But when the American preachers gathered a congregation in woods or shady grove or under the spreading limbs of a stately oak, they imaged the experience in reverent terms. For June 21, 1779, Garrettson noted: "I was to preach at the Sound. In the morning I intended meeting the society at eight o'clock; but such a croud gathered that I declined it; and preached a sermon. At twelve about 1500 gathered and the Lord made bare his arm under the spreading trees."* Other instances of his sylvan preaching we

---

on down to Tioga Point, and housed with Captain Clark. We have made forty-seven miles to-day.

Saturday. We must needs come the Northumberland road; it is through an awful **wilderness.** We stopped at Eldred's; they are English, and disciples of Priestley. Alas! Read and prayed in the woods. I leave the rest to God. If the cry of want of order came from God, the appointment of the Genesee Conference was one of the most judicious acts of our episcopacy. We stationed sixty-three preachers, and cured some, till then, incurable cases. In the last three days and a half we have ridden one hundred and forty miles: what mountains, hills, rocks, roots, and ruts! Brother Boehm was thrown from the sulky, but, providentially, not a bone broken. *Sabbath, 29.* In the **wilderness**; but God is with us. Wretched lodging, and two dollars! Whilst busy in writing, John Brown came and took us to his cabin. We forded the swollen and rapid streams three times; the Loyalsock was the worst. We have spent the remainder of the day in reading, singing, and prayer. The rains had increased the streams, so that we kept our retreat on Monday. *Tuesday.* At the fordings we found drift logs obstructing the way: the stream was very full, and our toil through it great. Two active, bold men, with the aid of a canoe, got us and the horses safe over. Thunder and rain, and an awful mountain, were now before us; but God brought us safe to Muddy Creek. Deep roads and swollen streams we had enough of on our route to Northumberland on Wednesday. After waiting two hours at Morehead's ferry, on Thursday morning, we got over the Susquehannah...

Asbury, *Journal* 3: 342–43; cf. JLFA 2: 643–45.

* *American Methodist Pioneer*, 85. That same summer, Asbury, while confined in Delaware, noted for July:

"*Friday*, 23. Arose, as I commonly do, before five o'clock in the morning, to study the Bible. I find none like it; and find it of more consequence to a preacher to know his Bible well, than all the languages or books in the world—for he is not to preach these, but the word of God. I preached at G. Bradley's, in the **woods**, to about two hundred people, on Acts xiii. 26. Had considerable freedom. In the evening, at G. Moore's, on Rev. xxi, 6–8. Great liberty; the serious people much affected." Asbury,

have already detailed. It continued to be a Methodist impulse. Thomas Coke, ordained by John Wesley as superintendent, soon to join in ordaining Francis Asbury to that episcopal office, and sent by Asbury on an American preaching tour, noted for November 1784, "Annamessex-Chapel, Somerset, Monday 22. I preached to a tolerable congregation in a forest. It is quite romantic to see such numbers of horses fastened to the trees. Being engaged in the most solemn exercises of religion for three or four hours every day, and that in the middle of the day, I hardly know the day of the week: every one appearing to me like the Lord's-Day."[45]

Jesse Lee, like Garrettson a key leader and an almost-bishop, recorded that on Sunday June 20, 1784, "I preached at Coles, but the congregation was so large, that the house would not hold them, of course we had to look for another place; we got under the **shade** of some trees, where I spoke with great freedom, and with a heart drawn out in love to the souls of the people; and I felt a longing desire to be instrumental in bringing their souls to God."[46] Another important leader, Ezekiel Cooper, described the second day of a 1787 quarterly meeting on the Trenton Circuit in these terms:

> *Sunday*, 24. Love-feast began between eight and nine o'clock. We had the preaching-house well stowed with friends, and a glorious time we had. I don't know that ever I know the people to get under a better way of speaking than they did to-day. The Lord's Supper was administered between ten and eleven o'clock; then we went into the open woods to preach, where we had near about two thousand people. We,

---

Journal 1: 317; cf. JLFA 1: 306–07. The next month, he reported, "*Sunday morning*, 15. Read the law delivered by Moses, and our Lord's sermon on the mount; preached at nine o'clock at Boyer's; then went to the church at Dover; and preached in the **woods** at three o'clock on Acts xvii, 30. I was plain and faithful; but the people will, and will not. Our own people do not keep so close to God as they ought; this injures the work." Asbury, *Journal* 1: 321; cf. JLFA 1: 310.

Note here the outdoorsy biblical references—to Moses and Jesus. And in September, Asbury noted, "*Sunday*, 12. I preached to the people, who came to church, at Mr. Bassett's door, on Gal. ii, 19. In the afternoon, in the **woods**, to the most people I ever saw here, and had liberty; some living emotions appeared amongst the people: we revive again! I had a very different feeling to what I had the last time I was here. I hope we shall yet grow in Dover."

Asbury, *Journal* 1: 325; cf. JLFA 1: 312–13.

the preachers, got into a wagon, and then the speaker stood in a chair, so that we could both speak to and see the people. I preached the sermon from Acts xx, 31, 32. I had a field opened to me, and both the people and myself were affected. The power of the Lord rested on us. I don't think I ever saw so large a congregation in the woods behave so well; every one appeared to be still and attentive, an awe rested upon them, and I am persuaded that much good was done. Brothers Mills and Cromwell exhorted, and not in vain. After preaching I was, I believe, nearly an hour in bidding the friends farewell. I don't know that ever I bid so many people farewell, by shaking the hand, in one day before.[47]

William Colbert, who left ten journal volumes extending from 1790 to 1838, recorded numerous instances of preaching to congregations in the woods, typically rendered in emotionally positive terms. On Sunday, September 20, 1801, he indicated that much of a quarterly meeting had been conducted "under the beautiful trees…at Bowen Meetinghouse."[48] For a July 1802 quarterly conference on the Herkemer Circuit (the judiciary level for a circuit and below that of annual conferences), he entered this description:

Sunday 4 A glorious morning. Many of the friend[s] spoke with life and power in the Love-feast. The Lord displayed his power. One man who had been under conviction was so wrought upon, that he lost the use of his limbs, and was brought to experience the goodness of God, (I trust) in the conversion of his soul. After the Love-feast we took the congregation into the woods. To me it was pleasingly romantic, to Behold the people seated on the oldlogs, and in their waggons, Beneath the lovely shades of the stately Maple and Beach Trees listening to the joyful sound of salvation. I stood in the Waggon, and preached to them from Acts 16 ch 30, 31. Brothers Wilkerson Hoyer and Willy exhorted. The Lord was present, but more power fully at the administration of the sacrament. Numbers were brought on their knees, crying for mercy and one was brought to rejoyce in the God of her salvation.[49]

A month later for the Albany Circuit, Colbert reported: "we had recourse to the woods, and beneath the lovely shades of Beach, and Hemlock on a gradual descent we fixt a large and descent congregation on the eminence above us." A week later, for another quarterly conference, he recorded:

Su 22 This morning in the Love-feast we have had a blessed time, many spoke feelingly: and at the close of my account of the work of God round the District, which I gave them according to promise, the Lord made bare his arm...five were brought to rejoice in the God of their salvation. As our friends nearly fill'd the house, we had to take a large congregation into the woods. It is truly delightfull to see hundreds worshipping the Majesty of heaven beneath the lofty shades.[50]

By this time, as the next chapter indicates, Methodism had begun adopting the camp meeting.[51] The preachers often positioned a warm weather quarterly conference (sometimes termed a quarterly meeting) in a camp meeting. And so sylvan congregations became a common, indeed in many places, a regular feature of Methodist life. Recollections of camp meetings could invoke cathedral comparisons. Here, for instance, Charles Giles recalled his first camp meeting:

According to our expectations, we found the forest converted into holy ground, and, temple-like, consecrated to the worship of God. Rough seats, arranged with due design, were prepared to accommodate the worshipping assembly. On one side of the ground an elevated platform appeared, built of logs and floored, which was designed merely for the sacred rostrum. The forest trees, like lofty columns, stood in the order in which nature had placed them, whose wide-spread arms, intersecting, formed verdant arches high over the hallowed ground, waving gently as the winds played among the branches. The place was delightful.[52]

One feature of the camp meeting had already been institutionalized in the earlier outdoor quarterly conferences—they were biracial. Colbert described the segregated character of indoor services and the space made for both white and black when the congregation moved under the trees. For a quarterly meeting, the 22nd and 23rd of May 1790 (typically two days, with business affairs and preaching on the first day and multiple services on the second), Colbert noted, "Sunday 23d Brother Childs and I went out into the woods and preach'd to a number of black and white people."[53] For a July 18, 19, 1801 Salisbury quarterly conference with five preachers laboring, Colbert reported, "Sunday 19 This morning the black peoples Love-feast was held and after theirs the white peoples—it was a blessed time in both Love-feast's. Brother Ware preached in the woods...Brothers Larkins, and

Milbourne Exhorted."[54] On October 3 and 4, of the same year, Colbert presided at the Somerset quarterly conference, "Sunday 4 This morning the house was crouded with white friends I was sorry there was no room for the poor blacks. We had a good Love-feast. The people spoke well, after which I preached to a large congregation under the trees..."[55] In the cathedral-like forest or woodland gathering, whites and blacks could worship together, much as they trafficked together in other public spaces.

"And often the wilderness was my closet, where I had many sweet hours converse with my dear Lord"

In April 1779, Freeborn Garrettson reported extending his circuit into wilderness areas, in "places, I had none to converse with, at first, who knew the Lord; yet Jesus was sweet company to me in my retirements. And often the wilderness was my closet, where I had many sweet hours converse with my dear Lord."[56] Garrettson had begun the practice of sylvan devotions before becoming Methodist and continued it as a Methodist preacher. In mid-June of 1779, he conceded that "This morning I was much tempted. I walked about the field and in the woods, and could not enjoy the comfort that I desired." In late December, he noted, "I retired in the wood, spent some time in prayer to God to grant a blessing on the day."[57]

By early 1780, sharing with other Methodists the suspicion, harassment, and persecution awarded the movement on suspicion of collaboration with the British troops, Garrettson experienced dreams, nightmares, and visions and sought solace where he could find it. To be arrested that very evening, he recorded for February 25, "Saturday 25, my spirit was solemn and weighty: expecting something uncommon would turn up. I withdrew to the woods, and spent much time before the Lord. I preached with freedom to a weeping flock.[58] Also threatened with arrest during the Revolution, Benjamin Abbott reported, "When we arrived at the place appointed," [for him to preach]" he found "about two hundred horses hitched." He continued, "I also hitched mine, and retired into the woods, where I prayed and covenanted with God on my knees, that if he stood by me in this country, I would be more for him through grace, than ever I had been. I then arose and went to my horse, with a perfect resignation to the will of God, whether to death or to jail."[59]

In the same time frame (July 1780), Asbury, who recorded many such spiritual episodes— typically in the woods—noted while in North Carolina:

Tuesday, 18. Rode to Kimborough's, sixteen miles, crossed Neuse River. Many Baptists to hear; they were serious, and I spoke feelingly, and aimed at their hearts, from Romans viii, 24-26. I met brother Poythress, much cast down; the people are lifeless in religion; but, bless the Lord, I have had a good entrance, and a comfortable sense of the divine presence. After dinner, I was alone in the **woods** an hour, had sweet meltings, came back and wrote these lines for future consolation.[60]

Henry Boehm, a traveling companion of Asbury's, reported that after the 1805 Baltimore Conference, "I had the company of James Hunter and Henry Smith. Where we stayed over night we went into the woods, and there we wrestled and prayed together for a deeper baptism of love. Heaven met us in the grove, and we felt it none other than God's own house and heaven's gate. After riding together three days we separated."[61]

To some extent, a very small extent, the preachers resorted to the woods of necessity as Asbury explained: "I retired to read and pray in the woods, the houses being small, and the families large."[62] Preacher-in-training, Jacob Lanius, later echoed Asbury's complaint and rationale—the resort to the woods sometimes had to do with convenience as well as its accommodation of the spiritual life:

After dinner I took Dr. Mosheims History of the Church and went to the grove and spent the remainder of the evening in reading meditation and prayer. We often find it necessary in this new and frontier country thus to retire because the people have but one room in the general and a fortune of children who surround us crying and hollering to such an extent as to render it impossible to read and understand and very often we are interrupted by a question or a statement from a good brother or sister which the rules of ministerial and Christian etiquet require us to attend to.[63]

However, the resort to the "garden" forest for some began long before they became preachers and might have been forced outside by cramped quarters. Their conversion experiences and calls to ministry came as they prayed and meditated in the woods. "Wrestling Jacob,"[64] one of Charles Wesley's most important hymns, a favorite of John and esteemed by fellow hymnist, Isaac Watts, well might have been similarly claimed by the preachers who, like Jacob, had to fight spiritually to find favor with God.

No rock for a pillow, nor a ladder reaching to heaven, the Americans found themselves wrestling with "the Man that died for me" in the forest. Accordingly, Methodists experienced there the counterpart to Jacob's transformation, namely Christian conversion. Ezekiel Cooper so described his spiritual pilgrimage (in 1781):

> I was diligent in searching the Scriptures, and in private prayer; my understanding in divine things increased, and the more clearly I saw the state of my own heart. For months I went bowed down in mourning before the Lord, believing there was mercy for me, but not knowing how to secure it. By night I walked the fields in meditation, and brokenness of heart; or, when all were sleeping, would frequently pour out my soul in supplication. In the spring and summer seasons I made the woods my constant resort, walking and meditating, or reading and praying, sometimes prostrate on my face.

His emotional and spiritual anguish continued:

> One day, as I was walking alone in the woods, I felt great encouragement. I knelt down and prayed fervently. Presently I had an opening to my mind of the infinite fullness of Christ, and of the willingness of the Father, through his Son, to receive me into his favor. I had such confidence in the merits of Christ and the mercy of God that I laid hold of the promise, felt my burden removed, and a flood of peace, love, and joy break forth in my soul. I was now enabled to call Christ Lord, by the Holy Ghost sent down from heaven. I am assured, to the present moment, that at that time the Lord forgave me all my sins, and owned me for his adopted child. My heart was enlarged toward all mankind. I was ready to conclude that I could convince any or every body of the great truths and necessity of religion. I wanted an opportunity to warn the world, especially a number of my irreligious friends. But I found them not to be so easily convinced. "I work a work," said God, "which ye will in nowise believe though a man declare it unto you."[65]

Stith Mead also tracked his conversion experience in sylvan, "Wrestling Jacob," terms. He reported, "walking together with a friend in a grove to converse about salvation." He recalled that a little later he prayed in "a lonesome thicket of the woods." And after his conversion he found himself and direction for his life "one evening as I was kneeling by a tree in the wood."[66]

Charles Giles made "the wilderness my place of retirement" as he sought "salvation from sin, which lay heavily on my agonizing soul." There, he continued, "beneath the arms of the forest trees, I first bowed my soul and body, then in the attitude of devotion, to confess my sins to God, and to pray for mercy." His response, when his brother, Nicholas, his "whole family, and almost the entire neighbourhood, together with many in the adjoining settlements, became subjects of the blessed work?" Sylvan applause: "The wilderness and solitary places were glad. The trees clapped their hands, while the valleys echoed the sound of the triumphal songs of free grace and free salvation." Hardly a surprise that Giles experienced a woodland call to the ministry: "One memorable day, while I was under the lofty branches of a gigantic elm that stood near my father's house, which, for some reason, was left standing when the forest was hewn down around it, the Spirit of God came down upon me, and, in a mysterious manner, called me to preach the everlasting gospel, by a perceptible, inward voice; to which I responded, by expressing a willingness of mind to do whatso-ever my Lord and Master required at my hands." He regarded that tree as consecrated land: "The place distinguished by this moving occurrence appears still solemn to me; and I often contemplate on it with emotions of awe and delight, though the memorable tree, the ancient elm is not there."[67]

Similarly, John Kobler resorted to the woods for spiritual nourishment. In late December 1790, he reported, "I retired into a wood where I had deep impressions of Divine things." In June, Kobler noted, "Wednesday. June 15. This morning I feel a great hunger and thirst after righteousness. I retired into a wood where I found the Lord to be very precious to my soul, the very trees of the wood is praising of him, much more reason honor I who am a Brand plucked out of the fire." And for "Tuesday, Sept. 23. This morning I retired into the wood, where I had sweetness in com-muning with my beloved Savior." He read scripture, notably the letters of Paul to Timothy. Perhaps, the woods served as a place for reverence be-cause it served so well as resource for collective praise. Between these latter two times of personal communion, Kobler had transformed wood-land into cathedral: "Monday, July 11 at (Js-Ns) here preached to a large congregation on a hill side under a cluster of peach-trees."[68]

The preachers retired to the woods not only to deal with their personal spiritual struggles but also to equip them for challenges in ministry. John Young took to the woods to steel himself to deal with a large congregation "some about half drunk and as stupid as the ox by setting up all the night before gambling, a horse race being in the neighborhood the day before."

Feeling awful, he "retired in the woods alone, and poured out my soul to the Lord, and craved assistance from him that was able to save all that put their trust in him. I found help, and took courage, and went to the house."[69] William Colbert took to the woods in mid-August 1799 to prepare himself to deal with the death of the daughter of David Griffiths, Grace Griffiths, who had died "after a long and painful affliction." "Thursday 15 This morning retired into a little copse of woods, and spent a few moments in composing the few following lines on the departure of the unblemished Grace Griffith: (after which I went preached her funeral)."[70] Abner Chase reported that the new preacher on the Saratoga Circuit in 1801 "retired to a grove" distraught after an "indecently noisy" love-feast concluding "that Methodism was ruined for ever for him."[71]

In the early nineteenth century, George Brown's spiritual struggles took him to "secret places, mostly in the barn and in the woods," where he prayed "for mercy night and day." On his way into ministry, he attended a camp meeting and heard an African American, "a capital preacher," whose sermon convinced him that he "was a poor, miserable sinner, in great danger of losing my soul." Following the sermon, he reported, "I went to the woods, and sought a secluded place for prayer, for my distress was so great that it wonderfully exhausted all my physical energies. To this private place in the woods I resorted for prayer at the close of every sermon, from Thursday until Tuesday, eating but little, and sleep had well-nigh departed from me." He camped under an oak to hear the preaching, back-and-forth from "the bower of prayer in the woods and root of the oak in the congregation" until the last sermon, from Nicholas Snethen, his brother's support and penitential words from an "aged minister" brought him "in my soul a peace hitherto unknown."[72] In the early nineteenth century, David Lewis retired to a grove several times, praying for a neighbor. Finally, in an encounter with the man, he said "you are on the margin of conversion; and if you will go with me into the grove, we will engage in prayer, and God will pardon your sins." They did and the woods worked wonders.[73]

Sylvan meditation featured in calls to ministry. For instance, in 1805, E. F. Newell wrestled with "the question of duty, as to preaching the Gospel." "I oft retired to the shade of a large spreading pine, surrounded by a thicket of smaller growth," he reported, "where I poured out the anxieties of my souls to God."[74] Similarly, in late 1813, Thomas Morris, newly appointed to be a class leader (an office that led him to the preaching ministry), resorted to the woods to prepare himself for the task:

About this time the class-leader having moved away, and the little
class in that neighborhood being in a somewhat low condition, the
new preacher, Rev. John Cord, appointed Morris to fill the vacancy,
and handed him the class-book with the request that he would con-
vene the members once a week, and hold a class-meeting. This appointment was received with much fear and trembling. During the
week he retired into the woods, kneeled by the side of a fallen tree,
spread out the class-book before him, read the first name, and
prayed for him, and so on through the entire list, asking for grace
and wisdom to say profitable words to them all on the ensuing
Sabbath. The class was a small one, and the members, scattered
over a wide territory, did not usually all meet together at one time;
but on the following Sabbath there was a good attendance, and the
Master was present with them to impart strength and comfort.[75]

The same year, another bishop-to-be, Henry Bascom, also found the woods
important in steeling himself for ministerial tasks:

September 7, 1813. I was appointed by the Western [Ohio] conference to Deer creek circuit. Sept. 30, arrived at my circuit. Oct. 1, 2, 3,
and 4, I attended a camp meeting in the neighboring circuit, and
tried to preach and had a pretty good time. Oct. 6, filled my first appointment on my circuit—felt very low in spirits, the people being
dull and dead. Resorted to the woods and prayed, though sorely
tempted to believe the Lord had no work for me to do here. Returned
to the house and held family prayers—felt my sorrows measurably
dissipated, and light and glory began to break into my soul.

Oct. 10...Went to bed and slept cold and uneasy—rose but little
before sunrise, prayed with the family—retired to the woods, where
I found the Lord precious. Read the Bible, and some of Fletcher's
masterly productions—wrote some letters, and so spent the
morning before preaching. Help me, Lord, to-day.
Oct. 13. Rose very early—fled to the woods and prayed—fed my
horse, prayed with the family—ate my breakfast, and started for my
next preaching place. After riding about six miles, met the man at
whose house I was to preach, and he informed me there would not
be any one at home; so I rode through the neighborhood until I
found a place to preach at, and to lodge at. Sent round and called in

the neighbors to preaching. These people appear kind, but prodigiously filthy, and filthiness I hate. At twelve o'clock I preached to about fifteen souls, on the danger of neglecting salvation.

Next morning was sorely tempted, wrestled in prayer at my bedside, then went to the woods and prayed until I felt better, returned and prayed in the family; read some in the Bible, my old companion, also a sermon of Rev. Freeborn Garrettson on the union of the graces, an excellent piece of work. At twelve o'clock tried to preach to about a dozen people, and believe good was done.[76]

His biographer indicated that Bascom frequently resorted to the woods to prepare himself for ministerial duties.[77]

I have no doubt but that there will be a glorious Gospel-day in this and every other part of America

In late June and early July of 1781, in successive journal entries, Asbury brought the three sylvan experiences into a vision of a continent indeed reformed and overspread with scripture Holiness:

In journeying through this mountainous district I have been greatly blessed, my soul enjoying constant peace. I find a few humble, happy souls in my course; and although present appearances are gloomy, I have no doubt but that there will be a glorious Gospel-day in this and every other part of America. There are but two men in the society at Lost River able to bear arms; they were both drafted to go into the army: I gave them what comfort I could, and prayed for them.

Saturday, 30. I got alone into a barn to read and pray. The people here appear unengaged: the preaching of unconditional election, and its usual attendant, Antinomianism, seems to have hardened their hearts. *Sunday, July* 1. More people attended preaching than I expected: I had some liberty in speaking, but no great fervour; neither seemed there much effect produced. I retired to read and pray in the woods, the houses being small, and the families large.

Friday, 13. For some days past my congregations have not been very large, which is in part owing to the harvest-home....

Monday, 16. We set out through the mountains for quarterly meeting. It was a very warm day, and part of our company stopped after thirty miles' traveling; brother William Partridge and myself kept on until night overtook us in the mountains, among rocks, and woods, and dangers on all sides surrounding us: we concluded it most safe to secure our horses and quietly await the return of day; so we lay down and slept among the rocks, although much annoyed by the gnats.[78]

Traveling through the wilderness and experiencing its dangers and discomforts, Asbury lived the challenging, confessional, and cathedral dimensions of his experience of the American forest, recognized that the unseeing eye would find "present appearances" to be "gloomy," but looked with his spiritual vision to "a glorious Gospel-day in this and every other part of America." In other places as well, Asbury hinted that the ordeal of the wilderness, the Word preached in arbor or shady wood and sylvan devotional solitude had become one complex spiritual and redemptive reality for himself, for the people called Methodist, and for all who responded to a redemptive Wesleyan message. This theologizing of the woodland experience we take up in chapter 3. Perhaps it was premonition of that threefold conjunction that made Methodists adopt camp meetings spontaneously and immediately, make them very much their own, promote them feverishly, and programmatically transform wilderness sites into cathedrals for preaching, praise, and prayer. To that transition we now turn.

2

Cathedraling the Woods

*Their Quarterly-meetings on this Continent are much
attended to. The Brethren for twenty miles round, and
sometimes for thirty or forty, meet together. The meeting
always lasts two days. All the Travelling Preachers in the
Circuit are present, and they with perhaps a local Preacher
or two, give the people a sermon one after another, besides
the Love-feast, and (now) the Sacrament.**

SO NOTED THOMAS Coke, selected and shipped off by John Wesley to be
co-superintendent with Francis Asbury for the new Methodist Episcopal
Church. A close confidant of and lieutenant to Wesley, intimately and extensively knowledgeable about British Methodism in all its particulars,
Coke experienced the American quarterly conference as something
novel, significantly different from Mr. Wesley's provision for governance

---

* Thomas Coke, *Extracts of the Journals of the Rev. Dr. Coke's Five visits to America* (London,
Printed by G. Paramore; and sold by G. Whitfield, 1793), 34–35. Bishop Coke preceded this
April 1785 entry with a little "wilderness" experience of his own:
   Friday 8. According to my plan I was to preach in a Church called *Royster's* Church atnoon.
After riding about twenty-five miles, I got, as I found afterwards, within a furlong of the
Church; but the Church being out of sight in an immense Forest, and the path which led to
it hardly trodden, and having no guide, (the person who was to accompany me, having dis-
appointed me) I rode about eighteen miles more, backwards and forwards, generally on the
full stretch, and found it at last by the direction of a Planter, whose Plantation was the only
one I saw for some hours. When I came there, which was two hours after the time, there was
nobody to be seen. I returned to the Planter's, who gave me and my horse some refreshment, and recommended me to go to one Captain *Philps*, a Methodist about five miles off.
After travelling till nine at night, and expecting frequently I should be obliged to take up my
lodging in the Woods, with the assistance of two Negroes and two shillings I found out the
house. I now was informed that I had not been published in *Royster's* Church, or any part of
that Circuit, the two Preachers not having been at the last Conference, and the neighbouring
Preachers not having sent them a copy of my Plan. However our Brother *Philps* and his family and several other friends intended to set off the next morning for a Quarterly-meeting
about sixteen miles distant.

of a circuit and from British Methodist practice. It differed in duration, in size, and, one should add, in evangelistic magnitude! The American quarterly meetings, particularly those in warm weather, sometimes drew crowds far beyond the capacity of small meeting places, necessitated out-door worship, and then produced revival in the American woods. That Coke recognized the American quarterly meeting as distinctive is impor-tant. When he arrived in the new nation in 1784, the Americans had al-ready expanded the Wesleyan prototype from an intimate, internal affair to which leadership came to an open, public, crowd-eliciting extravaganza. In so doing, they had begun a dramatization and an institutionalization of their threefold experience of the forest or woodland. American Methodism completed and stabilized that appropriation and institution-alization with camp meetings.

To hold quarterly meetings, and therein diligently to inquire both into the temporal and spiritual state of each society

So the "Large" *Minutes* charged Wesley's assistants, his preachers who over-saw circuits (a role, as we shall see, that would fall to ordained elders in the American church and earn them the title of "presiding elder").* Wesley's renewal movement generated and/or appropriated social structures for

---

* Shaded material was omitted by the first *Discipline* from the "Large" Minutes. MATERIAL IN CAPS ADDED.

Q. 42. What is the business of an assistant?

A. (1.) To see that the other preachers in his circuit behave well, and want nothing. (2.) To visit the classes quarterly, regulate the bands, and deliver tickets. (3.) To take in or put out of the society or the bands. [NEW 4: TO APPOINT ALL THE STEWARDS AND LEADERS AND CHANGE THEM WHEN HE SEES IT NECESSARY.] (4.) To keep watch-nights and love-feasts. (5.) To hold quarterly meet-ings, and therein diligently to inquire both into the temporal and spiritual state of each society. (6.) To take care that every society be duly supplied with books; partic-ularly with "Kempis," "Instructions for Children," and the "Primitive Physic," which ought to be in every house. O why is not this regarded! (7.) To send from every quar-terly meeting a circumstantial account to London of every remarkable conversion and remarkable death. [TO SEND AN ACCOUNT OF HIS CIRCUIT EVERY HALF YEAR TO ONE OF THE SUPERINTENDENTS.] (8.) To take exact lists of his societ-ies every quarter, and send them up to London. [AND BRING THEM TO THE CONFERENCE] (9.) To meet the married men and women, and the single men and women, in the large societies, once a quarter. (10.) To overlook the accounts of all the stewards.

religious formation, encouragement, guidance, and discipline somewhat haphazardly.[1] With this formational template, colonial Methodists struggled and implemented as and where possible. Small confessional, gender- and marital-status specific "bands" were to be overlapped with geographically organized discipline-charged "classes," in which Methodists held membership. Where classes proliferated (in cities), classes and bands aligned with a society. In theory, bands, classes, and societies met so as not to compete with local Anglican services. Wesley deployed his preachers—the lay preachers and any clergy who cooperated with the Methodists—regionally in preaching circuits, meeting societies, and classes and preaching for Methodist groups, in public places, and in churches (if permitted). And Wesley called together his preachers to confer with him, creating the annual conference.

Q. 43. Has the office of an assistant been well executed?

A. No, not by half the assistants. (1.) Who has sent me word, whether the other preachers behave well or ill? (2.) Who has visited all the classes, and regulated the bands quarterly? (3.) Love-feasts for the bands have been neglected: neither have persons been duly taken in and put out of the bands. (4.) The societies are not half supplied with books; not even with those above mentioned. O exert yourselves in this! Be not weary! Leave no stone unturned! (5.) How few accounts have I had, either of remarkable deaths, or remarkable conversions! (6.) How few exact lists of the societies! (7.) How few have met the married and single persons once a quarter!

Q. 44. Are there any other advices which you would give the assistants?

A. Several. (1.) Take a regular catalogue of your societies, as they live in house-row. (2.) Leave your successor a particular account of the state of the circuit. (3.) See that every band leader has the rules of the bands. (4.) Vigorously, but calmly, enforce the rules concerning needless ornaments, drams, snuff, and tobacco. Give no band ticket to any man or woman who does not promise to leave them off. (5.) As soon as there are four men or women believers in any place, put them into a band. (6.) Suffer no love-feast to last above an hour and a half; and instantly stop all breaking the cake with one another. (7.) Warn all, from time to time, that none are to remove from one society to another without a certificate from the assistant in these words: (else he will not be received in other societies). "A. B., the bearer, is a member of our society in C.: I believe he has sufficient cause for removing." I beg every assistant to remember this. (8.) Every where recommend decency and cleanliness: cleanliness is next to godliness. (9.) Exhort all that were brought up in the Church, to continue therein. Set the example yourself; and immediately change every plan that would hinder their being at church at least two Sundays in four. Carefully avoid whatever has a tendency to separate men from the Church; and let all the servants in our preaching houses go to church once on Sunday at least. [READ THE RULES OF THE SOCIETY, WITH THE AID OF YOUR HELPERS, ONCE A YEAR IN EVERY CONGREGATION, AND ONCE A QUARTER IN EVERY SOCIETY.]

The Works of the Reverend John Wesley, A. M., ed. John Emory, 7 volumes (New York: Published by B. Waugh and T. Mason for the Methodist Episcopal Church, 1835), 5: 226–27. See Tigert, *Constitutional History*, Appendix VII, 569–71.

Over time, Wesley gradually integrated these layered meetings into something of a national system (and a template, at least, for colonial Methodists). In effect, Methodism came to be organized and governed through conversational, conferring, or conference-like gatherings. Annual conferences gathered the preachers—in Britain by Wesley's invitation, in America by being made a full member of conference. As conference ended, the preachers would receive their appointment, for Americans the two-, four-, or six-week circuit on which they would serve for the new conference year. The quarterly meeting (and "meeting" rather than conference was Wesley's preferred term) attended to the spiritual and financial affairs of the circuit. In Wesley's day, an "assistant" oversaw its proceedings and preachers and stewards (the financial officers) were expected to attend. Class meetings met weekly. They gathered the Methodist folk by gender and spiritual progress. And each was overseen by a class leader.

Had Wesley known that his movement would generate an American church and later also British churches needing a proper ecclesiology, he might have been well advised to use the word "conference" for each of these levels. In so doing, he would have recognized that each functioned effectively and appropriately when it capitalized upon conversation about matters spiritual, both collective and individual. He actually identified Christian Conference as one of five "instituted" means of grace (along with prayer, searching the Scriptures, the Lord's Supper, and fasting). But he used the phrase "Christian Conference" to mean carrying on conversation graciously and deliberately. Just such caring exchanges were to characterize every level of the Methodist system. Indeed, his "Large" *Minutes* and the first American *Discipline* began with that explicit mandate:

It is desired, That all Things be considered as in the immediate Presence of God:

That every Person speak freely whatever is in his Heart.

Question 1. How may we best improve the Time of our Conferences?

Answer 1. While we are conversing, let us have an especial Care, to set God always before us.

2. In the intermediate Hours, let us redeem all the Time we can for private Exercises:

3. Therein let us give ourselves to Prayer for one another, and for a Blessing on our Labour.[2]

Starting the American *Discipline* in such a seemingly curious manner might have occasioned theological reflection that developed "Christian Conference" formally into an ecclesiology, touching practice and structure at every level. However, that did not happen. Wesley had generated directives, rubrics, structures, and practices, originally to facilitate missional effectiveness within the Church of England, not to frame policy for and elaborate a theology of "church." That presumption would have signaled, if not constituted, a break with the Church of England, the formation of a new ecclesial entity, a schismatic venture. Wesley sought renewal, certainly in his British context. Indeed, the entire system came into being and was designed to reform the Church—the Church of England—and Methodists were explicitly committed not to separate into another church. For Wesley, it would have been duplicitous and destructive to systemize his renewal counsels, practices, and gatherings into a formal ecclesiology. That would have said, "We separate. We are a schismatic British church."

And in 1784, when he and Coke conspired to ready materials for an American church, they were too preoccupied with more practical issues to undertake the theologizing that would have positioned "Christian Conference" in an ecclesiology. Nor was the 1784 Christmas Conference competent or capable of such a task. Practicalities dominated as Asbury's brief account illustrates. Noting that he and Coke "were unanimously elected to the superintendency" and exhibiting his ordination certificate, Asbury reported,

> Twelve elders were elected, and solemnly set apart to serve our societies in the United States, one for Antigua, and two for Nova Scotia. We spent the whole week in conference, debating freely, and determining all things by a majority of votes. The Doctor [Coke] preached every day at noon, and some one of the other preachers morning and evening. We were in great haste, and did much business in a little time.[3]

So neither Wesley nor the Americans "theologized" the programmatic structures he put in place into a doctrine of the church. American Methodism inherited organizational features that it, in good Wesleyan fashion, treated pragmatically rather than ecclesiologically.[4] The elders ordained in 1784 and given oversight over circuits and societies became, by later rubric and practice, presiding elders. Their role in circuit quarterly meetings, on paper, remained that scripted by Wesley.

Quarterly-meetings on this Continent
are much attended to

The American circuit, governed itself, as per the Wesleyan template, through quarterly meetings (or quarterly conferences), overseen on the American side (in the MEC) by presiding elders. This office, implicit in the first *Discipline* and regularized by the first General Conference, that of 1792, reassigned inherited roles expected of Wesley's "assistants."[5] Expected at quarterly meeting were the presiding elder, the preachers assigned to the circuit (typically appointed in pairs, a senior and junior), and the lower echelons of Methodist leadership—local preachers, exhorters, stewards, class leaders—who were licensed by the quarterly conference, and accountable to it. At quarterly conferences, the preaching plan for the circuit would be established, assignments for local preachers and exhorters made, and appointments for the traveling preachers confirmed. Money would be collected, appropriately called "quarterage." And quarterly conferences would deal with disciplinary and other issues arising out the classes, the lowest level of conferencing and the membership level.

In its organizational or business functions and mandated attendees, the American quarterly conference differed little from the British model. The latter, borrowed from the Quakers, initially by John Bennett, one of Wesley's preachers, and then regularized by Wesley,[6] looked *inward*. Wesley or his assistant took stock of finances (stewards reporting) and of spirituality (class leaders reporting). It often included other spiritually inward events, as for instance, watch nights and love feasts. The latter service, a simple meal of bread and water, featuring testimony, was to include only members and those exploring that possibility.[7] So Wesley reported for May 4, 1753, "We had the first General Quarterly Meeting of all the stewards around Newcastle, in order thoroughly to understand both the spiritual and temporal state of every society."[8] Though such gatherings would commonly permit public preaching, by design quarterly meetings took the temperature of the Methodists. On two or three occasions Wesley mentioned preaching to crowds the next day or so but those "field" preaching events were not integral to or connected organizationally to the quarterly meetings. "Field preaching" meant going where and when a public might gather or be gathered rather than expecting the crowd to come to a Methodist event. "Multitudes" gathered to hear Wesley on many occasions. He counted crowds of a thousand or more auditors some fifty times. More typically, his journal recorded "multitudes," employing that term roughly a hundred and fifty times, often with a qualifier like huge, countless, great, or large. And sometimes the crowd was hostile or included ruffians bent on causing the Methodists trouble. Such indifferent or troublemaking elements were not welcome to the British quarterly meeting. It was for members. It looked *inward*.

By contrast and by the mid-1770s, American Methodists had made the quarterly meeting an *outward*-looking affair. The Americans turned the quarterly conference from a disciplinary organizational meeting into a two-day, crowd-eliciting occasion. The template, given extensive treatment by Jesse Lee in his *Short History of the Methodists* and cited already,[9] occurred in an area of Virginia served by the Anglican Devereux Jarratt, who found the Methodists a congenial, welcome, and supportive presence. Asbury so noted early in 1776:

> Monday, February 5. Having attended the several appointments in the way, I came to S. Y.'s, and met the preachers collected for the quarterly meeting. With mutual affection and brotherly freedom we discoursed on the things of God, and were well agreed. After Mr. J. had preached, he and Mr. C. administered the Lord's Supper. There was much holy warmth of spirit in our love-feast.

A week later, Asbury reported that Jarratt had agreed to attend the next annual conference.[10] In the summer of 1776, Thomas Rankin, then Wesley's General Assistant for America, joined George Shadford in revival-producing itinerating.[11] Both Rankin and Jarratt wrote Wesley describing the area-wide revival and a two-day quarterly meeting, Jarratt mentioning that it extended over two days, Rankin noting that Jarratt "received us with open arms." Rankin continued, describing the event's artificial grove:

> On Tuesday, 30, was our quarterly meeting. I scarce ever remember such a season. No chapel or preachinghouse in Virginia would have contained one-third of the congregation. Our friends knowing this, had contrived to shade with boughs of trees a space that would contain two or three thousand persons. Under this, wholly screened from the rays of the sun, we held our general love-feast. It began between eight and nine on Wednesday morning, and continued till noon. Many testified that they had "redemption in the blood of Jesus, even the forgiveness of sins." And many were enabled to declare, that it had "cleansed them from all sin." So clear, so full, so strong

was their testimony, that while some were speaking their experience, hundreds were in tears, and others vehemently crying to God
for pardon or holiness.

About eight our watch-night began. Mr. J. preached an excellent
sermon; the rest of the preachers exhorted and prayed with divine
energy. Surely, for the work wrought on these two days, many will
praise God to all eternity.[12]

In its staging and outward orientation, the two-day, crowd-eliciting quarterly meeting began the process of integrating and institutionalizing the
preachers' threefold experience of the American woodland. A brush or
bough arbor might have looked or felt like a pretty crude cathedral, but
other quarterly meetings did take to more sanctuary-like groves. The love
feast, though communal, was theoretically confined to members and those
deemed to be Methodist-compatible or on the way to membership. It featured testimony and included prayer, hymn singing, a collection, and a
simple meal of bread and water. The love feast provided the spiritual
space, emotional intensity, and reflective exercises that had taken preachers into sylvan confessionals. The most spiritually intense and focused
practice of Methodism, it highlighted quarterly meetings.[13] And wilderness? It was partly tamed when arbors were created or a parklike grove
selected for preaching. But, as we will see more dramatically with camp
meetings, the quarterly meetings—in attracting crowds, including many
unconverted persons—achieved a kind of Methodist encounter with worldliness, human wildness, and the "natural man."

"Shall we recommend our quarterly meetings to be held on Saturdays and Sundays when convenient?"

In 1780, the American *Minutes* in its curious Wesleyan question format,
asked "Shall we recommend our quarterly meetings to be held on Saturdays
and Sundays when convenient?" and answered, "Agreed."[14] In the late
1770s, the two-day pattern of quarterly meetings became more widespread
and Virginia Methodists again initiated the innovation of holding them
over a weekend.[15] So positioned in the week, the two days could best attract
a gathering. For a quarterly meeting that year, at Thomas Chapel, Delaware,
Freeborn Garrettson noted: "Blest be God it appeared as if the whole

country came together." He reiterated those words for a quarterly meeting at Bolingbroke. At others that year he estimated crowds of 1,000, 1,500, "between two and three thousand," and "near 4,000." Asbury, who attended the first of these, confirmed Garrettson's statistics, "Our little chapel with galleries, held about seven hundred; but there were I judge near one thousand people."[16]

Neither the *Minutes* nor the preachers in their journals, to the best of my knowledge, journaled the causes of or reasons for making the American quarterly meetings public affairs or for the crowds, in fact, to gather. One can guess. Colonial America had long responded to scheduled revivalistic preaching and especially the dramatically successful, publicity-driven Methodist version thereof, that of George Whitefield. Also, Methodists might well have copied from other religious groups in the areas of Methodist strength—Delaware, Maryland, Virginia—Quakers, Presbyterians, and the several German bodies. Quakers functioned with monthly and quarterly meetings. Presbyterians brought the tradition of revivalistic "sacramental seasons" or sacramental occasions from Scotland, a religious smorgasbord, functioning highly successfully in what has been known as the First Great Awakening.[17] The German religious movements had their own "great meetings."

Furthermore, in the gentry-dominated societies of the upper south and Chesapeake—laced together by waterways and largely wanting the towns that provided communal coherence in old and New England—settlers had become accustomed to gather for special occasions and specific times. Court days, quarter races, cock fights, dances, musters, elections, wharf-side business, and Anglican services occasioned social interaction. Community occurred. Happened. Came and went. Action or event rather than space defined the social, economic, political, and religious orders. Yet another scheduled happening, the quarterly meeting, fit well into established patterns of community and community building.

A number of the event-ceremonies popular in the south and the Chesapeake region exhibited and reinforced the values and preoccupations of the gentry. Such ritualized, patriarchal community—the established religion of southern society, it has been suggested—demanded deference rather than prayers. And even prayers could not escape the gentry's embrace, control of vestries, and endeavor to make the colonial Church of England sacralize class. Methodism challenged this patriarchy, its disciplines proscribing genteel practices and customs—finery, cards, dances, gambling, overindulgence, tobacco, distilled alcohol. Members of the gentry, incensed over the affront, sometimes threatened, and occasionally roughed up Methodist preachers. Beverly Allen, drawing crowds in North Carolina and Virginia in 1781, reported that

> The old, the young, the rich, the poor, were bowing to the name of Jesus. The fine, the gay, threw off their ruffles, their rings, their earrings, their powder, their feathers. Opposition indeed there was, for the devil would not be still. My life was threatened, but my friends were abundantly more in number than my enemies. Some gentlemen of the greatest abilities opposed, but God did truly make the weak to confound the strong, and the foolish to confound the wise, &c. For every mouth was soon almost stopped, and some of my enemies became my friends.[18]

Freeborn Garrettson, a traitor to his class, recorded a number of such frightening episodes.[*]

The Methodist quarterly meetings, in both their internal proceedings and public events, proved especially powerful demonstrations of Methodism's repudiation of genteel patriarchy. The assistants (and, in the new Methodist Episcopal Church, the presiding elders) presiding at the inward-oriented disciplinary quarterly meetings proceedings were charged, "Vigorously, but calmly, enforce the rules concerning needless ornaments, drams, snuff,

---

[*] Ezekiel Cooper noted persecution of Jonathan Forrest and William Wren in and around Annapolis and then gave a litany of wartime persecution of Methodists:

> "In Prince George's county, P. G., a preacher, was, by a mob, shamefully maltreated; 'honored,' according to the cant of the times, 'with tar and feathers.' In Queen-Annes, Joseph Hartley, was bound over, in penal bonds, of five hundred pounds, not to preach in the county; Thomas Segar, yet living, was one of his sureties.—In the same county, Freeborn Garrettson, was beaten with a stick, by one of the county Judges, and pursued, on horse back, till he fell from his horse, and was nearly killed.—In Talbott county, Joseph Hartley, was whipped, by a young lawyer, and was imprisoned a considerable time. He used to preach, during his confinement, through the grates, or window, of the jail, to large concourses of people, who, on Sabbath days, used to attend to hear the prisoner preach.... In Dorchester, Caleb Pedicord, was whipped, and badly hurt, upon the public road; he carried his scars down to the grave.—In the same county, brother Garrettson, was committed to jail. In Caroline, a preacher (T. C.) was taken up in a lawless manner, and put into the custody of the sheriff, to be taken to jail [but discharged]... In the same county, Joseph Foster, the father of Thomas Foster... was brought before the court, arraigned at the bar, and thrown into troubles, expenses, and costs."

Ezekiel Cooper, *The Substance of a Funeral Discourse... on the Death of the Rev. Francis Asbury* (Philadelphia, 1819), 86–88.

and tobacco. Give no band ticket to any man or woman who does not promise to leave them off."[19] These Wesley directives had more bite in the gentry-dominated upper South than they did in the more graded British class structure. In Britain, Methodist discipline and social critique confronted a complex class order—merchants, new industrialists, and layers of nobility—not the gentry alone. By contrast, in the largely rural, agrarian upper South and Chesapeake region, Methodist disciplinary codes seemed to single out a single dominant class, the gentry. The public services of quarterly meetings equally dramatized a countercultural response to genteel ceremony. They did so by example, welcoming all, including slaves to the event. And they did so by precept, proclaiming through the Wesleyan doctrines of universal atonement, liberty, antislavery, and free will that all—rich and poor, male and female, white and black—are children of God.[20] The welcome, affirmation, and acceptance that slaves, lower and middling class whites, and women heard at quarterly meetings doubtless had much to do with the events' popularity. Hearing a freeing and enabling message, they came.

Another factor in the appeal of quarterly meetings, perhaps, had to do with the fact that it gathered preachers. These young men had one proven talent. They could preach and at every opportunity did. A meeting that brought together a number of preachers—exhorters, local preachers, traveling preachers, presiding elders—could then produce multiple sermons if many of their number were given a chance to speak. Clearly that happened. Taking advantage of the occasion for a preaching festival doubtless had something to do with America's sparse population and distances. At some point, the circuit size in thinly populated colonial America, time needed for travel, and opportunity to make the event evangelistically useful led to two-day quarterly meetings featuring much preaching and an array of services. And once quarterly meeting had become patterned as a preaching festival, it could and did attract numbers.

A great concourse of people attended the ministry of the word

So Asbury reported for an April 1779 quarterly meeting. For August 1780, he recorded:

> *Saturday,* 5. Our quarterly meeting began at Henley's preaching-house. I preached on Coloss. i, 27-29, then brother Bailey, Ivey, and Morris spoke, there was some reviving among the people. We lodged at John

Lee's—my mind was much drawn out; we retired to an old log-shop, and prayed frequently, and found our hearts sweetly united together.

Sunday, 6. We had a great meeting, love-feast at ten—very warm weather; a log-house, covered with long shingles; the sun beating through. At one o'clock preaching began, I spoke on Eph. iii, 16-18, to about five hundred people; was blest, and the word went with power. Some were moved, some hardened, yet I hope good was done and the work will revive.[21]

As Asbury's account perhaps implies, the first day typically included the business portion of quarterly conference—preaching assignments (appointments), collections, licensing, disciplinary matters—but included some preaching. The second day featured early morning love feasts (held separately for African Americans and whites), preaching, the Lord's Supper (after 1784 when Methodists were ordained or earlier with Anglicans celebrating), more preaching, and other services (baptism, wedding, or memorial) as needed.[22] Asbury recounted going to a late fall 1780 quarterly conference at Barratt's Chapel with a cooperative Anglican priest, Samuel Magaw, but without indicating whether Magaw celebrated Communion.* Ezekiel Cooper rode through eight inches of snow toward a February quarterly meeting, the weather perhaps explaining why no baptisms were sought in an otherwise colorful occasion:

Sunday, 11. Meeting began about eleven o'clock. The Rev. Mr. Whatcoat preached, and administered the sacrament, after which Mr. Benjamin

---

* JLFA 1: 386–87 for November 3–6, 1780:

"While tarrying after dinner, Dr. Magaw came in. I went home with the Doctor, and was kindly received. The Doctor's intentions were not to go to the quarterly meeting; but having this opportunity, I went and took him along. It was one o'clock before we arrived; about three hundred people had been waiting for us. Mr. Magaw preached an excellent sermon on "Who shall ascend the hill of the Lord?" Brothers Hartley and Glendenning exhorted. We all stayed at Mr. Barratt's; Mr. Magaw prayed with much affection: we parted in great love.

"*Sunday*, 5. We had between one and two thousand people; our house forty-two by forty-eight, was crowded above and below, and numbers remained outside: our love feast lasted about two hours; some spoke of the sanctifying grace of God. I preached on John iii, 16-18; a heavy house to preach in: brother Pedicord and Cromwell exhorted.

"*Monday*, 6. I preached to about four hundred people on 2 Chron. viii, 18, and had liberty: I spoke of the necessity of getting and keeping the power of religion: William Glendenning exhorted afterward; then we parted.

Abbott preached. Of all times, under preaching or prayer, I was now most plagued with laughter to hear the old man so queer in many expressions concerning the sinners. He may properly be called a son of thunder. We, the preachers, lodged at Mr. Dilks's.

Monday, 12. Love-feast began at nine o'clock. The Lord was with us indeed in a very powerful manner. I have not seen such a day for a long time. At eleven o'clock public service began, at which time a corpse was brought into the preaching-house, the sight of which called aloud, "Be ye also ready." After Mr. Sparks and Mr. Whatcoat were done speaking the corpse was interred. Then two young people were joined in wedlock. I think the most solemn wedding I ever saw. Some are dying, others marrying, but soon we shall all be laid in the silent grave. A little after, I preached; then brother Brush concluded the meeting. I have not a doubt but that many dear souls were much profited by the services.[23]

Like Asbury, Freeborn Garrettson provided countless accounts of crowd-gathering quarterly meetings, as for instance this one for a Dover meeting of May 1783:

Saturday 17. Quarterly Meeting began at (Thomas) W(hite's).

Sunday 18. Was a very high day to many souls. I do not think there were less than two thousand souls. After the house was filled, three of the preachers took the remainder of the people in the woods. Two of my brethren spoke in the house before me. Just as I began, they were dismissed in the woods, so that I had the whole congregation. I was obliged to speak so loud in order for all to hear, I got somewhat hoarse, but glory to God; it was a sweet time to me and many others.[24]

Ezekiel Cooper also recorded instance after instance of huge quarterly conferences. The following report, for May 1785, mentions the roles of African American Harry Hosier, a highly accomplished and much-loved black preacher, and of bishop-to-be Richard Whatcoat:

Sunday, May 15. Our quarterly meeting began. We had, I do expect, three thousand souls present. We held it at Dudley's Brick Preaching-house. The house was very large, but would not hold all the people.

Some gathered under the trees, and so we had preaching in both places.

Monday, 16. Love-feast began at nine o'clock; the house was almost full of members of society. Then preaching, in and out of doors, began at twelve o'clock. Brother Whatcoat preached within, Brother Cloud outside. George Moore gave an exhortation in, and Harry, a black man, exhorted without. It was a good time.[25]

Worship in the forest permitted biracial congregations, though not always black and white preachers. (The end of this chapter treats Methodism's biracial appeal, its limitations, and the important place of sylvan settings in sustaining biracial gatherings.)

[N]ot less than two hundred were converted during the sitting of our conference

So reported Richard Whatcoat for the General Conference of 1800. He recorded:

At our General Conference, held at Baltimore, in Maryland, May the 6th, 1800, I was elected and ordained to the episcopal office. We had a most blessed time and much preaching, fervent prayers, and strong exhortations through the city, while the high praises of a gracious God reverberated from street to street, and from house to house, which greatly alarmed the citizens. It was thought that not less than two hundred were converted during the sitting of our conference.[*]

---

[*] Whatcoat continued,

"On the 1st of June we held a conference at Duck Creek Cross Roads, in the state of Delaware. This was a glorious time; such a spirit of faith, prayer, and zeal, rested on the preachers and people, that I think it exceeded any thing of the kind I ever saw before. O, the strong cries, groans, and agonies of the mourners! enough to pierce the hardest heart; but when the Deliverer set their souls at liberty, their ecstasies of joy were inexpressibly great, so that the high praises of the Redeemer's name sounded through the town, until solemnity appeared on every countenance: the effect of which was, that on the Thursday following, one hundred and fifteen person joined the society in that town, while the divine flame spread greatly through the adjacent societies. We visited our societies, and passed on through Philadelphia.

Our conference began at New-York the 19th of June, 1800, and closed the 23d; a few souls were converted.

Conferences—quarterly meetings, annual conferences, even this general conference—became revivalistic occasions, as this last and the above reports indicate. A revival, after all, prospers with crowds, just what the warm weather conferences, especially the quarterly meetings produced. Indeed, one might argue that crowds constitute one of the prerequisites for popular or general revivals.[26] Such a tight connection of revival to conference must have seemed obvious to Jesse Lee. He conceived his *Short History of the Methodists* as a story of revivals and so told of one quarterly conference after another, punctuated by the occasional revival carried by an annual conference. So for 1787, Lee attributed to quarterly meetings a considerable revival in the same area in southern Virginia on which he had reported ten years prior:

> At one quarterly meeting held at Mabry's chapel in Brunswick circuit, on the 25th and 26th of July, the power of God was among the people in an extraordinary manner: some hundreds were awakened;...one hundred souls were converted....Some thousands of people attended....

> The next quarterly-meeting was held at *Jones's* chapel in *Sussex* country, on Saturday and Sunday the 27th and 28th of July. This meeting was favoured with more of the divine presence than any other that had been known before....

> Soon after this, some of the same preachers who had been at the quarterly-meetings mentioned above, held a meeting at Mr. F. Bonners, ten miles from *Petersburg*, where a large concourse of people assembled; and the Lord wrought wonders among them on that day. As many as fifty persons professed to get converted....

> They had another meeting at *Jones-Hole* church; about twelve miles from *Petersburg*, and many people assembled...On that day many souls were brought into the liberty of God's children.[27]

In Jesse Lee's narrative, Methodism transitioned from quarterly to camp meetings naturally and seamlessly. Writing of the year 1801, he observed, "About this time CAMP MEETINGS were first introduced." As Lee

---

P. P. Sandford, *Memoirs of Mr. Wesley's Missionaries to America* (New York: G. Lane & P. P. Sandford for the Methodist Episcopal Church, 1843), 372–73. There is also a very thorough discussion in *Those Incredible Methodists. A History of the Baltimore Conference of the United Methodist Church*, ed. Gordon Pratt Baker (Baltimore: Commission on Archives and History, the Baltimore Conference, 1972), 88–90. See also on this revival, Lee, *Short History*, 271–73.

explained, the camp meeting evolved out of circumstance, a necessary way of providing accommodations when crowds gathered numbering far more than the local homes could bed down. "The ministers," he said, "were obliged to preach in the woods, and some of the people to lodge on the ground in order to be at the meetings the next day."[28]

Methodism had prospered with revivals driven by crowds drawn to multiday meetings. Their little chapels and homes inadequate for the numbers, they had taken to the woods. "Methodists would go forty and fifty miles to quarterly meetings," David Lewis explained. "These were," he insisted, "our great festivals. Here we renewed our covenants with God and his people, obtained encouragement and strength in our souls, and rejoiced together in the salvation of God."[29] The age of miracles having passed and unable to replicate Jesus' ability to feed multitudes with a few loaves and fish, Methodism discovered that camping solved acute feeding and housing challenges.[30]

"What is a Camp Meeting?"

So queried a Methodist defender of the institution in 1810 (apparently the publisher John Totten?):

> It is a body of christians, christian ministers, preachers and exhort-
> ers, assembled in an appointed grove, or some other convenient
> place, where they form a regular encampment, for the express pur-
> pose of spending a few days and nights together, in preaching, ex-
> hortation, hearing the word of life, prayer, praise, and other religious
> exercises; which are allowed by all sects and denominations of
> christians under heaven, to be means of grace, instituted by Christ
> himself, for the promotion of his own kingdom, in the awakening,
> conversion, edification, and sanctification of the souls of men, in
> order to their being prepared for heaven, as well as for usefulness
> in this life: and none dispute their natural tendency thereto, who
> believe the divinity of the gospel of Christ Jesus.[31]

Totten's roughly fifty-page defense of camp meetings did not agonize over patent rights. Nor did Lee, who published his *Short History* the same year, worry about camp meeting authorship. Neither of them spilled ink trying to press camp meeting origins back into the eighteenth century and Methodist large-meeting practices. And both recognized camp meetings as having quickly spread over the entire Methodist landscape. Later interpreters would mistakenly construe them as frontier phenomena and argue about who invented camp meetings and when. And virtually all who have treated them, beginning perhaps with Totten, have dealt with the emotionalism and spiritual displays (crying, shouting, jerking, falling) and with the crowds of disorderly or disruptive that congregated around or outside the camps.[32]

Order and organization proved essential in the camp meeting's cathedraling the woods. So Lee illustrated in the "Conclusion" to his *Short History*, describing camp meetings with five points. The first three of these detail the creation of these temporary sylvan cathedrals and serve well for descriptive purposes here:

1. With regard to the laying out the ground: we have two, three, or four acres of land cleared of the under growth, in an oblong square, sufficient to hold as many tents as will be erected. We then have the front of the tents on a line on each side, and at each end. Back of the tents we have a place cleared for the carriages to stand, whether they be waggons, carts, or riding carriages; so that every tent may have the carriage belonging to it in a convenient position. Just back of the carriages we have the horses tied and fed. Before the tents we generally have the fires for cooking, and to help in giving light at night to those who are walking about. But when it is not convenient to have the fire in the front of the tent, it is placed behind it.

2. We have one or two stages erected; if we have two, one is near the one end of the ground, and one other near the opposite end; but both within the lines whereon the tents are fixed. At each stage we have a sufficient number of seats to contain the principal part of the attentive hearers: who are requested to sit according to our form, the women on one side, and the men on the other. The stages are placed at such a distance from each other, that if necessity should require it, we might preach at each stage at the same time. Or in case there should be a great degree of life and power among the people at one stage, we might without interrupting their devotion in singing and praying, withdraw to the other stage and preach to as many as might wish to hear.

3. We have the ground within the tents illuminated at night by candles, which we fix to the stage, the trees, and other places prepared for the purpose. These candles, with the light of the fires, keep the whole ground sufficiently illuminated. On some occasions, I have seen at these

meetings as many as 120 candles burning at the same time. These lights in a dark night, when the evening is calm, add greatly to the solemnity of the meeting.[33]

The undergrowth clearing dealt with one aspect of wilderness, the natural—taming wilderness into cathedral-like shady grove. Lee's fourth point might be seen as treating another wilderness challenge, an enduring or constitutive challenge—that from human threat. So, camp meetings needed a watch of men who walked the camp "all night through" to "prevent disorderly persons" from mischief. Wilderness of spirit, then, of a human rather than botanical character. Shady grove? That was what camp meetings were all about. Lee's fifth rubric covered that. The schedule: meals and the various services—at sunrise, at 10:00, at 3:00, and at "candle light"—a trumpet calling the camp to worship. The trumpet also bid the camp to a dawn confessional or garden experience. After one long blast, "the people in all their tents begin to sing, and then pray, either in their tents, or at the door of them, as is most convenient."[34] Though noting that this signature practice had "never been authorized by the Methodists, either at their general or annual conferences,"[35] Lee made clear by the way he shifted his revival narrative from quarterly to camp meetings, that the latter had become an established feature of the Methodist system.

Methodists, listening to the voice of God, in those evident indications of the Divine will

Camp meetings brought together the three Methodist experiences of the American woodland. They created, for a few days, a cathedral-in-a-grove, a community ordered as clearly around its central tabernacle as in any European city. They permitted garden-like, confessional times during which individuals and families could wrestle with the spiritual challenges that the grove preaching induced. And always they dealt with wilderness— the natural wilderness tamed by clearing the underbrush, the human wilderness of mischief makers and liquor sellers and ruffians constrained by the guards or watch, and the spiritual wilderness faced by those "unconverted" who came, perhaps under the pressure from mother or spouse. Cathedral, confessional, and challenge or shady grove, garden, and wilderness, the camp meeting united what Methodist preachers had long experienced as they reformed the American continent. When Methodists saw the camp meeting they recognized it immediately as theirs. Not only theirs,

but providentially given! So John Totten construed Methodist appropriation of what he conceded had had Presbyterian origins and an ecumenical
first chapter—an appropriation that he compared explicitly to John
Wesley's own providential guidance in adopting essential features of the
Methodist system:

> But the Methodists, listening to the voice of God, in those evident
> indications of the Divine will, by his providential and gracious in-
> troduction of camp-meetings, have ever since, by suitable prepara-
> tions, and regular appointments, continued to pursue the same
> practice; and as the fruit thereof, God has given them a rich harvest
> of souls, whom he has awakened and brought to the saving knowl-
> edge of himself under this institution; and still continues by this
> means to add to their number.[36]

For Totten, as for Wesley and Methodists generally, slain-in-the-spirit body
count evidenced "clear proof" that their wilderness warfare had been divinely guided. Persuaded by the eloquence of his case for the providential
character of Methodist camp meetings, Totten repeated the above sentence word for word, in his third edition of *A Collection of the Most Admired
Hymns and Spiritual Songs, with the Choruses Affixed; as Usually Sung at
Camp-meetings, &c. To Which is Prefixed, a Concise Account of the Rise of
Camp-meetings, And some Observations Relative to the Manner of Conducting
Them.* After the word "Methodists," Totten added "in the different parts of
the United States," so acknowledging that camp meetings had become
connection- or system-wide.[37]

They bring provisions with them, pitch their tents in the woods, and there continue for days

The origins and authorship of camp meetings have been and doubtless
will remain contested, definition itself providing no small part of the unclarity. For our purposes, we can credit Presbyterians with initiation of multi-
denominational encampments in the summers of 1800 and 1801 in the
Cumberland region of Tennessee and Kentucky and most notably at Cane
Ridge, Kentucky. However, Methodists immediately recognized their
value. William McKendree, then presiding elder of the Kentucky district
and later to be bishop, championed them and so informed Bishop Asbury.
Asbury, Ezekiel Cooper, and others communicated the revivalistic import

of camp meetings to Bishop Coke and through the (British) *Methodist Magazine*[38] to the Methodist world, construing them as part of revivals taking place across the continent. Asbury wrote, "By accounts from Cumberland, according to elder M'Kendree, the work goeth on among the Methodists and Presbyterians." Cooper, the Book Agent (Methodism's publisher) and at the communication center of the church, sent Coke two letters in 1801. In the first, he spoke of "a general revival almost throughout the United States" and "a glorious work of God in the western country, among both the Presbyterians and Methodists." In the second, Cooper reiterated the news that the "work of religion goes on in a glorious manner in many parts of the United States." He then informed Coke of "a great and glorious Revival in Tennessee and Kentucky, among both Presbyterians and Methodists, who join in Christian fellowship, and help each other in the blessed work." He continued:

> Some of our Ministers, and some of the Presbyterian Clergy, join as a band of brothers to make war against the kingdom of the Devil; and the fruit of their joint labours is wonderful. Their meetings continue for days together; the people come from far in their wag-gons, &c. to their great meetings: They bring provisions with them, pitch their tents in the woods, and there continue for days, worship-ping the Lord together. The cries of the penitents, the praises of the saints, and the acclamations of the assembled multitude, make the woods ring with melodious sounds.[39]

By his travels, conference to conference, and through extensive correspond-ence, Asbury (and Cooper) knew the Cumberland area camp meetings to be especially effective aspects of revivalistic activity across the Methodist system.

By late 1802, Asbury had turned from observer and reporter to pro-moter. He directed Methodist leadership to establish camp meetings in connection with annual conferences and quarterly conferences. He wrote the presiding elder of the Pittsburgh District:

> The campmeetings are as extraordinary in North and South Carolina, and Georgia, as they have been in Cumberland and Kentucky; hun-dreds have fallen, and many have been soundly converted....

> I wish you would also hold campmeetings; they have never been tried without success. To collect such a number of God's people

together to pray, and the ministers to preach, and the longer they stay, generally, the better—this is field fighting, this is fishing with a large net.

And he wrote George Roberts of the Baltimore Conference:

The campmeetings have been blessed in North and South Carolina, and Georgia. Hundreds have fallen and have felt the power of God. I wish most sincerely that we could have a campmeeting at Duck Creek out in the plain south of the town, and let the people come with their tents, wagons, provision and so on. Let them keep at it night and day, during the conference; that ought to sit in the meeting.

Zachary Myles of Baltimore informed Coke, "Mr. Asbury wrote word to our preachers, to make preparation for the erection of a Camp within two miles of this City, at our next Conference in April."[40] By such instructions, Asbury routinized camp meetings across Methodism, not just in the sparsely settled West but also in the East and at Methodism's very heart, the Baltimore area.[41] By 1810, he was anticipating some six hundred camp meetings.[42]

Our strong lunged men exerted themselves until the whole forest echoed, and all the trees of the woods clapped their hands

So reported Thomas Sargent for an 1804 Baltimore area camp meeting. It culminated in Sabbath services drawing "at the lowest calculation eight thousand souls," led by thirty ministers, and yielding "not less than fifty converted." Sargent conceded, "I am reconciled to camp-meetings fully; but it was what I saw and felt of the great things of God's power that reconciled me."[43] Asbury had instructed his presiding elders to detail "the most pleasing and interesting things of the work of God," intending to publish those in the Methodist magazine or in a book.[44] A revival of the church's second attempt at a serial, the *Methodist Magazine* (1797–98), was not in the cards.[45] Instead, such reports as came in appeared in 1805 in *Extracts of Letters Containing Some Account of the Work of God Since the Year 1800*. The book bore the subtitle "Written by the Preachers and Members of the Methodist Episcopal Church to their Bishops." Arrayed chronologically (roughly), the accounts document the transition from quarterly meetings to camp meetings and camp meeting quarterly conferences.

By 1804, Asbury's respondents, like Sargent, tended to feature the dramatic, so dwelt on camp meeting results, and, like quarterly conference accounts previously and generally, neglected to say much about the business of concurrent quarterly meetings. However, a late 1802 Kentucky report detailed the convergence of quarterly and camp meeting. The respondent, Mark Moore, took note of religious fervor in cooperative Methodist-Presbyterian meetings. "The work was pretty general though the circuit," he observed, "by the time the quarterly meeting commenced," a Friday. "On the day appointed," he continued, "I was on the ground by ten o'clock; the people were then collecting and forming camps." After the Friday services and more services Saturday morning from two stands, Moore noted, "in the afternoon we returned to some distance from the camp, to do the business of quarterly conference, leaving Mr. Canady a Presbyterian minister and several of our preachers to attend the stand." The "blessed effects of this meeting"? By Moore's reckoning: two thousand gathered, some hundred and forty "struck down," an unknown number converted, "shrieks of the distressed," shouts of those "raised from the depths of misery," at night, persons "lying silent as death and their friends wailing round them," and one sinner so joyful in being "delivered from the load of guilt," that "he brake forth in loud songs of praise; he leaped, he shouted free grace, free grace" and generally kept others from sleeping.[46]

Another report from Virginia in late 1804 observed that "the work is principally carried on at our quarterly and camp meetings" though the correspondent, James Ward, worried "that the jirks will check the work." Ward, then presiding elder for the Greenbrier District, listed meetings, covering much of the conference year for his several circuits, intermixing large meetings of various sorts:

Our first quarterly-meeting was in this circuit at Moffit's meeting-house...

The next was at Edward Mitchel's, Bottetourt...

The next big meeting was on Indian Creek, at Bethel...

The next Saturday, quarterly-meeting began for Greenbrier circuit, at Mount

Tabor...

The next was in Old-Town, Alleghany circuit...

The next was a camp-meeting...in Bottentourt circuit

On Saturday, quarterly meeting began for Bottentourt circuit...

The next was a camp-meeting in this circuit, on Lenvill's Creek (nine days)...

Our next was a camp-meeting in Munroe, at Rehoboth, Greenbrier circuit. Here we had brother Jesse Lee with us, who was also with us at Salem quarterly-meeting..."our meeting continued six days, and we calculated on fifty converted."

The next was a camp-meeting at the Big Levils..."some began to jirk, which seemed to stop the progress of the work"...

The next was a quarterly meeting in Pendeton circuit, which lasted three days...

At the next camp-meeting in Bottetourt, on the old ground...[47]

Stith Mead, presiding elder in 1805 for the Richmond District, set out his "camp and other meetings of magnitude" for his five circuits in tabular form. One column gave the dates of such meetings, twenty-three in all, from late March 1804 to April 2, 1805. A second identified the site (community, chapel, or circuit). A third provided a body count, those converted for each meeting, 1,086 total. The last listed the number who joined the church, 538 total.[48]

One of the longer and more richly detailed reports, somewhat out of place in the volume chronologically (dated December 1803) came from Samuel Coate, who served Baltimore that year. Held fifteen miles out of the city "in a grove or forest in a very retired situation, it lasted three days and attracted 1,000 to 1,500 week days" and "about five thousand or upwards on the Sabbath." Coate concluded rhapsodically and reverentially on the camp meeting scene at night:

The appearance of the place at night, was truly solemn, and at the same time romantic. While going to it, along a meandering path through a thick wood, you would hear the preaching, singing, and other exercises, some distance off; but at length, all of a sudden, you would be struck with the sight of a large congregation of people, a whole train of fires around, candles and lanterns hanging to the trees in every direction, and the lofty oaks, with their spreading boughs forming a canopy over your head, and every thing conspiring with the solemnity of the night to make the place truly awful.[49]

Might a first nighttime experience entering a medieval cathedral have elicited comparable awe?

Voted that we have Camp Meeting at our next Qrt

So a May 1811 Smithfield, New York quarterly conference made a decision that had been and would be replicated again and again for much of the nineteenth century.[50] Before and after the Civil War, a Georgia circuit routinely minuted, "The third Quarterly Conference for the Richmond circuit was held at the Richmond Camp ground Sept. 1st 1851"[51] For a while, particularly where accommodations were limited, Methodists situated annual conferences alongside of camp meetings, as per Asbury's 1804 directives. He jotted, for instance, the following for the 1808 Western Conference, meeting in Tennessee.

> *Saturday, October 1.* I began conference. I preached twice on the Sabbath day, and again on Tuesday. Our conference was a camp-meeting, where the preachers ate and slept in tents. We sat six hours a day, stationed eighty-three preachers, and all was peace. On Friday the sacrament was administered, and we hope there were souls converted, and strengthened, and sanctified.

Camp meetings met in connection with the 1810 Philadelphia, New England, and Genesee conferences.[52] And later western conferences, particularly initial ones, would be held in camps, as Jacob Lanius reported for the Missouri Conference in 1832 and 1833 and S. R. Beggs for the first (1840) meeting of Rock River Conference.[53]

More typically, Methodists structured camp meetings in relation not to annual conference but to the staple of local Methodist religious life, quarterly meetings. They had become, as we have noted already, two-day, multifunction, highly liturgical, often crowd-gathering events. Once the camp meeting emerged and had the church's blessing, routinely and for several decades, quarterly conferences across the whole church voted to hold one of their warm-weather sessions as a camp meeting. So Methodists could speak of a "quarterly meeting conference," as did James Finley, who was licensed to preach at one in 1809, or of a "quarterly camp meeting," as did S. R. Beggs, decades later when licensed to preach "at the local conference at a quarterly camp meeting near Salem, Indiana."[54] So Jacob Lanius, serving in Missouri between 1840 and 1841 on the Cape Girardeau District,

Missouri Conference, referred to "quarterly camp meetings." At the end of the conference year, he reported "a harvest to the church and to my own soul. The work of God revived at all the quarterly camp meetings except one, held on Greenville circuit. The aggregate of conversions & accessions to church during the last round is near 100 we think."[55] In consequence, preachers spent a considerable portion of their time, particularly in the summer, in going to neighboring (or conducting their own) camp meetings. Lanius, for instance, attended successive camp meetings (in different places) from late July 1836 through to mid-September, breaking then "in order to get to conference in time," only to attend two more thereafter.[56] Peter Cartwright narrated the ministerial chapters of his life story, *Autobiography of Peter Cartwright* and *Fifty Years as a Presiding Elder*, as one camp meeting after another, indicating that he spent his entire summers in camp meetings. He neglected to mention that he did so because of his office. As presiding elder he was obliged to preside at the quarterly meeting/camp meetings for his circuits.[57] Typically, he and others attended those of other presiding elders as well.

Cartwright's colorful stories of faith and fisticuffs have imaged camp meeting as a western affair and all but totally obscured their relation to quarterly conferences. The business portion, when the camp meeting "housed" a quarterly meeting, did not make for good yarns and/or was privileged. Nor did the eastern camp meetings yield the drama that some of those in the west elicited. Camp meetings, however, blossomed as much in the east, where they served to put increasingly urbanized Methodism in touch with its fervid past as in the frontier where they served well to command the attention and to create the community around the Methodist message and program requisite for individual transformation and corporate formation.[58] As Nathan Bangs reported, speaking of 1807, "In the older states the camp meetings were multiplied, and attended with the most happy consequences, particularly in Maryland, Delaware, Virginia, and Georgia."[59]

Their successful introduction in the east was welcomed and celebrated by Bishop Asbury, and especially by those from Methodism's heartland, Delaware, where William Chandler served as presiding elder:

Some of my northern letters have come in: they bring good news; camp-meetings at Albany, New-York; at Lebanon, Vermont; in the New-Hampshire districts; all successful. But O, the wonders of Doctor Chandler's report! He says his authority bids him say, that at Duck Creek camp-meeting five hundred souls; at Accomack camp-meeting four hundred; at Annamessex chapel, in the woods, two hundred; at Somerset, Line chapel, one hundred and twenty; at Todd's chapel, Dorset, two hundred; at Caroline quarterly meeting, seventy-five; all, all these profess to have received converting grace![60]

This Asbury entry and perhaps the letter as well did not break out the attendees and conversions by race, perhaps fittingly. Camp meetings—combining physical aspects of wilderness, grove, and garden, staging events in manners suitable to those patterns of Methodist experience, and locating whites and blacks physically accordingly—sustained Methodism's efforts to evangelize both races even as the church came to terms with an increasingly racialized society.

What Methods can we take to extirpate Slavery?

So Methodism's first *Discipline* (of 1785) posed the commitment that signaled its resolve to be a biracial church.[61] It answered:

> We are deeply conscious of the Impropriety of making new Terms of Communion for a religious Society already established, excepting on the most pressing Occasion: and such we esteem the Practice of holding our Fellow-Creatures in Slavery. We view it as contrary to the Golden Law of God on which hang all Law and the Prophets, and the unalienable Rights of Mankind, as well as every Principle of the Revolution, to hold in the deepest Debasement, in a more abject Slavery than is perhaps to be found in any Part of the World except America, so many Souls that are all capable of the Image of God.
>
> We therefore think it our most bounden Duty, to take immediately some effectual Method to extirpate this Abomination from among us: And for that Purpose we add the following to the Rules of our Society:

Then followed a five-stage program for manumitting slaves (to be freed at birth or by their reaching specified ages), for record-keeping by preachers of members' slave-holding and commitments to manumission, and for excommunication of the recalcitrant. To be sure, Methodism qualified the radical resolve by deeming the rules "to affect the Members of our Society no further than as they are consistent with the Laws of the States in which they reside" and by giving Virginians two years "to consider the Expedience of Compliance or Non-Compliance with these Rules."[62]

Such qualifications would gradually erode Methodism's abolitionist resolve and eventuate in the 1844 split that yielded a church for the slave
states, the Methodist Episcopal Church, South. But despite the drift from
the 1785 commitment, many white Methodists, particularly in Maryland
and Delaware, chose to free their slaves.[63] Methodist preachers continued
to preach liberty, to invite African Americans into membership, and to
identify and travel with black preachers. The egalitarian commitments of
early Methodism, truly remarkable for their time, should not be obscured
either by their incompleteness or by the church's steady march into racialized patterns.

Illustrative of Methodism's biracial nature and practices were the travels
and experience of William Colbert. A few excerpts should indicate that
Methodism sustained its biracial ministry, at least in part, by resorting to
the outdoors and to the forest, first in quarterly conferences, later in camp
meetings. For a May 1801 quarterly meeting, Colbert noted a number of
conversions and that "12 whites & 15 or 16 blacks joind." In a July quarterly
meeting in Salisbury, Colbert reported preachers participating included
[Thomas] Ware, [Edward] Larkins, Milbourne, and Addison, as well as himself: "Sunday 19 This morning the black peoples Love-feast was held and
after theirs the white peoples—it was a blessed time in both Love-feasts.
Brother Ware preached in the woods... Brothers Larkins, and Milbourne
Exhorted." For [Sept.]. he noted, "Friday 11...At night met a black class,
joind 12 in society and maried a black man and woman." For another quarterly meeting on Sunday the 20th he reported much of it "under the beautiful trees...at Bowen Meetinghouse." The Lord's supper was apparently in
the house. In the evening Boehm spoke, "after which I administer'd the
sacrament to a large number of black people and a glorious time we had
with blacks and whites. I have join'd 6 whites and 1 black to day." October
3rd and 4th for the Somerset quarterly meeting, he noted, "Sunday 4 This
morning the house was crouded with white friends I was sorry there was
no room for the poor blacks. We had a good Love-feast. The people spoke
well, after which I preachd to a large congregation under the trees." For a
later quarterly meeting, again at Bowen's Meetinghouse, attended by Ware,
Larkins, Ryan, [Henry] Boehm, as well as Colbert, the latter noted:

Sat. "At night we had a glorious Love-feast among the blacks.

Sunday 14 Brothers Ware, Larkins and Ryan preached to as many as
the house would hold, and Bro. Boehm and myself took the Black

people in the woods. I preached ... Brother Boehm gave an exhortation: and indeed we had a great time, many tears were shed and many joyful shouts were heard. We left them shouting the praise of God, and went to the Meetinghouse.... we then administered the sacrament and held a Love feast, and a glorious time we had. It is not according custom to hold Love-feast after preaching but I believe it would be best on many accounts."*

---

* A Journal of the Travels of William Colbert, Methodist Preacher: thro' parts of Maryland, Pennsylvania, New York, Delaware and Virginia in 1790 to 1838, 10 vols., Typescript 4: 15, 25, 34, 35, 37, 68.

Between 1804 and 1805, Colbert served as presiding elder on the Chesapeake District (Philadelphia Conference) and in that office attended its quarterly meetings. Some excerpts from his journal attest his continuing efforts to build a biracial church:

Sunday 5 [August 1804, Brick Meetinghouse, Kent?] This morning we had a joyful time with the Black people in their Love-feast. Many of them spoke the wisdom from above. After them we had an excellent time with the white people at their Love-

feast which we closed with the sacrament....

Centerville Queen Anns circuit

Saturday 18 ... [night] The black people were carried away in extacies.

Sunday 19 O the glories of the black and white Lovefeast this morning....

Saturday 25 Began our Quarterly meeting in Chestertown ... [night] Here the blacks made a great deal of noise.

Sunday 26 This morning we had a very large number of Black people in the Lovefeast, who were so very noisy that I had to cease speaking in prayer I suppose before I had spoken one minute ... a joyful season it was, which was succeeded by the white peoples Lovefeast which was a time of refreshing from the presence of the Lord.... I have finished my first round on the district, and to God be all the glory ascribed good times I have had.

Centerville 19 [January 1805] Thos. Smith preached ... Henry Hosure [Harry Hosier] a black man spoke after him with life and power, and after him I felt freedom in speaking for about ten minutes.

20 Tho' the weather has been very unpleasant,—cold, and dreary we had a joyful season this morning in the Love-feast: both whites and blacks spoke with the wisdom from above and animation. After the Love feast, I preached ... and after me George Moore preached ... We dined at Joshua Kennards and at night Henry Hosure a black man; commonly call Black Harry gave us an excellent discourse from Rev. 3d ch. 20th v. This is not a man made preacher. It is really surprising to hear a man that cannot read, preach like this man. I gave an exhortation after him, and returned to Joshua Kennnards.

Chester Quarterly Meeting

26 ... At night I heard Henry Hosure a black man preach with life from Eph. 5 ch 8v. I sang and prayed after him ...

27 ... In the afternoon Our black friend Henry Hosure preached from Matt. 6 ch 20th he spoke with life and power. I spent the evening in singing a while at my good friend McKennies who is a merchant, and a rich respectable man, but not of so

Early Methodism was biracial but hardly free from racism—unable to see its way to fully credentialing the Richard Allens and Harry Hosiers, segregating its meetings when gathering both races, and subjecting African American congregations and classes to white oversight. Facing such discriminatory patterns, Richard Allen had already pulled out of St. George's and set in motion the dynamics that would yield the African Methodist Episcopal Church. But if Methodism's biracial policy and practice were far from ideal, it endeavored to live into its own preachments of universal atonement. And even as it came to terms with slavery, Methodist preachers sought freedom in the spirit, if not in the flesh, and outdoors if not indoors. Indeed, the outdoors of quarterly or camp meetings—where black and white mingled every day—singing, praying, testifying, exhorting, and preaching continued to dramatize Methodism's biracial commitments long after segregation had become normative indoors. Richard Bassett wrote the Methodist bishops to report on just such a biracial event, indoors and out.

Dover, June 15th, 1802.

OUR annual meeting commenced on Friday evening, the 5th inst; being the evening before the time intended. At candlelight our house

---

narrow a soul as to think a black man not good enough to sit by his fire, and at his table. I was very much affected at some of part of the experience of Henry Hosure, which he in private conversation related...

[Chester circuit February]

Wednesday 6 We were invited to dine at Thomas Battens, where we spent the afternoon, and at night heard Henry Hosure a black friend preach from Isaiah 3 ch 10 v. The people were affected. I spoke after him, and conclude the Meeting. We lodged at James Batten.

Thursday 7 We had a disagreeable ride from James Battens to Wm. Hunters, where Henry Hosure preachd again for us from Heb. 4 ch 11th v. I gave an exhortation after him. William Ross prayed and concluded the meeting...

Friday 15...At night attended a Black & white Lovefeast at Zoer [Zoar, Philadelphia, Hosier the founding preacher]. The congregation was of various colours, and the speaking very extraordinary....

Monday 18 at night we held a Love feast in Bethel [Philadelphia, Richard Allen's congregation]. The house was crouded, and many spoke with life and power.

Tuesday 19...Preached at St. Georges...Henry Hosure a black man gave a powerful exhortation after me...

Tuesday 26 This afternoon I started with Alward White and Henry Hosure, a black preacher from Wilmington for Baltimore. We din'd at Newport...

A Journal of the Travels of William Colbert, Typescript 5: 35, 39, 41, 63, 65, 27, 68, 69, 75.

was filled, and the word of God began to be dispensed. It was a solemn time among the people professing godliness. Prayer meeting next morning at sunrise, a large meeting; and a gracious time, many of God's people were filled with his goodness.... Sunday morning at sun-rise the black people's love-feast began, and a precious time it was amongst them; a vast body of them were collected, and their conduct was unexceptionable; God verily is no respecter of persons.

Love-feast for the whites, commenced at half past eight o'clock, and our holy and good God was in the midst of us;... the congregations this day had they been numbered were seven thousand souls.... On Tuesday after preaching, the sacrament was administered: this was the most gracious, solemn, and rejoicing time I ever saw. I conclude there were not less than between twelve and fifteen hundred came to the Lord's table, white and coloured people. In this exercise many sinners were cut to the heart, and powerful convictions took place; most of which I believe ended in sound conversions; and many backsliders were reclaimed. Oh! the astonishing goodness of the all-wonder-working God.[64]

James Jenkin wrote the bishops two years later, naming the several outdoors, biracial extravaganzas "camp meetings." He gloried that "All Souls were made Subjects of the work, male and female, whites and blacks, rich and poor." (He also noted that camp meetings do not escape terrible racist events.)

Wilmington, North Carolina, October 18th, 1804....

The last camp-meeting is just over last Monday, in Bladen circuit, by brother Gauteer's: ten preachers, and about Sixteen hundred people. This exceeded all that I ever saw. The work broke out the first day, and increased rapidly until we left the ground. The Lord rode forth, conquering and to conquer. The devil's kingdom fell like lightning to the ground.... All Souls were made Subjects of the work, male and female, whites and blacks, rich and poor. From the hoary-headed Sinner, to children of nine years old, were the subjects of this blessed work. Many Sinners had to fly from the ground or fall under the power of God. One Sinner that had been burning the negroes that were down, at last fell himself, and never rose till he was happy in God. We suppose that there were three or four hundred christians. About twelve hundred sinners, and out of twelve hundred, one hundred found the Lord.[65]

The expressive emotional, physical, and rhetorical responses that camp meetings elicited, especially among African Americans, have led some historians to argue for African origins or an important African dimension to camp meeting spirituality and to the similar highly emotional patterns generalized from camp meetings into popular American revivalism.[66] Assessing that argument lies beyond the concern of this study. Suffice it to say here that the openness of worship under the trees and the space configured behind the preachers' stand for African Americans kept alive, albeit in segregated fashion, the biracial signature of early Methodism. Indeed, the considerable "black" space in camp meetings permitted them more opportunity for independent and expressive religious actions, far more so than other worship occasions, including even the earlier large, outdoor quarterly conferences. Hence, the notice given to the expressive modalities of African American spirituality, including especially the ring shout.[67]

Indeed, Cynthia Lyerly finds in camp meetings one of several attractions that Methodism held for slaves. Methodists services generally, but camp meetings especially, allowed slaves to "meet relatives and friends from neighboring plantations, find spouses and spread family and neighborhood news." Too, such inclusive gatherings registered an implicit theological or spiritual judgment on slavery itself, conveying in dramatic form that African Americans (also) belonged in the kingdom of God. And third, she suggests, implicitly in camp meetings as well as in evangelism of slaves generally lay a judgment on "the values of a slaveholding society" and a proclamation of Christian "virtues of the weak and powerless."[68]

Even where slavery stamped religious separation most starkly—as in the Methodist Episcopal Church, South—the slaveholders made space for African Americans at camp meetings. Indeed, at its first general conference, that of 1846, the MECS in a ten-point program for ministry with "the people of colour" dictated: "At our camp-meetings let such accommodations be furnished at the back of the stand, or pulpit, as shall be convenient for the holding of prayer-meetings among the coloured people, as is usual with the whites, in front of the stand."[69] So Charles Johnson observed. "Most of the slave owners were of the opinion that religious instruction would keep their workers servile and obedient. And as for the bondsmen, there was no question of their love for camp meetings."[70] A northern Methodist, an observer and critic of slavery, provided a contemporary judgment to that effect:

Camp-meetings in the South are held almost exclusively by the Methodist churches. The primary design of these meetings was the glory of God and the salvation of souls. They are generally held in the summer time—in some central position, on an elevated spot, shaded with beautiful oak and hickory trees, and where water can easily be obtained....

Behind the pulpit, and separated by a board fence, is the place allotted for the colored people, who labor under the disadvantage of not catching the inspiration which darts from the eye of an earnest orator, or beams from a countenance irradiated by heavenly enthusiasm....

But by no class is a camp-meeting hailed with more unmixed delight than by the poor slaves. It comes at a season of the year when they most need rest. It gives them all the advantages of an ordinary holiday, without its accompaniments of drunkenness and profanity. Here they get to see their mothers, their brothers, and their sisters from neighboring plantations; here they can sing and jump to their hearts' content.

When properly conducted, more can be said in favor of camp-meetings than against them. I have witnessed scenes at these meetings, morally grand and sublime—scenes which can never be blotted from my memory. Campfires blazing in every direction with heart pine wood; the groans and the sobs of penitent sinners; the shout and the rapture of the new convert; the rejoicing of friends; the deep, melodious, organ-like music welling from a thousand African throats—all conspired to elevate the soul to Christ, "who sitteth at the right hand of the Father."[71]

[D]eep, melodious, organ-like music welling from a thousand African throats

Northern Methodism—though its support for the Civil War and its efforts at interracial ministry immediately thereafter might appear to have been of a different character—had long made the camp meeting a study in segregation and racism. Perhaps, ministry across racial lines, in that day, appeared to be of necessity a ministry out-of-doors and under the trees. So Jacob Lanius of the Missouri Conference explained in an April 1834 journal entry:

I have recently determined to pay more attention to our slave population than I have hitherto done. Great and mighty are the efforts now being made for the salvation of the world. Missionaries are now going to almost every part of the world, some to Africa and the various islands of the earth and others to the natives of the far west, and yet others to the negroes of the south engaged in making sugar, but nothing is done for the slaves on our Circuit. If they attend our regular appointment for the whites the houses are so small that they are compelled to remain out doors, and receive little or no benefit from the preaching, and again if a man preaches in acceptable style to the whites the slaves cannot understand him. It really seems to me that as Christ died for them as well as for us they ought to be attended too. And I variable believe that I shall be as amply rewarded for being instrumental in converting a poor son of Africa as for the salvation of a crowd of Europeans. In executing my determination I expect to receive the reproach of the proud and haughty white man, but I want to save souls, as well the black as the white. After preaching three hours and quarter on baptism during the day at night I preached the funeral of 2 black men to the negroes we had a good time. The crowd was praising God. Three negroes joined the church. This encouraged me to follow my resolution.[72]

A camp meeting, including but segregating African Americans, was reported for 1842 in Maryland, with about five hundred whites and about the same number "colored," one third of them perhaps free. The two races tented and worshiped in a circle, one half white, the other black, with "a sort of pole fence that divided the grounds of the blacks and the whites at preaching hours." The whites, the white Methodist indicated, "would sometimes mingle with the blacks at their prayer-meetings; the blacks were the life of camp-meeting," their singing especially so. "The meeting grew better and better, and the last night I was bathing and swimming in the ocean of love. It was a Pentecost to me and many others. There was little or no sleeping in the camp that night." About 3:00 am the blacks were marching about "singing a farewell hymn" and "they were joined in song (not in procession) by the whites, which made the welkin ring."[73]

As a personal aside, I might mention that in the twenty-first century I attended one of the five camp meetings held annually near Charleston, South Carolina. Three white, two black, they sustain the racial "prejudices" to which Lanius alluded and Henry documented. I should perhaps qualify this judgment by noting that the white camp meeting I observed permitted in a black man to call whites to worship by blowing a six-foot horn, and its cooks, working slavishly on the outer edge of the eight-sided, wooden, two-story, wood-chip or straw floor, nineteenth-century "cabins," were all black. My personal experience, as well as through extensive reading, indicated that camp meetings had proved to be a highly serviceable for American Methodism. They made place for African Americans. In places and at times, as noted above, they gave space, time, and air sufficient for African Americans to exercise a kind of spiritual leadership. But, like everything else in Methodism, camp meetings could not and did not rise above the wilderness of racism.

[N]orthern letters have come in: they bring good news; camp-meetings

Jesse Lee narrated the history of American Methodism as a series of conference and quarterly conference revivals. For the period after 1802, he centered the Methodist story on camp meetings. And as we noted, he concluded his narrative (for 1809) with a short overview of the camp meeting, its staging, rules, layout, rhythms, and order.[74] Camp meetings could be celebrated for their redemptive love and experienced assurance, as did Fanny Lewis for one near Baltimore in 1803.[75] But others reacted negatively to their emotionalism and display (crying, shouting, jerking, falling) and to the crowds of disorderly or disruptive that congregated around or outside. Methodists found it necessary to order them carefully and also to defend them against critics within and without, as did John Totten.[76] The institution needed denominational defense because it had become a regular feature of Methodist religious practice.[77] So Finley, looking back, affirmed, "Much may be said about camp meetings, but, take them all in all, for practical exhibition of religion, for unbounded hospitality to strangers, for unfeigned and fervent spirituality, give me a country camp meeting against the world."[78]

As a mechanism for effective evangelization, ordering and celebrating in frontier settings, camp meetings served well to continue and nationalize Methodism's orientation to extend over, indeed to conquer the continent and its many peoples. And for that continental conquest, it served well to commit to the church's itinerating leadership—bishops, presiding elders, preachers, and exhorters—a sense that nothing constrained them. Indeed, as Dee Andrews notes, "The elevation of circuit riders as a caste apart—and above—their coreligionists began with the camp meeting."[79] However, ironically because of the way in which camp meetings elicited and celebrated the emotional expression of all gathered, they sustained and even enhanced the role of women in evangelistic outreach (a topic to which we return in chapter 4).[80]

To reiterate: Camp meetings brought together the three Methodist experiences of the American woodland. They created, for a few days, a cathedral-in-a-grove, a community ordered as clearly around its central tabernacle as in any European city. They permitted garden-like, confessional times during which individuals and families could wrestle with the spiritual challenges that the grove preaching induced. And always they dealt with wilderness—the natural wilderness tamed by clearing the underbrush, the human wilderness of mischief makers and liquor sellers and ruffians constrained by the guards or watch, the spiritual wilderness faced by those "unconverted," who came, perhaps under the pressure from mother or spouse, and the wilderness they created by bringing black and white together (and later Native Americans as well). If cathedrals to escape the world of sin, the camp meetings nevertheless returned Methodism to fundamental questions about what it meant to be the church, who belonged therein, and under what conditions would all humanity be welcomed.

3

A Church Spread into the Wilderness

March 9th. I have again entered into my romantic way of life. For there is something exceedingly pleasing in preaching daily to large congregations in immense forests. O what pains the people take to hear the gospel! But it is worthy of all pains. 11th. I am now come among the Peach trees: and they are in full bloom. Truly they assist a little, under the Supreme Source of Happiness, to make the heart gay.

It is one of my most delicate entertainments, to embrace every opportunity of ingulphing myself (if I may so express it) in the Woods. I seem then to be detached from every thing but the quiet vegetable Creation, and MY GOD. The Ticks indeed, which are innumerable, are a little troublesome: they burrow in the flesh, and raise pimples, which sometimes are quite alarming, and look like the effects of a very disagreeable disorder. But they are nothing when opposed to my affection for my Lord.

Yea, I'll carve thy passion on the bark:

And every wounded Tree
  Shall drop, and bear some mystic mark
That Jesus died for me.
  The Swains shall wonder, when they read
Inscrib'd on all the Grove,
  That Heaven itself came down and bled
To win a mortal's Love.*

---

* Thomas Coke, *Extracts of the Journals of the Rev. Dr. Coke's Five visits to America* (London, Printed by G. Paramore; and sold by G. Whitfield, 1793), 147. The verse Coke cites from Isaac Watts.

Inscrib'd on all the Grove, That Heaven itself came down and bled To win a mortal's Love

As he traveled through the forest in 1791 from Savannah to Augusta, and to a Georgia conference, Bishop Thomas Coke meditatively brought together the shady-natural-cathedral grove and confessional-garden themes and, perhaps one might say, one aspect of wilderness challenges (ticks):

> "something exceedingly pleasing in preaching daily to large congregations in immense forests" (shady grove),

> "detached from every thing but the quiet vegetable Creation, and MY GOD" (confessional-garden),

> "The Ticks indeed, which are innumerable, are a little troublesome: they burrow in the flesh, and raise pimples, which sometimes are quite alarming, and look like the effects of a very disagreeable disorder" (wilderness).

Coke, the only Methodist laboring in America with formal theological training, provided both in prose and poetically what would have been an absolutely wonderful starting point for woodland-oriented doctrines of creation, soteriology, and ecclesiology.

These doctrines of God's work and corresponding ruminations on God in God's three persons (Father, Son, and Holy Ghost) might well have been extrapolated out of Methodism's encounters with the American forests. How so? Coke's "the quiet vegetable Creation and MY GOD"? Might it point to and encourage Methodist reflection on creation and on God the Creator, on God's providence, on God's rule? And that "every wounded Tree" declared "That Jesus died for me"? When the groves and shady forests gathered folk to hear of their salvation and to learn that Christ claimed them, might the trees or events bear some Christ mark, some reminder of the true cross, some token of their forgiveness from sin, some welcome into his kingdom, and some grounds for a Christology? For Methodists, the grove would speak of the atonement and its universality. The woods would testify that Jesus died for all, for you, for me. And would peach trees "in full bloom" with assistance from "the Supreme Source of Happiness" constitute some sylvan-based operation of the Holy Spirit and motivation to reflect thereon? Might all Methodists, like the preachers, find the solace and also the conviviality of the woods both opportunity for and reflection on the Holy Spirit? So the performances with and indeed the forest itself would attest the Trinity. The several-fold engagement in and with the American woods would enable Methodists to experience and glorify the triune God. And even the ticks might indeed point to "very disagreeable disorder," to the good creation marred by sin and evil and to the needed renewal brought through law and gospel. Implicit in Methodist experience of the American forests lay the potential for profound reflection on God-in-three-persons and on the extraordinary way in which Methodism lived its theology.[1] First, some reflections are given here on doctrinal possibilities or tendencies that American Methodists, with the guidance of Coke and Wesley, might have developed into a full-fledged Trinitarian scheme. Then sections explicitly attend to patterns and emphases that might have yielded formal doctrines of God, Christ, and Holy Spirit.

God's Design, in raising up the Preachers called Methodists

Had Coke committed himself, as had Asbury, to the American movement and stayed to exercise intellectual leadership, the Methodist Episcopal Church might have made early headway in thinking theologically about itself, about the new American society, about the natural order and the world, and about God-in-three-persons. Coke could have drawn on his own experiences of the American forest and on John Wesley's several efforts to elaborate God the Creator and a doctrine of creation to frame a woodland theology for American Methodism (on Wesley's doctrine, see the next section). Coke's extensive publications suggest he would have been capable of such an effort. His writings, some sixty, included brief items (sermons) but also a four-volume *Commentary on the Holy Bible*, *A History of the West Indies* (also in four volumes), the 1798 *Discipline* with its elaborate commentary, a major treatise on justification, and *Four Discourses on the Duties of the Gospel Ministry*.[2] Coke, however, traveled too widely and ambitiously over trans-Atlantic Methodism to devote himself to intellectual leadership of American Methodism. He aspired to lead all of Methodism. Fittingly perhaps, he died endeavoring to spread Methodism across the globe, while on shipboard leading a missionary cohort to India. And long before then, in trying to head Methodism on both sides of the Atlantic and journeying back and forth, Coke frustrated the Americans. To curb any notions he might have had about initiative-taking, the Americans in 1787 rewrote the answer to the question in the *Annual Minutes*, "Who are the superintendents?"— "Thomas Coke (when present in the States), and Francis Asbury."

Before and after Coke appeared on the scene, self-educated Asbury sol-diered on. At places, he made his own efforts to meditate on Methodism and the American woodland. In the 1781 wilderness statement with which chapter 1 concludes, we noted that Asbury brought together the challenging, confessional, and cathedral dimensions of his experience of the American forest. He had recognized that the unseeing eye would find "present appear-ances" to be "gloomy," but looked with his spiritual vision to "a glorious Gospel-day in this and every other part of America." In other places as well, Asbury hinted that the ordeal of the wilderness, the Word preached in arbor or shady wood and sylvan devotional solitude had become one complex spir-itually energizing but challenging reality for himself, for the people called Methodist, and for all who responded to a redemptive Wesleyan message. He was living, if not articulating, a doctrine of God. Writing not from the Alleghenies but from Georgia in November 1799, Asbury observed:

> *Thursday,* 21. We rode sixteen miles, sometimes through the naked woods, to Redwine's; where we had an unexpected congregation in the solitary woods. I held forth on, "The Son of Man is come to seek and to save that which was lost." The house was open, but the peo-ple were simple-hearted, and very kind.[3]

Here, Asbury seemed to theologize, in threefold fashion, his wilderness ride, the solitude that beckoned to prayer, and the congregation in the wood. He did so by preaching that Christ came to save the lost.

Too much the evangelist and too committed to call congregations to conversion and holiness, Asbury did not frequently resort to the outdoor scenes of Old and New Testament, contemporize them, and employ scrip-ture's places and events typologically in his preaching.[4] Asbury lived too much in the present, too much for the future, too much in saving souls, too much for his people, too much committed to bringing in others, to wander in and through the Scriptures away from redemptive texts. Instead, he knew himself and the Methodist preachers to be Spirit-led in his and their wandering over the continent, across the American landscape, and through its wilderness. So traveling—itinerating to preach—prompted his spiritual musings and the occasional threefold reflection. In Tennessee in October 1800, he observed:

> *Thursday, 30.* We rode slowly on to Starr's, twenty-two miles, and had a heavy shower of rain on our way. From Monday morning to

Thursday afternoon we have made one hundred and thirty miles; we have experienced no stoppage by water-courses, and have found the roads of the wilderness, their unevenness excepted, pretty good. And here let me record the gracious dealings of God to my soul in this journey: I have had uncommon peace of mind, and spiritual consolations every day, notwithstanding the long rides I have endured, and the frequent privations of good water and proper food to which I have been subjected; to me the wilderness and the solitary places were made as the garden of God, and as the presence-chambers of the King of kings and Lord of lords.[5]

Asbury had lived by, embodied, actualized the Methodist mission statement:

"What may we reasonably believe to be God's Design, in raising up the Preachers called Methodists?" *Answ.* "To reform the Continent, and spread scripture Holiness over these Lands. As a Proof hereof, we have seen...a great a glorious Work of God."

For almost five decades, across the states, and through the woodlands, Asbury had rode, preached, and prayed—reforming the continent and spreading scripture holiness over the American countryside and through its forests. If ever anyone made wilderness into the garden of God and so made God present, Asbury was the man. And he, along with his fellow itinerants, left hints and clues from their woodland experiences that a colleague, more theologically trained, might have developed into doctrines of creation, redemption, and new creation and into full-fledged Trinitarianism. John Wesley had already provided solid foundations on which they might have built.

The Wisdom of God in the Creation[6]

"The renewal of the creation and the creatures through the renewal in humanity of the *image of God*," affirms Theodore Runyon, "is what Wesley identifies as the very heart of Christianity."[7] A polymath who sought to provide his preachers and people with compilations of the theological and scientific wisdom of the ages, Wesley extracted the best of the spiritual writings in his fifty-volume *Christian Library*[8] and of scientific enquiry in the several volumes of *A Survey of the Wisdom of God in the Creation: or A Compendium of Natural Philosophy*. To doctrines of creation and of the

New Creation, Wesley returns again and again in the *Sermons* that—along with his *Explanatory Notes Upon the New Testament*—functioned as theological lodestones for Methodism. Americans had access to editions of Wesley's *Sermons* essentially from the beginning, Robert Williams having taken it upon himself to function as publisher and had been reprimanded for doing so on his own. His initiative was, however, understandable as then and thereafter the *Sermons* constituted the basic theological text for Wesleyanism. When established as a denomination, the Methodist Episcopal Church set up its own publishing enterprise, the *Sermons* standard fare. And the MEC published its own edition of the *Survey* by the point at which it was developing camp meetings into a program.

Methodism might well have taken Wesley's counsel to meditate upon nature and to have reaped theologically from its engagement with American flora and fauna. So Wesley advised:

> By acquainting ourselves with subjects in natural philosophy, we enter into a kind of association with nature's works, and unite in the general concert of her extensive choir. By thus acquainting, and familiarizing ourselves with the works of nature, we become as it were a member of her family, and participate in her felicities: but while we remain ignorant, we are like strangers and sojourners in a foreign land, unknowing and unknown.

And again:

> By acquainting ourselves with the various subjects in natural philosophy, we disarm nature, as it were, of her terrors, and she assumes a smiling aspect, where superstition bedecked her in frowns: we can behold her inviting where before she appeared forbidding; her horrors are converted into charms, to the mind that can contemplate her in her appropriate characters.[9]

Wesley's confidence in the instructive value of nature rested on an extraordinarily robust doctrine of providence, a theological posture that might have surprised Calvinists familiar with the equally strong Wesleyan attacks on predestination. Indeed, Wesley's statements on God's providence might be taken by the careless reader to be headed in Calvin's direction. For instance, in the sermon "Spiritual Worship," Wesley reflected in providential terms on 1 John 5:20, an affirmation that Christ was both true God and eternal life. He affirmed that Christ was with "God from eternity," "the sole Creator of all things," "also the *Supporter* of all things that he hath made," "likewise the *Preserver* of all things," "the true '*Author* of all' the *motion* that is in the universe," "the *Redeemer* of all the children of men," "the *Governor* of all things," and "the *End* of all things." Wesley extended the providential theme to Christ's office as eternal life. Not only will he be eternal life but he is now, posited Wesley:

> He is now the life of everything that lives in any kind or degree. He is the source of the lowest species of life, that of *vegetables;* as being the source of all the motion on which vegetation depends. He is the fountain of the life of *animals,* the power by which the heart beats, and the circulating juices flow. He is the fountain of all the life which man possesses in common with other animals. And if we distinguish the *rational* from the animal life, he is the source of this also.[10]

Since God's handiwork reflects God's nature and glory, Wesley instructed followers to reflect on the good creation. In "God's Approbation of His Works," Wesley commented on Genesis 1:31:

1. When God created the heavens and the earth and all that is therein, at the conclusion of each day's work it is said, "And God saw that it was good." Whatever was created was good in its kind, suited to the end for which it was designed, adapted to promote the good of the whole and the glory of the great Creator. This sentence it pleased God to pass with regard to each particular creature. But there is a remarkable variation of the expression with regard to all the parts of the universe taken in connexion with each other, and constituting one system: "And God saw everything that he had made; and behold, it was very good!"
2. How small a part of this great work of God is man able to understand! But it is our duty to contemplate what he has wrought, and to understand as much of it as we are able.[11]

Our duty to contemplate what he has wrought

Had the Americans been driven to reflect formally and theologically on their threefold experience of the American forest and a doctrine of God implicit therein, Wesley might have indeed provided guidance. His insistence on the fall with Adam and Eve and the continuing taint of original sin could well have informed American reflection on humanity's persistence in personal, sinful wilderness, absent or before the redemptive experience of prevenient grace, forgiveness of sins, and the new birth (conversion). For Wesley, "The Wilderness State" might betoken as well the post-conversion state of regeneration, a period of self-analysis often beset with doubt and confusion. In the sermon so entitled, Wesley considered that wilderness entails loss of faith, love, "joy in the Holy Ghost," of "that peace which once passed all understanding," and of "power over sin." The inner travail recapitulated for the individual what Israel experienced after the Exodus.

> After God had wrought a great deliverance for Israel by bringing them out of the house of bondage, they did not immediately enter into the land which he had promised to their fathers, but "wandered out of the way in the wilderness," and were variously tempted and distressed. In like manner after God has delivered them that fear him from the bondage of sin and Satan; after they are "justified freely by his grace, through the redemption that is in Jesus," yet not many of them immediately enter into "the rest" which "remaineth for the people of God." The greater part of them wander more or less out of the good way into which he hath brought them. They come as it were into a "waste and howling desert," where they are variously tempted and tormented. And this some, in allusion to the case of the Israelites, have termed "a wilderness state."[12]

And if the Americans did not draw on such explicit treatment of wilderness by Wesley, they certainly would have had much to work with in his continuous meditation on the taint of original sin.

Similarly, Wesley's guidance on the shady grove as site for Methodist preaching of salvation from and forgiveness of sin might have come from his many sermons in one way or another treating prevenient grace, the forgiveness of sins, the new birth, justification, and regeneration. For instance, in "The New Birth," Wesley affirmed:

> If any doctrines within the whole compass of Christianity may be properly termed fundamental they are doubtless these two—the doctrine of justification, and that of the new birth: the former relating to that great work which God does *for us,* in forgiving our sins; the latter to the great work which God does *in us,* in renewing our

fallen nature. In order of time neither of these is before the other. In the moment we are justified by the grace of God through the redemption that is in Jesus we are also "born of the Spirit"; but in order of thinking, as it is termed, justification precedes the new birth. We first conceived his wrath to be turned away, and then his Spirit to work in our hearts.[13]

American Methodists took Wesley's evangelical doctrines to heart, preached them consistently, dwelt on them in their outreach to the unconverted in quarterly and camp meeting settings, and might have done more to theologize their sylvan worship services.

So also, Methodists might have taken counsel on theologizing their retreat to the woods for garden-like prayer, study, and meditation from Wesley's sermons dealing with sanctification, eternal life, the resurrection, and the final judgment; for instance, those on "Christian Perfection," "The General Deliverance," and "The New Creation."[14] Americans certainly sustained Wesley's signature insistence—holiness, perfection, sanctification, perfect love. They might have found interesting his speculation that the final and full restoration promised humanity would extend to "the brute creation." In "The General Deliverance," Wesley conjectured that "All the beast of the field, and all the fowls of the air, were with Adam in paradise. And there is no question but their state was suited to their place: it was paradisiacal, perfectly happy." Adam's fall damaged the entire creation not just humanity:

> As all the blessings of God in paradise flowed through man to the inferior creatures; as man was the great channel of communication between the Creator and the whole brute creation; so when man made himself incapable of transmitting those blessing, that communication was necessarily cut off. The intercourse between God and the inferior creatures being stopped, those blessings could no longer flow in upon them. And then it was that "the creature," every creature, "was subject to vanity," to sorrow, to pain of every kind, to all manner of evils.

Further, Wesley insisted, the restoration (new heavens/new earth) promised in the book of Revelation would extend to the whole creation:

> The whole brute creation will then undoubtedly be restored, not only to the vigour, strength, and swiftness which they had at their

creation, but to a far higher degree of each than they ever enjoyed. They will be restored, not only to that measure of understanding which they had in paradise, but to a degree of it as much higher than that as the understanding of an elephant is beyond that of a worm.

Animals would experience humanlike restoration also for their affections, liberty, and appetites. "No rage will be found in any creature, no fierceness, no cruelty or thirst for blood." So alluding to the vision of Isaiah 11:6-9, Wesley affirmed, "In the new earth, as well as in the new heavens, there will be nothing to give pain, but everything that the wisdom and goodness of God can create to give happiness." Then Wesley speculated,

> May I be permitted to mention here a conjecture concerning the brute creation? What if it should then please the all-wise, the all-gracious Creator, to raise them higher in the scale of beings? What if it should please him, when he makes us "equal to angels," to make them what we are now? Creatures capable of God? Capable of knowing, and loving, and enjoying the Author of their being? If it should be so, ought our eye to be evil because he is good? However this be, he will certainly do what will be most for his own glory.

Such views, Wesley thought, might lead the reader "to imitate him whose mercy is over all his works," counsel well suited to meditation in the woods, physically seated in God's good creation. He continued, urging readers to consider God's future for his animals in "the brute creation":

> They may soften our hearts towards the meaner creatures, knowing that the Lord careth for them. It may enlarge our hearts towards those poor creatures to reflect that, as vile as they appear in our eyes, not one of them is forgotten in the sight of our Father which is in heaven.... Yea, let us habituate ourselves to look forward, beyond this present scene of bondage, to the happy time when they will be delivered therefrom into the liberty of the children of God.[15]

Wesley offered no conjecture here on how the plant world (trees, woods, and forests) might look in the new paradise but certainly it too would have Edenic qualities, making it suitable for praying and giving glory to its Creator.

Further, might Americans have been guided to theologize their mission to reform the continent and reflect on their diverse sylvan experiences by drawing on Wesley's sermon, "On God's Vineyard"?

> The "vineyard of the Lord," taking the word in its widest sense, may include the whole world. All the inhabitants of the earth may in some sense be called "the vineyard of the Lord," who "hath made all nations of men to dwell on all the face of the earth, that they might seek the Lord, if haply they may feel after him, and find him." But in a narrower sense the vineyard of the Lord may mean the Christian world; that is, all that name the name of Christ and profess to obey his word. In a still narrower sense it may be understood of what is termed the reformed part of the Christian church. In the narrowest of all one may by that phrase, "the vineyard of the Lord," mean the body of people commonly called Methodists.[16]

Deeming Methodism "the vineyard of the Lord," Wesley then sketched out the nature, mission, and commitments of the movement. The conceit that Methodism was God's vineyard would have provided American Methodism a Wesleyan and biblical starting point for drawing together the several experiences of the forest, for theologizing camp meetings and structuring them into the church's polity, and for grounding scripturally its mission to reform the continent.

To make the necessary sacrifices, and to enter impartially into the good of the whole[17]

American Methodism perhaps failed to take advantage of Wesley's guidance on thinking about nature, woods, and wilderness and the doctrinal implications thereof. But, in some ways, it seemed headed toward different, arguably more significant ideas, certainly more expansive ideas (geographically and sociologically). A contrast in the imaging of the basic Wesleyan/Methodist term "connection" hints at the different direction. The American "Minutes" initially bore a title reflecting the original British notion, that of a connection around John Wesley, "Minutes of Some Conversations between the Preachers in Connection with the Rev. Mr. John Wesley." After organization as a church, the new MEC retitled its annual statistical ingathering, "Minutes Taken at the Several Annual Conferences of the Methodist Episcopal Church."[18] Increasingly, the Americans lived into their missional understanding of the connection, not as centered around Wesley or, in the American case, around the bishops, but instead expanding to the continent and requiring commitment therefore, from one and all, to the sacrifices necessary for such an audacious mission.

With just such a radical notion, the bishops constructed their 1798 commentary on the *Discipline*. Bishops Coke and Asbury dwelt in several places, with great care, and at some length on the priority of connectional, holistic, and missional purposes over those interests of person and place. We excerpted in the first chapter a lengthy but just a small part of a much longer argument from the bishops that their authority to appoint and deploy the preachers served the church's continental missional orientation. In the statement heading this section, the bishops indicated why Methodism did not constitute its general and annual conferences with (lay) representatives from the individual circuits or congregations. Here, too, they contrasted the missional good of the whole against local self-interest. Why not the inclusion of laity in a representative church polity? We answer, they affirmed, "It would utterly destroy our *itinerant plan*. They would be concerned chiefly, if not only, for the interests of their own constituents." The bishops continued, "They could not be expected, from *the nature of things*, to make the necessary sacrifices, and to enter impartially into *the good of the whole*."[19]

Such a notion of connectionalism oriented Methodism to missionizing the continent, to tracking the sprawling American population, to extending ministry to frontier settlements, and to braving the wilderness. It recognized no boundaries to its work, indeed, to itself as a church. It refused to bind its ministry to locale but would appoint and itinerate preachers broadly. And in quarterly conference and camp meetings, Methodism dramatized itself and its offer of salvation in a specific locale in a strange, unbounded fashion, inviting the world, as it were, to its services. In its unwillingness to set boundaries around itself, Methodism made a curious and important theological and ecclesiological statement. It thought of itself as *church-without-boundaries*.[20]

By contrast, in thinking about the relation of the church to its society, to culture, to the state, to nature, and to the world, theologians and church leaders have tended, I believe, to construe the two realms, however they interrelate, as realities, as entities, as systems, as bounded. So for instance, to consider church and culture, one might conceptualize them initially as distinct, separate, distinguishable. They might then be viewed as relating, coinciding, or interpenetrating in various ways, as H. Richard Niebuhr instructed

us. They might be set over against one another—Christ against culture—
yielding a sectlike opposition to culture and society or an atheistic state intent on stamping out religion. One might govern the other, Christ over
culture or culture over Christ (Christ transforming culture or Christ of culture, in Niebuhr's phrasing). Their relationship might be paradoxical or
Christ set above culture. If their relations might be various and overlapping,
nevertheless in such conceptualizing both Christ and culture, church and
society are deemed self-contained or bounded. Similarly, at least for explanatory purposes, interpreters have tended to contrast church and state,
church and society, Christianity and the world, humanity and the rest of
nature.[21] Having thereby bounded some aspect or aspects of the realm of
grace, the theologian can then explore the several ways in which church and
culture, grace and nature relate or interpenetrate. This reflex to distinguish
religion from the contexts in which it functions has been reinforced in the
U.S. context by separationist readings of the First Amendment and careless
use of Thomas Jefferson's image of a wall between church and state.

Early American Methodism lacked such a fully developed sense of itself as bounded. Nor did it treat society, culture, the nation, or the world as
bounded, as realities to stand over against. For their lack of clarity, especially about the United States as nation—for their 1784 framing of their
mission in North America in relation to "the Continent" and "these
Lands," not the new American republic—the Methodists might be for-
given. After all, whether the Revolution would yield a single viable nation-state remained something of an open question. In 1784, the newly
freed colonies operated under the Articles of Confederation, a constitutional project in need of some serious attention. Still, long after 1784, at
least insofar as they heeded Bishop Asbury, the Methodists continued to
see through the nation—not to see the nation but to see through and beyond it to the peoples and terrain to be evangelized! So I argued earlier in
"Views of the Nation: A Glass to the Heart,"[22] invoking Asbury's image to
suggest that though they labored strenuously to evangelize within and beyond the expanding nation, Methodists' vision focused on souls to be
saved and on the kingdom to be built. In an 1806 letter, Asbury affirmed:

> All the prospects of this world are dead to me. I feel not a wish for
> creatures or things. The glory of the Kingdom of Christ, the organi-
> zation of a primitive Church of God, these are my objects; was it
> possible to set a glass to my heart, you should see them engraven
> there by the word & spirit of the living God.[23]

My earlier effort to understand Asbury's larger agenda argued that he and early Methodism lacked what those in the Reformed tradition, New England Puritans (Congregationalists) and Presbyterians, offered the new nation, namely a theology that recognized and distinguished the distinctive civil and religious realms.

Here we can press that further to suggest that the "wilderness" motif and notions of continent and lands extended the unclarity and ambiguity about the arena in which Methodism operated to society and culture as well as to state (or nation-state). None of these three terms—society, nation, culture—offered boundaries to Methodism's sense of its operating arena. None, from their vantage point, stood over against Methodist efforts. None conjured up an entity or realm to be addressed or petitioned. None suggested a social or ideational system that might be reformed. To be sure, Asbury and Coke paid visits to George Washington, beginning in 1785, and in 1789 wrote the president formally on behalf of the Methodist Episcopal Church to celebrate his election.[24] And in 1800, General Conference issued a pastoral letter calling upon annual conferences to petition their respective states urging a gradual emancipation of slaves.[25] In various other ways, Methodists in fact recognized that they functioned in a nation and acknowledged the social order. Yet, they with Asbury indeed also saw through nation, society, and culture to the kingdom of God. And so they worked for the kingdom, evangelizing beyond the nation's boundaries in untamed wilderness, building up society where none existed through their disciplined classes and ordered circuits, and extending Christian culture to African Americans.

So Methodists engaged the new world and its peoples as complex, dynamic, mutable, and differentiated. So they dealt with various dimensions or aspects of the new land, its woodlands and wilderness as seemed most appropriate. Methodism's evangelistic presence in the woods, including its camp meetings, constituted an important, indeed, "vital record of Methodists' evolving self-image," "a self-portraying and self-fulfilling organization of space and time," "a metaphor of itself."[26] Its language about itself and its concerns betrayed, as another interpreter put it, four characteristics: "its experiential quality, its concrete representational vocabulary, the realism or sacramentalism of these representations, and a deliberate engagement of the non-definitional textures and multivocal possibilities of language." Or as he put it elsewhere, "Methodist camp-meeting language is primarily poetic; it seeks less to persuade than to capture and reflect on an elusive experience." He termed it a "vernacular language," not implying "an inability to think or to theorize but...a different mode of theorizing than that found in classic systematic theology." Instead Methodists "thought in a poetic mode with concrete images, actions, and objects rather than with abstract theological concepts."[27]

Although American Methodists did not follow Wesley's theological guidance or develop their own brief but promising comments into formal, explicit, and elaborate doctrines of wilderness, shady grove, and garden, we can tease out some possibilities from their activities and concerns. The following **wilderness** section treats themes of **God the Father**, creation, and church, corresponding to Wesley's notions of prevenient grace. Then under **shady grove** come **Christ**, redemption, and ministry (justifying grace). And the **garden** section deals with **Holy Spirit**, the Christian life, and the goal of holiness (sanctifying grace). The three sections also correspond roughly to three classic Methodist (and Reformed) touchstones of church and ministry (order, word, and sacrament). In comparable applied respect and for each doctrine, the emphasis falls not on a quasi-creedal formulation but on a lived theology, doctrine expressed in the day-to-day commitments latent in Methodist polity and practice. The "lived" and dramatized aspect of Methodism's camp-meeting theology has attracted a number of discerning studies. One, for instance, charts camp meetings' mapping of the Bible's experiential doctrinal landscape or portrayal of humanity's journey across space and time to God—Eden, Canaan, Temple, Pentecost, Heaven, New Jerusalem.[28]

The template for such a practiced theology lay, of course, in Scripture. But for Methodists Scripture guided best when it was turned into formulae for life and church order in the *Discipline*. At the heart of the *Discipline* were Wesley's "General Rules," which elicited the longest of Bishops Coke and Asbury's exegetical explanations[29] and which set forth the theological, ethical, and religious expectations for those who would "continue to evidence their desire of salvation." And perhaps the greatest test of its aspirations to live its doctrine of God, discipline its membership, and fulfill its redemptive continental and socially reconstructive mission came in Methodism's campaigns to bring into its membership (if not its leadership) Native Americans as well as blacks. The placement of the evangelistic outreach to Indians at the end of this chapter and to African Americans at the end of the last should indicate that these partial inclusions bear treatment but that Methodism could not find its path to making these peoples truly equal in the sight of God and within the church. Following a brief treatment of that effort, we conclude the chapter by acknowledging Methodism's sense that its wilderness had been conquered.

The wilderness and the solitary places were made as the garden of God, and as the presence-chambers of the King of kings and Lord of lords

Doctrine of God the Father

For this declaration by Asbury that concisely brought together the three aspects of Methodism's woodland experience, our chapter title, "a church spread into the wilderness," might serve as a convenient shorthand.[30] For he and his compatriots envisioned Methodism being unbounded, committed to spread into the wilderness, indeed intended to be made part of that wilderness. One recent interpreter deems it undeniable that "Methodists retreated to the forest for religious encounters.... [for] forests symbolized the transcendent."

> Things occurred in the woods that defied logic. It was a place of dread and devotion, fear and security, a place of instability which could simultaneously engender absolute confidence. Settler attempted to harness the natural environment through worship as much as hunting, felling trees, agriculture, or building water-powered mills."[31]

The wilderness presented "world" to Methodism as complex, dynamic, mutable, differentiated, but "world" of which Methodism was part. Methodists dealt with various dimensions or aspects of this wilderness as seemed most appropriate. To the wilderness *populace,* the people needing to hear the Gospel, Methodists proclaimed Arminian doctrines of prevenient grace, universal atonement, and forgiveness of sins. To *society* in wilderness condition and so under the dominion of class and caste, Methodists rendered a scathing critique dramatized and institutionalized in the Wesleyan classes, which made space for all and so countered societal privileges of gender, race, and class. To the wilderness *civitas,* the state, Methodists summoned the courage to attack slavery, to demand that its members free the slaves, and to preach liberty to the captives. To wilderness *culture* and cultural practices that encouraged finery, fancy dress, conflict, frivolity, and excessive consumption, Methodists offered Wesley's General Rules, a disciplined Christian life. To penetrate nature, the physical wilderness, the challenge of the North American **continent**, Methodists sustained Mr. Wesley's plan of itinerancy, deploying preachers as needed and where needed.

Something of that range of thematic aspects of a doctrine of God came through in one of the early defenses of camp meetings. Creation motifs suggested that participants in camp meetings were impressed by

> the eternal power and Godhead, as revealed in the works of nature, providence and grace, where the gentle zephyrs fan the noontide rays of the scorching sun, the evening shades prevailing, present the thousand beauties of the sky; pouring instruction from their Maker's hand; while the gospel proclaims the matchless love, and boundless condescension of all nature's God to guilty man; which all conspire to excite a devotion and humility, more sublime than that of the Psalmist, when induced to exclaim, "When I consider the heavens, the works of thy fingers; the moon and the stars, which thou hast ordained; what is man that thou art mindful of him? and the son of man, that thou visitest him? O, Lord, our Lord, how excellent is thy name in all the earth?"

The camp-meeting apologist proclaimed himself (Methodists generally?) struck "with such an amazing display of the infinite wisdom, power, goodness, and omnipresence of the great architect of nature, (who has carpeted the pavement of this his magnificent temple with verdure)." Not surprisingly, he regarded these dramatizations of the doctrine of God as providentially given. "Modern camp-meetings appear not to have owed their origin to any pre-election, or appointment of man, but to the interposition of the grace and providence of God."[32]

If Methodism's wilderness world proved multifarious or multifaceted, so also Methodism itself. With its roaming bishops, itinerant preachers, quarterly meetings, conferences, and general conferences that sat briefly and then dispersed, Methodism had no center and, as noted, no boundaries. Several dimensions of its complex *missional* nature corresponded to the fivefold aspects of wilderness (people, society, state, culture, continent—Zion, class meeting, quarterly meeting, connection, MEC). Each in its own way attested Methodism's search for God the Father.

Methodism spoke of itself as Zion. That biblical term claimed relationship to the new Jerusalem, to the kingdom, to Methodism as part of the redemptive/redeemed new order. In the class meeting, Methodists held their membership and insofar as they belonged to church, they did so through the class. The quarterly meeting, the business gathering for the circuit, came as close as any aspect to providing the markers that defined church—word, sacrament, and order. Methodism cohered as connection, as a system of doctrine, practice, and order oriented by fidelity to the Wesleys' discipline, hymnody, and theology. And as the Methodist *Episcopal* Church, the movement aspired, however gropingly, to be the new Anglicanism for the new American society. The wilderness and wilderness church correspondences, then:

People	Zion
Society	Class meeting
State	Quarterly meeting
Culture	Connection
Continent	Methodist *Episcopal* Church

To "be church," Methodism presented itself slightly differently depending on what dimension or aspect of the American landscape or the American forest it engaged. But whatever the aspect, Methodism engaged the new world *missionally*. It offered itself as church-in-mission.

So as **Zion**, Methodism labored to create the new people of God, the new Jerusalem, the new city of God in the American wilderness. The **class meeting** constituted one of the essential membership units that helped American society cohere as a society, a point that Donald Mathews once made. Holding membership in the class, Methodists made their contribution to social stability, order, and lawfulness.[33] The **quarterly meeting**, or quarterly conference, functioned within Methodism as did civil government on local, state, and national levels—playing judicial, legislative, and executive roles for the church and its members. By calling itself a **connection**, Methodism referenced the totality of its practices, structures, membership, and leadership; oriented itself by its Wesleyan standards; identified itself with Methodism(s) elsewhere; and recognized itself as a distinctive way of being a collective, a church. Connection corresponded roughly to the way in which culture stamped a society as distinctive. And as the **Methodist *Episcopal* Church**, the movement aspired to occupy a role on the North American continent like Anglicanism did in England and in the British colonies.

To distinguish the fivefold dimensions of Methodism and of the American landscape and to link them in the above fashion aids in our visualizing the complexity and dynamism of Methodism's practice of church. But the isolating and pairing also oversimplifies and makes overly neat what doubtless were impulses, attitudes, efforts, and ambitions that interplayed in more confusing fashion. The infrequently, but eloquently, evoked notion of Methodism as Zion, its eschatological vision, for instance, might as well apply to American society, culture, and continent as to the people. And to work for a new Zion meant energizing the full dimensions of Methodism's ecclesial resources—its classes, circuits, quarterly conferences, the conferences—indeed the whole connection of itinerating and local preachers that made up the MEC. On the other hand, some Methodists and Methodist leadership may have had little sense of anything above the class level. And when these folk moved west into the wilderness, they knew to reconstitute the movement and claim their identity as Methodists by forming new classes. Similarly, preachers who "located"—leaving the itinerancy to farm and raise a family—might have lost something of the grand visions of Zion, of the MEC's ambition to reform the continent and of a worldwide Methodist connection. But there were always new preachers to fill the ranks of the itinerancy, to carry the standard into western wildernesses, to take over the oversight of classes, circuits, and quarterly meetings, to gather in the annual and general conferences and to refresh the MEC's Zion-ward march.

Of the Church

Here, then, was a practiced ecclesiology that Methodism had not drawn and did not draw together into formal doctrines (of church and of God the Father). American Methodism had, to be sure, a proper, precise definition of church, one carried over from Anglicanism's thirty-nine "Articles of Religion" into the MEC's twenty-five. Article XIII. *Of the Church* specified, "The visible Church of Christ is a Congregation of faithful men, in which the pure Word of God is preached, and the Sacraments duly administered according to Christ's Ordinance, in all those things that of necessity are requisite to the same."[34] This cramped definition corresponded to very little in the expansive, missionary order that American Methodism had become. Class meetings most closely approximated the "Congregation of faithful men, in which the pure Word of God is preached." However, for "the Sacraments duly administered," Methodists would have looked instead to the quarterly meeting. And the formal definition lacked mention of the discipline of members and leaders that both class and quarterly meeting oversaw. Eventually, the church would come to claim word, order (discipline), and sacrament as ecclesial criteria (belatedly adding "service" as well). Most important, perhaps, was that the "Articles" doctrine did not even hint at the missional, connectional, continent-reforming, Zion-ward order that the Methodist Episcopal Church had become. Continent, not congregation, actually set Methodism's ecclesial horizons.

Had early Methodism had the theological leadership equipped and the inclination to theologize its practice of church and situate the definition from the "Articles of Religion" into a dynamic, evangelistic, redemptive doctrine, the term "connection" might have served best as a governing rubric both for the movement and for a proper doctrine of God.[35] "Connection" had the elasticity to cover these several dimensions of church practice and had the rootedness in Wesleyanism to gather in Methodist distinctiveness. However, for reasons that are not entirely clear, the General Conference of 1816, in crisis because of the death en route of its great leader, Francis Asbury, directed the editors of the *Discipline* to replace distinctive Wesleyan terms like "connection" and "society" with the traditional word "church." That move toward theological conventionality had its costs, among them losing a term that might better have captured the richness and dynamism of early Methodism's practice of church in the wilderness.

In not giving formal doctrinal expression to its effort to be a wilderness church with "connection" or some other term with similar elasticity, Methodism also failed to claim the distinctive use it made of its engagement with the world and made no effort to conceptualize its practice of church within a larger theological system or schema. Wesley, we noted, had plenty to say about God's creation, providence, the fall, and original sin. The Americans might, in engaging the wilderness, have drawn on Wesley to think about God the Creator, God's creation, nature, and the world and the place therein of the Methodist connection. Instead, they seemed to have taken basic Christian doctrines for granted, assumed them, as it were, focused instead on the soteriology that they undergirded theologically, and so pulled the world, nature, and wilderness into a practiced, but not conceptualized, ecclesiology. That direction can be seen in Asbury's earlier cited statement that provides the header for the prior section:

And here let me record the gracious dealings of God to my soul in this journey: I have had uncommon peace of mind, and spiritual consolations every day, notwithstanding the long rides I have endured, and the frequent privations of good water and proper food to which I have been subjected; to me the wilderness and the solitary places were made as the garden of God, and as the presence-chambers of the King of kings and Lord of lords.[36]

Asbury experienced the created world—so daily, so physical, so trying—in his untiring effort to reform the continent and spread scripture holiness over these lands and to make Methodism itself, as it were, "the New Creation." Other Methodist preachers, especially those appointed in the newer conferences, could well have echoed his sentiments. Church and world intermingled and overlapped. Early American Methodism lived and worked for a wilderness church, a redemptive order that would engage this new world—its people, its social and civic orders, its culture and its landscape—and reshape it. Key to this agenda was Methodism's distinctive pattern of ministry and a shady grove Christology to which we now turn.

Preach the ever-blessed gospel far more extensively through the sixteen states, and other parts of the continent

Doctrine of Jesus Christ

Wilderness cashed out the doctrines of God the Creator and creation into practices (multiple practices) of church. Preaching in **shady grove** might be taken as dramatizing Methodism's understanding of Christ, of the saving Christological doctrines of prevenient grace, forgiveness of sins, new birth, and justification, of an itinerancy committed to offering Christ, and therefore of *a theology of ministry*.[37] Such an obligation the Americans had carried over into their *Discipline* from Wesley's "Large Minutes." "What is the best general Method of Preaching? A. 1. To convince: 2. To offer Christ: 3. To build up: And to do this in some Measure in every Sermon."[38] This instruction heads in the direction of a theology of itinerancy but one would have to dig through Wesley's writings as through the writings of early American Methodists to flesh out theologically the practice by which he and they lived. Similarly, toward a theology of itinerancy, Bishops Coke and Asbury gestured in their 1798 commentary on the *Discipline* and from which we excerpted in chapter 1. *"Our grand plan, in all its parts,"* they affirmed, "leads to an *itinerant* ministry."[39] On the purposive, missional character of itinerancy they then dwelt at length. To illustrate, they might well have taken an exhibit from any one of a number of preachers' journals—the selection from Freeborn Garrettson's journal capturing well something of the itinerant drama (excerpted in the same section of chapter 1). The bishops' exegetical statements, the Garrettson selection, and Colbert's journal (which we exhibited liberally in chapter 1 and do so more below) trouble the image, widely held, of Methodist itinerancy as an individual, often lonely affair. In fact, itinerancy was and ought to be understood as a something of a collective enterprise as the bishops insisted. And noteworthy in the journal selections from Garrettson and Colbert was their repeated use of the plural pronouns "we" and "our" in describing their travels. Elsewhere, in commenting on itinerants' journaling, I have suggested that early Methodist itinerancy was communal, cooperative, missionary, appointive, connectional, commissioned, and covenantal.[40]

On several of these characteristics the treatment above of Methodism's wilderness ecclesiology and commentary in the first two chapters have already been sufficiently elaborated. In particular, we have dwelt at some length on the *missionary* nature of the *appointive* system of itinerancy, points on which Asbury and Coke dwelt. So also they emphasized its inherent and requisite *connectional* character, making it possible for them, as the ultimate appointive authority, to deploy the preachers where most needed, even across the continent. We will defer exposition of itinerancy's *covenantal* dimension to the next section.

Methodism understood its ministry to be *commissioned*. At the heart of the commission was traveling to preach Christ. And in traveling to represent Christ, to re-present Christ. Names conveyed the charge: "Travelling Elders" and "Travelling Deacons." Lest nomenclature or single clauses not suffice to outline duties, the *Discipline* appended the note: "No elder that ceases to travel, without the consent of the yearly conference, certified under the hand of the president of the conference, shall on any account exercise the peculiar functions of his office amongst us." A similar warning followed the brief outline for the traveling deacon. The *Discipline* specified eight quasi-episcopal duties for the presiding elder. The first was "To travel through his appointed district." One of the sixth duties of bishops was "to travel through the connection at large."[41] In various places in their commentary, Bishops Coke and Asbury claimed not only that Methodist bishops did and must travel but also that this had been the apostolic pattern. For instance, in the first section "Of the Origin of the Methodist Episcopal Church," the bishops defend the ordinations by John Wesley on which the church was founded, rejected the Romish doctrine of an "apostolic, uninterrupted succession of bishops," claimed the Methodist church to have "every thing which is scriptural and essential to justify its episcopacy," and aligned theirs with Timothy and Titus, whom they deemed "bishops in the proper *episcopal* sense" as "*traveling* bishops."[42] In their explication of Methodism's conference system, the bishops again reiterate the identification of Timothy and Titus as *"traveling bishops,"* asserting *"this* is the primitive and *apostolic plan."*[43]

Those commissioned to travel as deacons and elders did so *coopera-tively.* Itinerants were appointed two to a circuit, a junior and senior. The latter had oversight and was to model, teach, encourage, correct, counsel, and mentor the junior. Methodists had a name for the arrangement: "yoke-fellows." It was their system of theological education, presuming reading following Wesley's instructions and learning ministry in the saddle. So explained Joseph Trimble, converted while a student at Ohio University (Athens), of his subsequent theological apprenticeship in the 1830s: "There were no Theological schools at that day, for the training of the young men of the church for the work of the ministry in the Methodist Church. Indeed, some of the fathers desired them not, believing that the circuit system, with a senior and junior preacher, proffered the best possible advantages for theological study and for training the young men of the Conference to be useful ministers of the Lord Jesus. This was my school."[44]

This brush-college would loom large in the "croaking" of Peter Cartwright and other defenders of early Methodist training practices who touted the advantages of brush-seminaries over theological seminaries.[45] Just such counsel was received by S. R. Beggs, who had intended to take two years' schooling, but was dissuaded by the Rev. James Armstrong. "He held that I could better receive my education and graduate in the 'Brush College,' as most of our preachers had done."[46] A more even-handed recollection from Dan Young illustrates the system at its best:

> The following year (1806) I was sent to Barre Circuit, in Vermont. This to me was a memorable year. I had for my senior preacher that excel-lent and distinguished man of God, Elijah Hedding. I am sure I never saw a more worthy man. I was intimately acquainted with him for many years, and I know not that I ever saw anything in him that would have been inconsistent in St. Paul. An attachment had existed between us before we met in our work on the circuit, and when we met it very soon matured into warmest friendship and Christian love. He often remarked that our love was like to that of David and Jonathan. At the commencement of our work we entered into a mutual agreement to tell each other of all the errors and improprieties that we knew, saw, or heard of each other. This agreement was faithfully kept, to the advan-tage of both. We so arranged the circuit as to be often together at our meetings, in which we preached alternately. The one who heard

watched and noted all the errors of the one speaking, and gave him a faithful account of them. This was a great means of improvement. We had not labored long till a gradual but good work of God broke out nearly all round the circuit, which continued throughout the year.[47]

Preachers called one another "brother" and those who traveled together on a circuit, spending quality time together as well as time apart on appointments they set for one another, indeed developed deep, affectionate fraternal bonds.[48] At the center of those bonds and with them in traveling? Who but the one who centered, traveled with, and sent the original disciples, Jesus Christ. With and for Jesus, Methodists traveled. Like him, they traveled, albeit on horse rather than foot. Methodism and Methodist preachers particularly functioned with a lived Christology.

Conference

Illustrative of the theologically Christological and *communal* character of itinerancy (but also its cooperative, missionary, appointive, connectional, commissioned, and covenantal dimensions) and of early Methodism's wilderness fluidity and uncenteredness was the church's practice of holding annual conferences. Conference was the preachers' spiritual home. It was obviously a home with one another, but also with Christ. It functioned for them as the class meeting and love feast did for members. Like those Wesleyan institutions, conference sessions often included the highly bonding telling and hearing of one another's conversion, spiritual pilgrimage, and recent struggles with Christ.[49] This practice may have been something of an American addition to Wesleyan practice. Bishop Coke so intimated in a 1791 entry: "At each of our Conferences, before we parted, every Preacher gave an account of his experience from the first strivings of the Spirit of God, as far as he could remember; and also of his call to preach, and the success the Lord had given to his labours. It was quite new, but was made a blessing, I am persuaded, to us all."[50] At any rate, that *communal* spirituality honored the directives that Wesley had given for his conferences, directives carried over virtually verbatim in the American *Discipline*. By 1796, Wesley's instructions headed Section III "Of the General and Yearly Conferences":

It is desired that all things be considered on these occasions, as in the immediate presence of God: That every person speak freely whatever is in his heart.

Quest. 1. How may we best improve our time at the conferences?

Answ. 1. While we are conversing, let us have an especial care to set God always before us.

2. In the intermediate hours, let us redeem all the time we can for private exercises.

3. Therein let us give ourselves to prayer for one another, and for a blessing on our labour.[51]

The communal Christological spirituality that defined itinerancy and its shady-grove spirit was well captured in the camp-meeting hymn, "Children of the Heavenly King":

> *Children of the heavenly King,*
> *As They journey sweetly sing:*
> *Meeting in the verdant grove,*
> *Fir'd with flames of mutual love.*
>
> *Each the other now embrace,*
> *In the purest bonds of grace;*
> *Tell what Jesus Christ has done,*
> *T' make and keep their spirits one.*
>
> *Thus, while they each other greet,*
> *As upon the ground they meet,*
> *With one heart, one soul, one voice*
> *They in Jesus all rejoice*
>
> *Where they shall meet to part no more,*
> *But sing and shout their sufferings o'er.*
> *Beneath the shade of life's fair tree,*
> *In gayer fields, in higher glee.*
>
> *May I wish these encamp'd above*
> *Shout victory to redeeming love;*
> *Where God my sun and shade shall be,*
> *My All, to all eternity.*

Reproduced in and as part of the *Apology for Camp Meetings*, the hymn was broken between verses 3 and 4. There comments suggested that the hymn referenced the great ingathering who from the four corners "sit down in the kingdom of glory with Abraham, and Isaac, and Jacob, and all the holy patriarch, prophets, apostles, confessors and martyrs of the living God."[52] In the hymn itself, the "Children of the heavenly King" go from "verdant grove" to "Where God my sun and shade shall be." And it is Christ, as the first three stanzas indicated, who gathers camp meeting attendees as his children, makes and keeps their spirits one, and finally (perhaps implicitly) in "redeeming love" encamps them above for "all eternity."

The intense spiritual bonds between and among the preachers led eventually to American Methodism's following the British pattern and making the class-meeting hymn "And are we yet alive" a conference standard and using it to open annual conferences.[53] The first, third, fourth, and sixth verses capture well what conference meant to the itinerants:

> *And are we yet alive, and see each other's face?*
> *Glory and thanks to Jesus give for his almighty grace*
>
> *What troubles have we seen, what mighty conflicts past,*
> *fightings without, and fears within, since we assembled last!*
>
> *Yet out of all the Lord hath brought us by his love;*
> *and still he doth his help afford, and hides our life above.*
>
> *Let us take up the cross till we the crown obtain,*
> *and gladly reckon all things loss so we may Jesus gain.*

Until 1796, possessed neither of defined membership nor geographical boundaries, the called conferences brought together the preachers from one or two districts and then often dispersed them more broadly to circuits in other districts. Their malleable character really made the cohort of preachers into one *communal* connection. Illustrative of this, for instance, in 1800, according to one recollection, "Bishop Asbury requested that all the preachers who had labored in the West for any considerable time, should attend the General Conference, and 'receive their appointments in the old States; and a new set be sent to this division of the work.'"[54] By 1800, however, the fluid, ill-defined conference system had given way to some extent, and geographical order had been established. The 1796 General Conference had divided the Atlantic seaboard circuits among five conferences: New England, Philadelphia, Baltimore, Virginia, and South Carolina. Still, a sixth, the Western Conference, opened to the frontier,

Kentucky, Tennessee, and beyond. And further, with respect to both the western and northern wildernesses, General Conference provided for expansion, "*Provided*, That the bishops shall have authority to appoint other yearly conferences in the interval of the General Conference, if a sufficiency of new circuits be anywhere formed for that purpose."

The rationale for the new conference system, geographically defined where Methodism had put down roots but permitting new conferences as church and society expanded was missional—to maximize the effectiveness of an itinerancy committed to preaching Christ. General Conference explained "[T]hat the active, zealous, unmarried preachers may move on a large scale, and preach the ever-blessed gospel far more extensively through the sixteen states, and other parts of the continent; while the married preachers, whose circumstances require them, in many instances, to be more located than the single men, will have a considerable field of action opened to them; and also the bishops will be able to attend the conferences with greater ease, and without injury to their health."[*] The proviso permitting the bishops to create new conferences was reiterated by subsequent General Conferences up to 1832.[55] And create they did: seven by 1800, nine by 1812, eleven by 1816, twelve by 1820 (along with three provisos), seventeen by 1824, twenty-two by 1832, twenty-nine by 1836.[56] So Methodism endeavored to keep its conferences small, geographically as compact as possible, nimble, close to the people, effective in communal mission, and growing on its wilderness frontiers.

Other evangelical denominations, indeed Christianity generally, perhaps shared with Methodism a commitment to mission, and others typically are credited with inaugurating the modern missionary movement.

---

[*] *Journals of the General Conference of The Methodist Episcopal Church*, I, 1796–1836, (New York: Carlton & Phillips, 1855), 1796: 11–12. (Hereinafter this would be referenced JGC/MEC 1796: 11–12.) The first three reasons offered for the delineation of conferences on the landscape were:

"N.B. For several years the annual conferences were very small, consisting only of the preachers of a single district, or of two or three very small ones. This was attended with many inconveniences:—1. There were but few of the senior preachers whose years and experience had matured their judgments, who could be present at any one conference. 2. The conferences wanted that dignity which every religious synod should possess, and which always accompanies a large assembly of gospel ministers. 3. The itinerant plan was exceedingly cramped, from the difficulty of removing preachers from one district to another. All these inconveniences will, we trust, be removed on the present plan; and at the same time the conferences are so arranged that all the members respectively may attend with little difficulty."

Methodism, however, functioned with a missionary understanding of its ministry, especially so of its "conferenced" itinerants. Indeed, Methodism functioned long into the nineteenth century with a self-understanding that stood the typical evangelical Protestant ecclesiology on its head. The typical doctrine—patterned by Congregationalists in New England and Baptists elsewhere—viewed the church as built from the ground up, laity covenanting together to form a congregation and congregation calling a minister. First people and congregation, then minister. Methodism, by contrast, began with the preachers. First preachers, then people. Its purpose or mission statement, by the 1790s altered from Wesley's question-and-answer format still narrated Methodist history in terms of the preachers. It began with "the two young men," the Wesleys, then the American preachers, Philip Embury and others, and then the very slightly revised purpose statement, still framed in ministerial terms: "We humbly believe that God's design in raising up the preachers called Methodists, in America." American Methodism adhered to Wesley's admonition: "You have nothing to do but to save souls. Therefore spend and be spent in this work."[57] So "worn-out" became virtually formalized as a descriptor for those who itinerated, preaching Christ in shady groves.

In their dramatic encounters with and occasional meditation on wilderness, the American Methodists enacted a doctrine of God. Their preaching experiences in shady grove similarly yielded something of a dramatized or enacted Christology. And where but the garden-like woods could Methodists have sought holiness and quested for a deeper engagement with the Holy Spirit?

I retired into a wood where I found the Lord to be very precious to my soul[58]

Doctrine of Holy Spirit

So John Kobler noted in June 1790, expressing something of the covenantal spirituality that defined the itinerant life and that required times of garden solitude. Preachers broke away for prayer, meditation, disciplined reading, and soul-searching because itinerancy was itself a spiritual discipline, a journey of the soul, a pilgrimage guided by and in the Holy Spirit. Itinerancy had a physical and a spiritual dimension, both entailed by and entailing the rich social or fraternal bonds—communal, cooperative, missionary, appointive, connectional, and commissioned—that tied the itinerants to one another and together. That life in the spirit, in the Holy Spirit, came dramatically and graphically to expression in the forests and forested ministry.

On the camp meeting as a Spirit gathering, James Finley recalled looking back to the beginning of his ministry, to a camp meeting in the summer of 1809 and remembering a crowd and a "preachers' stand...filled with ministers."

> To this meeting the tribes of Methodism from all parts of the country repaired. It was the annual celebration of the feast of tabernacles, under the Christian dispensation. I had passed the Red Sea of repentance, and the wilderness of doubt and uncertainty, and now I was prepared to take my family and tabernacle on Mount Zion with the people of God.... Just before reaching the consecrated spot, our attention was arrested by the clear and melodious strains of the children of Zion, singing that memorable camp meeting song,
>
> "Stop, poor sinner, stop and think,
>
> Before you further go;
>
> Will you sport upon the brink
>
> Of everlasting woe?"[59]

The commitment to and empowerment of itinerancy—to the disciplined conference life in the Spirit, to relocate when and where the Spirit stipulates (the bishop's appointment), to itinerate as a spiritual vocation, to itinerate as the Spirit blows, to tabernacle on Zion—had and continues to have a claim on the life and lives of the preachers.[60] That commitment remained and remains beyond adequate theological exposition. To this day, candidates for the ministry of elders are asked, "Will you itinerate?" They must answer in the affirmative even if they and the conference members posing the question know full well that the answer probably will be compromised by a spouse's ministry, well-paying job, ill-health or caring responsibilities, children's schooling and activities, or by a myriad of other familial, economic, and employment issues. It's the minister's new Zion. So, the answer must be in the affirmative—"I will go where sent, my new Zion"—because the commitment to and empowerment of itinerancy claimed the candidate for and in Methodism's life in the Spirit and its doctrine of ministry.

When, in the nineteenth century, family, health, or economic vicissitudes required an itinerant to locate—that is to relinquish "his" traveling and membership in the conference—the loss had spiritual aspects for the fraternity of preachers and often spiritual turmoil for the minister, even though the many who located often continued a very active ministry in that "local" relation. Indeed, one might term these locations as a breaking of the Spirit. Those "locating," Bishop Asbury complained, included the "brightest ornaments" of the church. The local preacher office, derived from Wesley, was exercised under the authority of the traveling preacher and quarterly conference. For some, office served as temporary, the entry into itinerancy, for others a permanent bi-vocation, and for traveling preachers locating for family, health, or financial reasons a much reduced status. By 1796, the *Discipline* devoted a distinct paragraph to it. In 1789, the church authorized ordination of local preachers as deacons and in 1812 as elders.[61] The *Minutes* annually asked, "Who have located this year?" and then identified by name those who had left the "traveling" fraternity.[62] In their histories, Lee and Bangs somberly cited the number year by year.[63] The 1816 General Conference, echoing Asbury, reported on the loss to church through locations, of its experienced, trained, and pious "ornaments."[64] Indeed, within the cadre of local preachers, two-thirds of the Methodism's ministers in the nineteenth century, were individuals who had played such key leadership roles, as presiding elder, editor, or traveling companion to Asbury. Especially for such located preachers, who had enjoyed the status, voice, and suffrage in annual and general conferences, the loss of standing within the Spirit ministerial community as well as the loss of authority increasingly grated. Did not their numbers, experience, role, and work warrant some role and representation in those bodies within which ministry symbolized itself, where decisions were made and legislation passed for the church, and which gathered in the Spirit? Reformers so concerned led in the causes that produced division and the organization of the Methodist Protestant Church (lay empowerment and election of presiding elders serving also to galvanize the movement). Earlier, the refusal of the MEC to move African Americans beyond the status of local deacon proved one of the troubling issues in the emergence of the African Methodist Episcopal Church (1816). And episcopal Methodism employed the "local" relation until 1956 to placate women who had experienced calls to ministry. These and other strains or divisions (to which we return in the next chapter) had their spiritual dimensions and/or consequences. Dealt with on the surface politically and relationally, the locations and divisions shattered the Zion— the community in the Spirit—of which these "men" had become part.

Perhaps part of Methodism's difficulty, politically and intellectually, with the other ranks of ministry—class leader, exhorter, local preacher—lay in its failure to theologize its understanding of itinerancy and treat it formally in relation to the doctrine of the Holy Spirit. Bishops Coke and Asbury, in the exegesis to which we have several times called attention, certainly moved in the direction of a theology of itinerancy. Their 1798 exposition, however, was neither kept in print nor repeated. The official Disciplinary statement for deacons and bishops remained essentially that cited above for elders—to cease to travel, without consent, mean relinquishing "the peculiar functions" of the office. And so "traveling," or itinerancy, involved the vocational travel of the cohort of preachers—communal, cooperative, missionary, appointive, connectional, and commissioned—by which Methodism defined and displayed its distinctive understanding and practice of ministry. Itinerancy displayed a practice of spirited ministry, as we noted in the prior section. And preachers lived into it, grasping what it meant to be part of this particular and peculiar spiritual "fraternity" as they internalized its rhythms, rituals, patterns of interaction, taboos, and modes of communication. I discovered its unarticulated but powerful character when I set out to write an essay on the annual conference, found that there had never been just a history, and only gradually came to understand its incredibly rich, multidimensionality.[65]

Methodism's difficulty in "seeing" the richness of its practiced theology of itinerancy doubtless owed in no small measure to the easy equation of it with physical travel (space) and with the way that "traveling" appointments defined calendar (time). The latter especially became a yardstick by which some would measure whether Methodism retreated from or sustained itinerancy. Six months in the 1760s, later a year, then two and three, four when my dad entered ministry, and who knows now, the duration of appointments was readily legislated and documented. Methodism itinerant time certainly changed; so also the spatial aspects of itinerancy evolved. Into the nineteenth century, preachers traveled out from conference to their respective appointments, often with all those headed similarly, separating as the yokefellow teams rode to their respective circuits. Then junior and senior preachers traveled around the six- or four-week circuit. They traveled to appointments they made for one another (making appointments also for the presiding elder and sometimes for the bishop when either came onto their circuit). They traveled to their quarterly and camp meetings, the liturgical highpoints that defined calendar for their circuit. They traveled to similar events on other circuits. And then they traveled back to annual conference, again often joining a caravan of preachers in a Methodist pilgrimage to their spiritual home. The stationing of preachers in the cities and to specific congregations proved another way to measure Methodism's commitment to itinerancy or, by some lights, its retreat therefrom.[66] So collapse of circuits into stations worried some Methodists. If I am pressed, said George Cookman in 1839, with the question

> "What is the grand characteristic, the distinctive peculiarity of Methodism?" I would answer, It is to be found in one single word, ITINERANCY. Yes, sir, *this*, under God, is the mighty spring of our motive power, the true secret of our unparalleled success. *Stop the itinerancy, let congregationalism prevail for only twelve months—, Samson is shorn of his locks, and we become as other men.*[67]

In defining Methodism by its itinerant ministry, Cookman gestured beyond the sheer physical and even the vocational aspects of itinerancy toward its role or place in epitomizing Methodist spirituality. For as Wesley had construed it, sin-to-salvation was *via* perhaps more than *ordo*, at least a *via salutis* as well as an *ordo salutis*, a lifelong grace-enabled journal or travel from sin through repentance, forgiveness of sins, justification and new birth, regeneration to entire sanctification (holiness or perfect love).[68] Wesley's "scripture way of salvation" did not mark out different paths for ministers than for laity nor, as a good Protestant, elevate the spirituality of preacher over that of member. Nevertheless, with Pietism generally, Wesley and the Methodists expected its leaders to live the life they espoused. American Methodist preachers certainly sought to follow the path toward holiness, to face the challenges posed by wilderness of nature and of spirit, to listen as well as speak in the shady grove, to take full advantage of garden solitude, and to live in and for the Holy Spirit.

Holiness: Journeying and Retiring

Itinerancy was itself a spiritual and covenantal discipline, a journeying with the Holy Spirit, a journey in which the vocational and physical aspects of travel accompanied, reinforced, and even deepened the spiritual path. We can delineate the spiritual-vocational-physical travel with prepositions—upward, onward, inward, outward, and around.[69] At various places along the route a retreat to the woods might be needed.

Itinerancy meant first, traveling *upward*, along the long road to perfection, the *via salutis*, the path to the kingdom. The journals marked out this spiritual travel through wilderness, to grove, and finally to garden. They often started retrospectively, with the individual's early religious struggles, a recollection written after conversion and call, when already preaching and facing the inevitable doubts and feelings of inadequacy of early ministry. Within his longer Christian pilgrimage toward heaven, the itinerant then located his current inner vocational turmoil. Then the journals took up his further travels in the faith as well as into ministry. They carried the writer and reader through a physical landscape that also landscaped the writer's personal journey along the way marked out by John Wesley. Daily entries remarked on trials and tribulations on the road and also the struggles of the spiritual walk, on physical hardships and spiritual turmoil. Not infrequently, the itinerant needed a stop to bring the two travels into accord. He then retired to a woods or to a quiet room for solace, prayer, quiet. [Upward]

Second, one traveled into ministry, *onward*, in the way indicated above—by being taken on the road by another preacher who saw in the neophyte promise for ministry. Individuals who showed some signs of promise for the traveling ministry, as class leaders perhaps, would travel with the itinerant around the circuit, through wilderness and into groves, as a way of beginning the long road of ministry. That riding into one's call often involved travel out of and back into one's former life, its family context and worldly inducements. The call to preach sometimes battled the allure of home, society, security (old but still tempting retreats to familiar wildernesses). Not infrequently, preachers represented the temptations to quit traveling as from Satan. Physical and imaginative travel back home contended with the spiritual disciplines undertaken on the road and through the woods under the guidance of other preachers. Probationary riding spiritually needed the actual riding with one's yokefellow and other compatriots, the communal support of quarterly conference, the disciplines of the *Discipline*, and the road out of the world. Being drawn out spiritually, itinerancy began as an invitation to travel to test out one's calling. [Onward]

Third, itinerancy involved traveling *inward*—from distant quarterly conference to annual conference, the first of such trips being as one recommended on trial. Subsequent trips would be to have one's character assessed, to be examined for full connection, and then to play a role as a traveling preacher both in assessing others and being assessed. The journals record the itinerant's efforts to hold himself accountable to connectional expectations—of study, prayer, fasting. Itinerancy involved the annual travel into trial. And such inward journeys required use of the several means of grace, including the oft-noted retirement to the wood for prayer. [Inward]

Fourth, itinerancy meant traveling *outward* from conference to circuit, a journey away from one's brothers in ministry, a journey with them as long as possible, and then into what was often a new and strange region. Such entry and experience of loneliness while one's yokefellow went elsewhere on the circuit has given us the image of the solitary rider. This road took the itinerant into his vocation, into the exercise of his calling and quite literally through wilderness to grove and garden. [Outward]

And finally, itinerancy involved traveling *around* one's circuit, a journey that often recapitulated the prior kinds of travel. The first weeks on a new circuit would be strange, challenging, threatening, call-questioning, a spiritual wilderness. The itinerant would not know the people or their spiritual estate nor elicit their trust. Gradually, the promise of the circuit would appear as persons along the stops would respond to the itinerant and his ministry, particularly his preaching. By the end of the conference year, the preacher would take tearful good-byes at the fourth quarterly conferences, feel painfully the separation from the people whose spiritual journeys he had become part of, and head back to annual conference to receive another appointment and begin the wilderness-to-grove-to-garden cycle again. [Around] And so, we can affirm, that itinerancy was/is a covenantal, spiritual journey.

Itinerancy was, then, more than physical travel, more than circuits and circuit riders, more than complete turnover of appointments every year or every other year, more than just a man and a horse. It constituted a complex metaphor for a multifaceted ministry, a variety of journeys, and a corporate itinerancy—ministry carried on connectionally, as much with one's peers as apart from them. Itinerancy was communal, cooperative, missionary or evangelical, appointed/appointive/under authority, connectional, and commissioned. Covenantal at its heart, it entailed spiritual journeying, moments of garden solitude, times for claiming the Holy Spirit's guidance in living a disciplined life.

The Doctrines and Discipline of the Methodist Episcopal Church

By 1792, the bishops Coke and Asbury had incorporated Methodism's historical self-identification and its purpose statement of reforming the continent and spreading scripture holiness over these lands into a prefatory address to the church's *Discipline*, "To the Members of the Methodist Societies in the United States." "We wish to see this little publication," they proclaimed, "in the house of every Methodist, and the more so as it contains our plan of

Christian education, and the articles of religion maintained, more or less, in part of in the whole by every reformed church in the world." They continued with an exhortation drawn from Scripture, "Far from wishing you to be ignorant of any of our doctrines, or any part of our discipline, we desire you to read, mark, learn, and inwardly digest the whole."[70] For them and early Methodism, the *Discipline* put forth and explained the doctrines of Holy Spirit, Christ, and God the Father by which the people were to—indeed, must—live.

This counsel may be difficult for modern readers to fathom. United Methodism's *Discipline* by the twenty-first century had ballooned into an eight-hundred-page description of the church's labyrinthine organizational structure, complex procedures, and detailed duties. In Coke and Asbury's day, the *Discipline* indeed functioned as essentially a small pocketbook for living the Christian doctrine and the Christian life, individually and corporately, the preachers living a "disciplined" life and so ordering the lives of members. So, the first *Discipline* had followed the "Large Minutes" in putting Wesley's guidance for the life of preachers together in conference up front: "It is desired that all things be considered on these occasions, as in the immediate presence of God." And discipline had to do with life with the neighbor as well as in the Spirit, with ethics as well as spirituality. Nothing epitomized that social dimension of the disciplined life more than early Methodism's commitment to antislavery, to the making of a biracial community, and eventually to ministry among Native Americans—incredible challenges that the preachers undertook as implementers of the *Discipline*. (See chapter 2 on evangelism among African Americans and immediately below for Native Americans.) These were campaigns that Methodism found easiest when in sylvan settings. In outdoor gatherings for quarterly meetings and then in the camp meetings, Methodism could assemble black, white, and Native Americans, albeit even there often in segregated clusters.[71] When Methodists went indoors, worldly racist strictures ruled. But indoors or out, early Methodism perhaps best enacted its threefold doctrine of God in its outreach to African and later to Native Americans, and its efforts against slavery. So they proclaimed blacks to be children of and beloved by God. So they offered them salvation in Christ. And so they brought African and Native Americans into the community sustained by the Holy Spirit, into class and society.

Such outreach across racial, linguistic, and cultural lines might have occasioned deeper reflection by Methodists about the God who had created such peoples, about the Christ whom they preached, and about the Holy Spirit who they believed saved any and all of every race. We treat

Methodist efforts with Native Americans here, as with African Americans in the prior chapter, in acknowledging that neither missionary venture brought those converted fully into Methodism's families in the forest or indoors. The open, wall-less ministry in the woods did not embrace either people fully into the Christian family as would have their inclusion in a chapel or house. Camp meetings early, and balconies later, extended a less-than-full evangelistic invitation.

I ran to that cross and buried the tomahawk and scalping knife, and to-day you greet Mononcue as brother

So the Wyandotte chief preached at an 1833 Ohio camp meeting, one catering to both his people and whites. To the latter, through an interpreter, he was reported to have proclaimed:

> The time was, my white sisters, when you trembled at the sound of Mononcue's step. It was well, for Mononcue came with tomahawk and scalping knife, knowing only the war song and dance; but these men (turning to the preachers behind him) found me in the depths of my native forest, worshiping in the temples of my fathers; they told me of the cross of Christ by which the enmity of man to man is destroyed. I ran to that cross and buried the tomahawk and scalping knife, and to-day you greet Mononcue as brother.[72]

Methodism's belated missions to Native American peoples—launched between 1815 and 1816 to the Wyandottes on his own by John Stewart, himself part Native, part African American—constitute quite an ethically and socially mixed story. Catering more and more to their white constituents, Methodist preachers started late and proved unable to resist local, state, and federal initiatives to remove Native Americans from their traditional lands. Here I would only note that the forest and camp meetings served Methodism well, when and where it did reach out. Two early illustrations, one north, one south, should suffice.

Heroic on the outreach cause generally, James B. Finley, missionary to the Wyandotte and presiding elder, at several points in his history of that mission commented on the import of camp meetings and of their serving white and Native peoples. For instance, early in the 1820s, both he and

Mononcue, in summarizing the Christian message, ended on and stressed the Holy and Great Spirit. Finley reported "three hundred whites gathered from the different frontier settlements" and "Indians" whom he met separately "in a cabin." To the latter he proclaimed:

> In my address I tried to give them a history of the creation; the fall of man; his redemption by Christ; how Christ was manifested in the flesh; how he was rejected, crucified, and rose from the dead, and was seen by many; that, in the presence of more than five hundred, he ascended up into heaven; that he commanded his people to wait at Jerusalem for the Holy Spirit; and as we are sitting, so were they, when it came down on them like mighty wind, and three thousand were converted to God that day. At this they made the whole house ring with exclamations of wonder, (*waugh! waugh!*) and said, "Great camp meeting."

Mononcue spoke the next day, first to Native Americans, then through a translator to whites, saying the following:

> Fathers and brothers, I am happy this night, before the Great Spirit that made all men, red, white, and black, that he has favored us with good weather for our meeting, and brought us together, that we may help each other to do good and get good. The Great Spirit has taught you and us both in one thing—that we should love one another, and fear him. He has taught *us* by his Spirit; and you, white men, by the good Book, which is all one. But your Book teaches us more plainly than we were taught before, what is for our good.

In 1826, on invitation from Nathan Bangs to Methodism's Missionary Society, Finley took Mononcue along with Between-the-Logs east for that meeting and to promote Native American missions. There, too, camp meetings served for witness to the Holy Spirit and the Spirit's work.[73]

Another early, initially constructive and southern Methodist effort with a camp meeting signature, occurred among the Cherokees. Overseen by the Tennessee Annual Conference, the outreach built on occasional efforts that dated from 1815 and a conference ministry after 1823. William McLoughlin noted:

> The Methodist circuit riders, most of them young and themselves of little education, proved popular among the Cherokees when they

came into the Nation after 1823....The Methodists never established permanent mission stations; they lived with the Cherokees as
they traveled around the circuits. In addition, their Arminian theology, their exhilarating, spirited camp meetings, and their willingness to tolerate and give encouragement to "backsliders" who fell
into spiritual error made them seem more friendly in their evangelism than the stern authoritarians in the Calvinist denominations.[74]

In his several books on the Cherokee people, McLoughlin notes the importance of camp meetings in Methodist outreach and cites them as an
indicator of the church's advantage over other denominations working
evangelistically among them (Moravians, Baptists, Presbyterians, and
Congregationalists, the latter two via their cooperation through the American
Board of Commissioners for Foreign Missions). Several white preachers
married Cherokee women. Methodists early (within four years) began to
commission Cherokees to preach, putting one "on trial" as an exhorter as
early as 1826. And their camp meetings constituted a similar embrace of the
Cherokees as McLoughlin explained:

> The Methodists had another advantage over the more staid denomi-
> nations. Their camp meetings resembled in tone and excitement the
> all-night dances of the Cherokee religious tradition. Sometimes their
> camp meetings lasted all night. At a camp meeting the Cherokees
> recognized the same feelings of exhilaration or uplifting and sensed
> the same strong emotional force at work that they felt when their
> own people gathered to shout, dance, and sing in unison to the Great
> Spirit hour after hour. The Methodists' enthusiastic revival style out
> under the trees was a familiar mode of worship to the Cherokees.[75]

McLoughlin does not illustrate his comments but notes that "Usually each circuit rider held four camp meetings (and 'love feasts') each year on his circuit."
    The naturalness of forest or grove worship, including that of camp
meetings, to Native American Christianization was captured by William
Apess in his spiritual autobiography. At age nineteen, a camp meeting figured in what might be seen as his conviction and further forest gatherings
in his conversion. He recalled of the first:

> The camp meeting was a very happy one, I found some comfort,
> and enjoyed myself tolerably well. The parting scene was very

affecting—serious thoughts passed through my mind, as I gazed on this large number of respectable and happy people, who were about to separate, and meet not together again till the blast of the archangel's trump shall bring them in a twinkling to the judgment seat of Christ. And so it was, for we have never met altogether again—some have taken their everlasting flight.

When I returned home, I began to tell the family all about the camp meeting, what a blessed time we had, &c., but they ridiculed me, saying, we were only deluded. I attempted to exhort them to seek an interest in the sinner's friend, but to no purpose, as they only laughed at me.

When the time for which I engaged had expired, I went among my tribe at Groton.... Once in four weeks we had meeting, which was attended by people from Rhode Island, Stonington, and other places, and generally lasted three days. These seasons were glorious. We observed particular forms, although we knew nothing about the dead languages, except that the knowledge thereof was not necessary for us to serve God. We had no house of divine worship, and believing "That the groves were God's first temples," thither we would repair when the weather permitted. The Lord often met with us, and we were happy in spite of the devil. Whenever we separated it was in perfect love and friendship.[76]

After another camp meeting in 1818, at which "many a gracious shower of divine mercy fell on the encampment," Apess, then about twenty, sought and received baptism. Others, too, felt the showers of Methodism's forest outreach. He continued, "many a hitherto drooping plant revived, and many a desolate and ruined heart, was made the home of new, and happy, and heavenly feelings."[77]

Recently, Douglas Strong has echoed this observation of camp meeting compatibility with traditional patterns and applied it more generally to Methodist efforts with the various Native Americans. He notes, "Methodist class meetings offered Indians communal support while camp meetings built upon the same kind of emotional exhilaration they had known in their traditional spirituality."[78] Doubtless patterns of living in camps made Native Americans receptive to them and made this Methodist reflex effective in early evangelistic efforts. On the other hand, if camping seemed to white Methodists the Indian way, camp meetings might be indistinguishable from other dimensions of Native American life and from other efforts to

Christianize them. So William Graham noted, rather in passing, attendance at a camp meeting held among Choctaws in Arkansas in 1845 and within the Indian Mission Conference then just organized by Methodism.[79] The overlap or confusion of a people's tradition and a church's outreach may explain why camp meetings figure very modestly in standard denominational studies. One historian, for instance, noted helpfully, but just in passing, the importance of Methodist camp meetings among Native Americans in Michigan in the 1850s.[80] But why dwell? After all, this church's signature was in wilderness, grove, and garden ministries.

Glory to the Father, Son, and Holy Ghost ... never have I preached so much in demonstration of the Spirit

Methodism's signature—its sense of the presence of God—was in wilderness, grove, and garden ministries. As we noted above, the outreach across racial, linguistic, and cultural lines might have stimulated Methodists, were they more theologically trained, into formal doctrinal affirmations and theological treatises. They could have elaborated doctrines about the God who had created Native and African peoples, about the Christ whom they preached to these whom the society as a whole disdained, and about the Holy Spirit who they believed saved any and all of every race. In wilderness, grove, and garden—specifically in camp meetings that, as the next chapter shows, gradually found differing sylvan settings—Methodism demonstrated and dramatized its operative, if not doctrinally and systemically articulated, Trinitarian theology. Confessed if not published, lived if not creedal, proclaimed if not formalized, Methodists showed off and preached their orthodoxy. In such fashion, Alfred Cookman wrote his wife of an 1862 mid-Atlantic camp meeting:

> Oh, how much oppressed I felt in view of my fearful responsibility! But, glory to the Father, Son, and Holy Ghost, divine strength was made perfect in my great weakness, and I think that never have I preached so much in demonstration of the Spirit. Sinners were smitten on the right hand and on the left. The altar and tents were occupied with penitents and praying Christians; many souls were converted. One gentleman of forty years of age was awakened and converted while I preached. Not unto me, not unto me, but unto my blessed, blessed Saviour shall be all the praise and glory, now and forever more.

My own soul has been greatly refreshed and strengthened through the rich privileges I have been enjoying. I trust that I am more powerful to do for Christ than I have been. Glory to the Lamb![81]

In wilderness, grove, and garden, Methodism proclaimed and exhibited a Trinitarian theology. If not published, bound, and sold, it was an orthodoxy quite public, accessible, and operative.

4

Gardening the Wilderness or Machines in the Garden or Tending the Garden

"Let all things be done decently and in order" at camp-meetings, and they shall still be rendered a blessing, as they have heretofore been, to the souls of the people. There is greater danger at present arising from their degenerating into seasons of idle recreation, than of their being abused by ranting fanaticism. In the neighborhood of large cities, where the meetings are easy of access by steamboats, which ply constantly to and from the encampment, there is an alluring temptation for the idle and the gay, as well as for the luke-warm professors of religion, to go to the meetings as mere matters of amusement, and thus to make the nominal service of God a pretext to gratify a roving and inquisitive disposition. Whenever these and similar evils shall threaten to counterbalance the good, the friends of pure religion will either apply the corrective or abandon camp-meetings as a nuisance or as a means susceptible of an incurable abuse.[*]

Camp-Meetings.—This name has been given to a class of religious services held in the open air, and continued usually for from five to ten days. A grove is selected near some thoroughfare; within it, a stand or platform is built, and sittings arranged to accommodate several thousand people; around these, in the form of a square or circle, are pitched or erected tents to accommodate those who lodge

---

[*] Nathan Bangs, *A History of the Methodist Episcopal Church*, 4 vols.; 3rd. ed. (New York: T. Mason and G. Lake for the Methodist Episcopal Church, 1840–45), 2: 269–70. Volumes in the first edition appeared 1838–41.

upon the ground. Originally small cotton or cloth tents were used; subsequently small plank structures, and now, at some grounds, which are purchased and held by associations, neat and pleasant temporary buildings are erected.... Held, as they usually are, during the summer, and in a healthy location, they furnish a temporary retirement from the heat of large cities, and have thus been to some extent pro-motive of health. While there undoubtedly have been instances of persons attending these meetings for improper purposes, and there may have been scenes of disorder, espe-cially in the outskirts, yet the history of these meetings shows that wonderful reformations have been accom-plished by their agencies, and many intelligent and deeply devoted Christians have been spiritually edified.*

SO WRITING FOUR decades apart two of Methodism's most eminent church leaders, nationally visible activists, influential editors of the church's two main newspapers, institution-builders, college presidents—Nathan Bangs, Methodism's preeminent magazine and paper editor, and Matthew Simpson, the church's leading bishop—warned readers in eminently im-portant volumes that camp meetings could be either "scenes of disorder" or "wonderful reformations." Would the wilderness of hucksters and trou-blemakers violate the cathedral-like shady grove campsite and the rhythms and sanctity of the confessional-garden worship? And faced with the threatened violations should Methodism find other procedures and mech-anisms for spiritual renewal? Bangs effectively said "yes" in his four incred-ibly important volumes charting American Methodist history. "No," Simpson signaled in his thousand-page *Cyclopaedia*, celebrating ongoing, post–Civil War camp-meeting grandeur on Martha's Vineyard, at Rehoboth Beach, at Ocean Grove, and elsewhere.

So in predicting or finding the demise of camp meetings and of Methodism's bringing indoors its once-sylvan religiosity, Bangs proved to be at least premature. To be sure, the number held annually and the prominence of camp meetings in Methodism's rhythm changed. Once seemingly fea-

---

* Matthew Simpson ed., Cyclopaedia of Methodism. Embracing Sketches of its Rise, Progress, and Present Condition, with Biographical Notices and Numerous Illustration, copyright 1876, 4th rev. ed. (Philadelphia: Louis H. Everts, 1881), 162.

tured in every quarterly conference and celebrated around 1810 as reaching five to six hundred by Bishop Asbury, camp meetings gradually became
annual conference-sponsored, as we shall see, and radically reduced in
number.[1] Nevertheless, they continued (indeed into the twenty-first century) albeit acquiring differing identities and agendas.[2]

[W]onderful reformations have been accomplished by their agencies

Over the decades after the 1830s, camp meetings evolved into five related
but distinguishable garden, grove, and wilderness projects. They might be
termed **primitive, programmatic, perfectionist, popular,** and **progressive.**
For perhaps a majority of Methodism's leaders and participants, especially
outside the northeast, the camp meeting's **primitive,** unspoiled sylvan
character and revivalistic signature made them spiritually valuable and
eminently worth preserving. Stabilized, regularized, knit into local Methodist
conference patterns, they no longer featured the national Asbury-type leader
whose involvement would have made them widely known. Hence, perhaps,
Bangs's inattention to or ignorance of ongoing camp-meeting practices on
Methodism's various revivalistic fronts. The attraction of settings for the
fourth, popular type of camp meeting yielded just the vacation-like ambi-
ance that Bangs had feared. Exemplified best by Wesleyan Grove on
Martha's Vineyard, these became prominent after the Civil War. Bishop
Simpson regarded such as important enough to treat in his *Cyclopaedia*.
In addition to Wesleyan Grove, Simpson identified camp meetings serving
various religious purposes and becoming popular and fashionable spir-
itual resorts at Chester Heights near Philadelphia, on one of the Thousand
Islands, at Bay View in Michigan, and at Summit Grove near New Freedom,
Pennsylvania.

Camp meetings had proved useful for the **second, programmatic,**
extra-revivalistic assemblies earlier when they provided settings that might
be turned to one or another cause—denominational reform, temperance
revivals, campaigns that furthered or fought the Confederacy and eventually Sunday school conventions and even relief from hay fever and similar
diseases. This programmatic usage tended to be "for the moment" and
has largely escaped scholarly attention. A special instance of such utilitar-
ianism constituted the **third, perfectionist** or holiness pattern. Phoebe
Palmer and other holiness advocates went to camp meetings and found
them immensely useful for the promotion of Christian perfection, and led

eventually to the formation of the National Camp Meeting Association for the Promotion of Holiness. And **fifth,** a very different, at least faintly **progressive,** education-oriented, growth-in-the-faith religiosity came to typify Chautauqua, the Chautauqua movement, and Methodism's various camping and improvement programs.[3] To that we turn in the final chapter.

As we shall see, each of these camp-meeting styles came to terms with American wilderness in different ways and each had its own way of handling shady grove and the garden dimensions of its setting as well. Noting the contrast in terms of construal of "wilderness" perhaps suffices at this point. Primitive camp meetings seemingly sought to sustain a setting, accommodations, style, and religiosity as true to the **original wilderness** atmosphere as settling down and growing made possible. Second, camp-meeting programs, sites, and facilities—never textually embraced and covered by the Methodist *Discipline* so as to be fully under authority of presiding elders and bishops—lent themselves to various programmatic uses. Reform causes, for instance, attacked the **wilderness of bishops** (Methodist Protestants) or alcoholism (temperance crusaders).[4] The defenders or critics of established institutions (notably slavery) portrayed the opposition as hostile to societal order and representing a kind of wilderness—(cruelty or abolitionism). The third, perfectionist, sought holiness and the eradication of the **wilderness of sin** in various settings as we shall see, camp meetings being but one. By contrast, the fourth popular style sought sites void of and voided of the **wilderness of sinners**—hustlers, bullies, alcohol, and any other force, personnel, or activity that would disrupt decorum. It built for, programmed, and peopled its meetings in settings and with vistas that made for attractive vacations for an increasingly middle-class Methodism. Finally, the progressive style settings and programming inaugurated at Chautauqua and paralleled by various retreat and camping programs seemingly moved Methodism **beyond the wilderness of emotionalism and of a wilderness theology** that viewed conversion and hence revivalism of camp-meeting style as the Wesleyan way.

[E]ither apply the corrective or abandon camp-meetings as a nuisance

Writing in mid- to late-1830s and in the second of what would be his four-volume *A History of the Methodist Episcopal Church*, Methodist leader/historian/administrator Nathan Bangs stepped back from narrating events of 1809 and offered a fifteen-page description and defense of camp meetings (which we treated in chapter 2). Bangs seemingly had earned the right to interpret such rural phenomena. He had begun his ministry serving for a decade in the MEC's outreach to its Canadian frontiers. On camp meetings, Bangs moved beyond generalization. He provided a general overview of the camp-meeting phenomena and a six-page detailed description of one in which he had participated in 1818 on Cowharbor, Long Island. He made it clear that, though western in origin, they had been extended to "different parts of the country by previous appointment and preparation." He continued, "For this purpose, a grove is generally selected, in the neighborhood of good water, and, if possible, in such a place that the people may go by water, in sloops or steam boats." With a short, ten-point list of "rules and orders of the meeting," Bangs concluded: "In the city of New-York the entire arrangement and preparation of the meeting, providing tents, putting them up and taking them down, is under the superintendence of a committee appointed for that purpose by the presiding elder of the district, who also procure the steamboat to take the people to and from the meeting; and each person who chooses to go pay a certain amount, commonly about one dollar for passage, use of tent, fuel, straw, &c."[5]

The camp-meeting patterns that elicited criticism and upset the critics— the "annoyance" of hucksters, the presence of troublemakers, the events' emotionalism ("unseemly gesticulations and boisterous exclamations")— worried Bangs but far less than the threat that camp meetings would become "seasons of idle recreation."[6] And in his fourth volume of this history, Bangs took note of the appearance of protracted meetings, multiday (four or more) indoor revivalistic occasions, invented, he suggested by John Lord of the New England Conference in 1827, adopted across the country, and "borrowed" by Presbyterians, Congregationalists, and Baptists. "These meetings, in some places, have nearly superseded camp meetings, and probably will, if continued in many other places."[7] Validating his own judgment, camp meetings all but disappear in the period covered by this fourth volume, 1829 to 1840, the six or seven mentions typically recalling that some preacher had earlier been converted in the woodsy event. Similarly, the *Methodist Magazine*, founded in 1818 and continued under various names and with minor breaks to the present, carried forty-two reports or direct treatments from 1818 to 1827. The new Methodist mode of communicating across the church attended to camp meetings in the eastern states, along with Ohio, Illinois, and Ontario, and the fountains of the phenomenon, Tennessee and Kentucky. Bangs, as editor of the *Methodist Magazine* from 1820, doubtless played an important role in the apparent decision that camp meetings no longer remained news-worthy (?), valuable (?), or viable (?). Writing from its urban centers and deeming them no longer its frontiers, Bangs increasingly presented Methodism as city friendly and city-prepared. Were camp meetings rele-vant politically, socially, spiritually?

An Original Church of Christ[8]

If by the 1830s, small town and eastern Methodism had seemingly out-grown the need for annual sylvan drama of return (with its tune-ups or booster shots or evangelistic "killings"), Nathan Bangs might be credited with more than an observer's part in that play.[9] In his view, Methodism needed to appoint preachers in the urban areas to single congregations (to stations, as Methodism came to term it). He also encouraged the building of parsonages. Methodism, in his judgment, should come to look and act like a proper church with a ministry capable of caring for a maturing member-ship, particularly in the older and more eastern conferences. There the church had achieved stability—in membership, in contours, in ethos, in leader-ship. Methodism had created two major communication centers, in New York and Cincinnati; in the former, Bangs had played an important creative role. A *Methodist Magazine* (variously titled)[10] gave depth treatment to reli-gious matters and the *Christian Advocate* (NYC) and *Western Christian Advocate* (Cincinnati) reached the membership weekly. Out from the two centers poured books, tracts, Bibles, and Sunday school materials to be dis-tributed by the entire cohort of itinerants, functioning as colporteurs. A de-nominational and a women's missionary society (1819) with their conference and local auxiliaries (men's and women's) increasingly made Methodism aware of itself as a church with an evangelistic agenda. The church began dotting the landscape with colleges, depending on annual conferences to provide oversight and funding. Among such early conference efforts were Augusta in Kentucky (1822), McKendree in Illinois (1828), Randolph Macon in Virginia (1830), Wesleyan University in Connecticut (1831), Dickinson and Allegheny transferred to the Methodists in the 1830s, and in the same decade, Emory in Georgia, Emory and Henry in Virginia, Indiana Asbury University, and two women's colleges, Wesleyan in Georgia and Greensboro in North Carolina. No small part of the motivation for the college building was competition with other churches and fear that without their own insti-tutions, Methodist youth would attend the colleges, private and state, domi-nated by the Presbyterians and be lost to the faith.

Living competitively with the more established denominations entailed defending Methodist belief and practices. Letting camp meetings and their emotional turmoil drop from his view made apologetics easier for Bangs and his contemporaries. He would not fashion a doctrine of the church or of the church's mission out of Methodism's sylvan adventures. No wilderness or grove ecclesiology for him. Garden, perhaps, but what Bangs wanted was for Methodism to gain a proper sense of itself as a church and an appreciation of its own credible ecclesial practices.[11] So Bangs led the church in doctrinal disputes with Baptists, Presbyterians, and Episcopalians, especially the latter two. Indeed, Bangs, who led in Methodism's communication revolution in the 1820s and 1830s, had earlier established himself as Methodist spokesperson with four apologetic works that appeared between 1815 and 1820.[12] Also important in making Methodism ecclesiologically self-aware were its schisms. And by the 1830s, the Methodist Episcopal Church had been torn asunder by several divisions, including that by reformers who sought greater internal democracy for laity and local preachers and, failing to gain such, established the Methodist Protestant Church.

[N]ow calmly reposing under the shadow of His wing which formerly sheltered the children of Israel in the wilderness

Doubtless Methodism gained from its acquisition of greater ecclesiological self-awareness, reflected in Nathan Bang's 1837 *An Original Church of Christ*.[13] But if, with Bangs's affirmations Methodism had gained in theological acuity and precision, it had lost something of the dynamism and elasticity of its earlier wilderness practiced or implicit ecclesiology. In institutionalizing itself with media, missionary structures, and colleges, Methodism had embraced and found itself embraced by American society. Among the costs of this engagement had been the church's early commitment to abolition. Like its conference structure, Methodism's policy on race attested to both an early dynamism and gradual retreat therefrom. And to some appearances, certainly to Bangs, the camp meeting also belonged to Methodism's past.

In 1850, when he attempted a portrayal of Methodism (*The Present State, Prospects, and Responsibilities of the Methodist Episcopal Church*),[14] Bangs found no reason to mention camp meetings at all. And wilderness? Wilderness was a state that the church had, in many places and on many fronts, advanced beyond and, where not, was to be fully conquered. So Bangs challenged his Methodist readers to join with other evangelical churches in Christianizing America, a task he framed in sylvan terms— wilderness to be converted fully to grove and garden:

> I presume to say that there is not, nor ever has been, any country so favourable to the spread of the Gospel, and for the establishment of Christian and benevolent institutions, as the United States. Here the tree of liberty was early planted; here it has been watered, nursed, and pruned; here it has accordingly grown and flourished, until its spreading branches have extended all over our free soil, so that under its umbrageous foliage the weary sons and daughters of men may shelter themselves, while the stormy blasts are passing over the old world. Here also the Church of Jesus Christ was earlier planted, and it has imparted its sap to nourish the tree of liberty, and they have mutually supported and fed each other, and they are now calmly reposing under the shadow of His wing which formerly sheltered the children of Israel in the wilderness.

Having extricated the tree of liberty and the children of Israel from the wilderness—doubtless liberations like the first exodus guided by the arm of God—Bangs conceded that peoples needed to be missionized before their wilderness became grove and garden:

> But even here, under all these advantages, there are many vices to correct, and much infidelity to be conquered. The aborigines of our country are to be reclaimed, converted, and civilized; the slaves are to be emancipated and saved; and though the good work of convert- ing the natives has been begun with encouraging success, there remains much to be accomplished before the "wilderness shall blossom as the rose." ... It only remains, therefore, for the evangel- ical denominations to exert themselves unitedly, with becoming dil- igence and exemplary piety, that they may secure a complete triumph to pure Christianity in our own happy land.[15]

Being under God's wings may have freed (urban parts of) Methodism from physical wilderness but by the time Bangs so judged, Methodism had suffered multiple major divisions over race, slavery, lay rights, and other tree-of-liberty causes (AME, AMEZ, Wesleyan, Methodist Protestant,

MEC-MECS). Divisions, as well as its urban "maturing," took parts of eastern Methodism and the church's important interpreters away from true wilderness and intent, as we shall see, on "cultivated" grove and garden.

The strongest argument in favor of camp-meetings was the want of churches

Beyond whatever influence Bangs's writings had, various aspects of Methodist promotion, growth, and development factored into the decline of camp meetings. Certainly, as mentioned at the time, their apparent lagging conversion production and religious formation, clear conflict with rowdies and sellers-of-this-and-that, lack of advocates and advocacy, and various diversions factored in.[16] To some of this we turn below. The notice of and perhaps even some of the promotion of camp meeting to some extent died with the death of its champion, Francis Asbury. By surrounding his successor to centrality, William McKendree, with companion bishops, variously deployed, Methodism took away the single spotlight that Asbury's national itinerations and letters had given to various aspects of Methodism, camp meetings and forest ministry included. The explosion of the church across the continent made the routine sylvan affairs of new conferences no longer noteworthy.

A terribly important factor, implicit in Bangs's portrayal of Methodism, was (as noted above) its development of small town and city station churches and its maturation socially and economically along with American society generally. Increasingly, eastern and urban Methodists built substantial churches and made them station appointments. Such "charges" gravitated to a weekly rather than quarterly rhythm and to intracongregational rather than circuit ecclesial definition. With its own preacher, Sabbath worship services, internal leadership, and local financing—no longer just a stop on a six-week or sixteen-point circuit—such urban congregations or station churches could have their own quarterly conferences. For them, their required quarterly business sessions in warm weather as in cold had nothing to do with camp meetings. City churches no longer possessed early Methodism's combination of business and evangelism, its merger of quarterly meeting and camp meetings. As one defender of camp meetings observed, "[A]s great occasion, quarterly meetings have no existence in a considerable part of our country. Few attend them beyond the limits of the society where they are held, and we see no prospect of restoring them to their former greatness."[17]

Frontier and nonurban Methodism, however, continued to need the multipoint circuit and continued to relish camp meetings as congenial warm-weather settings for quarterly and camp conferences, as for instance in northern Pennsylvania and central and western New York.[18] Irish-born Andrew Carroll, whose family moved to Canada in 1829 and then on to Ohio in 1834, wrote a meditative account of his fourth camp meeting of 1836. Thinking somewhat of possible Irish readers he explained that camp meetings "come in August or September, or earlier, after the fatigue of a burning summer of toil, when we need to be revived by the Spirit of all grace the most of any period in the year." He insisted "that the religious exercises of a camp meeting are better calculated to draw our attention and our hearts to the cross of Christ than any other species of meetings." He continued:

> It is to hear preaching at 8 o'clock, A. M., and at 11 o'clock; then at 3 o'clock; then again in the evening at 7 o'clock; with prayer meetings interspersed between preaching hours; and as much secret prayer as time and circumstances will permit.
>
> Our friends in Ireland may wish to know about the actual condition of these meetings. Well, in the first place, you see a beautiful forest of beach, oak, and hickory-trees, with a splendid foliage; a spot of earth about one hundred or one hundred and fifty feet square, within the tents; those tents are built on each side of this square, either of boards or canvas; then around and outside of these tents is another row of tents, with a road or street between them; and so of the rest. At one end of this ground is the pulpit, which is made to seat some twelve or twenty preachers. Directly before the pulpit is an altar, four square, with an entrance into it in the front of the pulpit, and immediately at each corner, by the pulpit. It is an easier and better place to preach than any where else.

Indeed, the "beautiful forest of beach, oak, and hickory-trees" gave Methodists cathedral-like audio in Eden-like settings:

> The dense foliage and the tents around act as sounding-boards; and particularly the inspiration of the occasion, but yet more emphatically the inspiration of the Holy Ghost; and then,
>
> "Bright skies, so silvery, beautiful, and fair,

As if soft light from Eden wandered there;"

    While over head, and all around,

A thousand years their cloudy wings expand

Around me, and a dying glory smiles

O'er the far times."

— Byron.

These camp meetings are the paradise of believers, yea, the border-land of heaven. To repenting sinners they become the means of introducing them to the Fountain that cleanses from unrighteousness, and prepares them for the society of the blessed.[19]

The "paradise of believers, yea, the border-land of heaven"? As a religious practice to be explained or as a new spiritual experience—both perhaps operative for Carroll—the camp meeting needed to be noted and celebrated. But for many Methodists they became so routinized in the sacred calendar as to be presumed and not minuted. The ability now to access the vast library of digitized Methodist works and to do an online word search for "camp," "garden," "grove," and "wilderness" confirms what a few observers have noted—namely that camp meetings lived on through the nineteenth century, a reality documented in and to which we turn in this next section (and which readers already convinced may skip over or skim).[20]

These camp meetings are the paradise of believers, yea, the border-land of heaven

Perhaps sharing that celebratory note, the participant-observer of Georgia-Florida Methodism, echoed Carroll's injunction that repentance and cleansing from unrighteousness prepared sinners for the society of the blessed. However, he compared Georgia camp meetings of the 1820s not to Eden but to Jericho or some other war zone:

Ten thousand persons were supposed to have been present at one camp-meeting there, and it was no uncommon thing for over 100 to be converted during the four days. The great battle-fields of Methodism in the new purchase were the camp-grounds, and many were the victories won on them.

In those days of large circuits protracted meetings were not common, and the value of the camp-meetings was incalculable. Methodism advanced as the newer settlements advanced, rapidly.

And camp meeting sites participated in, perhaps furthered the settlements during those early years—"bush arbor, logs for seats, and a plain stand," then the "royal hospitality" of "shingle-roofed tabernacle, good seats, plank tents":

> In all the counties there was one, and in some of them there were two or more camp-grounds. In the new purchase the camp-ground was immediately selected. In 1825 the first camp-meeting was held in Monroe County, near old Mt. Zion, and in Upson near Thomas Maybrey's. Originally, just where the preacher and his leading members thought there ought to be a camp-meeting, the spot was selected. The work was all temporary, but afterwards there was a shingle-roofed tabernacle, good seats, plank tents, and royal hospitality; but in the new country the old plan was the first adopted—a bush arbor, logs for seats, and a plain stand. The presiding elder was in charge, and brought preachers from the country round about to aid him. A wonderful work generally was done.[21]

Arkansas launched camp meetings at least by 1821. The *Arkansas Gazette* reported them from 1825 and numbered nine in 1832.[22] One, celebrated by a hymn in its name, "Salem Camp-Ground," continued at least through 1878. And as we will note below, the Methodist Protestants found such settings congenial to further that cause in that state during the 1840s.[23] Similarly, one can find passing reference for the Southwest Missouri Conference to its camp meeting conferences for 1829, in Fayette for 1829, for 1834 "in Belleview valley," for 1835 "at Arrow Rock camp ground, in Saline county," and for 1847 for the then separate St. Louis Conference "at Ebenezer camp ground, in Green county."[24]

An Indiana preacher whose title page proclaimed him "For Fifty-five Years a Methodist Preacher" listed numerous references to camp meetings from the late 1830s on.[25] Another Indiana retrospective with numerous camp-meeting allusions attested their importance by devoting a chapter to the description of one and also including the following as subtitle: "Descriptions of Remarkable Camp Meetings, Revivals, Incidents and Other Miscellany."[26]

One further illustration from the 1840s came from the Central Illinois Conference in a treatment of the ministry of one its preachers. "Oh, those quarterly meetings in barns were times of power, never to be forgotten! Camp-meetings were held each year on his district with great success." And of a later point of the end of the final quarter of the appointment year, "The remainder of this Conference year his time was all occupied. He held several grove-meetings and attended a number of camp-meetings."[27]

The Lord's into his garden come, The spices yield a rich perfume[28]

In general, then, the more frontier or rural a conference, the more likely it would do its business in quarterly or annual conferences at camp meetings and the more likely they would find a place in the religious calendar that persisted after business came indoors. So camp meetings and Methodism's first-hand engagement with wilderness, grove, and garden prospered over the nineteenth century going west. And the judgment that camp meetings expired in the 1820s and 1830s perhaps betrays an eastern, Bangs-like perspective and attention to Methodist patterns. However, in places in the east they continued to retain something of their original character. John Allen of Maine was converted at a camp meeting of 1825 and died at one in 1887 at age 92. A local preacher in 1828; on trial in the Maine Conference in 1835; located in 1852; readmitted in 1857; located again 1860; in 1862 readmitted supernumerary; in 1863 chaplain in the Christian Commission—he resumed evangelistic activities until 1876. Several eulogies called attention to the fact that he "was a great lover of camp-meetings"—"converted at a camp-meeting, sanctified at a camp-meeting, and died at a camp-meeting, and in all attended 374 camp-meetings."[29]

Alfred Brunson touched on several of these points in an autobiography that covered his ministry, treating, for instance, two camp meetings per chapter in eleven of his chapters. And his judgment, rendered retrospectively, was that they created problems as well as saints, even though needed in frontier settings. Appointed Meadville presiding elder in 1833, he experienced conflict at two camp meetings that year. At the first, "one of the rowdies threw a brand of fire into my face." At the second, "rowdies troubled us here also. On Saturday night an explosion of gunpowder near the tents, as loud as a three-pound gun, shook the ground and tents." Brunson reflected on the experience with insight:

This circumstance strengthened my doubts as to the propriety of holding camp-meetings any longer.

The strongest argument in favor of camp-meetings was the want of churches; but now we had churches enough on each circuit for *Winter* meetings, and for neighborhoods without churches the barns in Summer, before harvest, made good temporary places of worship. Usually when a barn was to be thus used, the owner, as every good farmer ought to do in the Spring, cleared all the manure and mulch from about it. If the hay and barn-floor, and scaffold over the stabling are all cleaned out and seated, with proper precaution no accident of fire can occur. Every person leaving the barn after meeting at night, except such as sleep in it, an incendiary would have a poor chance to do mischief, if so disposed. I have held many, perhaps scores, of such meetings, and never knew or heard of one being burned in consequence of it.

Such meetings in a church or barn, need but little guarding against rowdies, and consequently but few, if any, called from the altar to guard the ground. The rowdies not having the woods to retreat to, fewer of them attend, or if they do, are under more restraint. Having had from twenty to one hundred conversions in four days, in churches and barns, with less expense and a smaller ministerial force than is required at a camp-meeting, the scale seemed to turn in favor of the former.[30]

Another form of rowdyism on which mainstream Methodism has seemingly not wished to comment was the importance of the camp meeting to three of its reform movements, each of which became a separate denomination—the Methodist Protestants, Wesleyans, and Free Methodists. To this we turn in the second major section below.

The commentator on Georgia-Florida Methodism noted when he reached the 1840s how camp meetings tracked the movement's maturation from wilderness affair, "the hard frontier work," to grove and garden settled church.

Up to this time, Georgia had never been without a frontier, and the Georgia Conference had held no session without appointing some of its members to the wilderness, and the opening of the Creek and Cherokee lands in Georgia, and of the whole of Florida to settlement had called for an unusual amount of this work. Forests were being cut down, new villages being built, and the times demanded energy and enterprise. It has been the glory of Methodism that her sons have never shrunk from the hardships of a new country, and that she has always been among the first in the newly opened land. It is this which has given her so strong a hold on the affections of the people. She did not wait for civilization to prepare the way for the Church, but the Church, going first, secured the blessings of refined life to the people....

The camp meetings were still in vigorous existence, though the protracted meetings in many of the country churches rendered them less a necessity. The people were better educated, and so were the preachers. Mercer University, Franklin College, and Emory, were well patronized, and there were high schools over the whole State.

The land had been well prepared, and the seed well sown. The laborers were toiling for a richer harvest, and the next decade will show still greater advancement.[31]

Similarly, the *Nashville Christian Advocate* reported for 1850 that "in Nashville, Methodism is decidedly in the ascendant, and Tennessee is a commonwealth of primitive, real 'camp-meeting' Methodists."[32] Five years later in its inventory of renewal efforts, the Methodist Episcopal Church, South, explicitly named as camp meetings the forty or so revivals reported for 1855.[33]

> Oh why in the valley of death shall I weep,
> Or alone in the wilderness rove?[34]

Twentieth-century conference historians, perhaps eager to document the progress of the body to which they belong, do treat forest ministries early in their narratives but drop attention to feature Methodism's organizational progress. This relative disinterest in or minimization of camp meetings might seem, if taken to be definitive, to chart their movement across the continent but systemic decline. For Central Pennsylvania camp meetings, Frederick Maser devotes two chapters (6 and 11) to camp meetings, "Camp Meetings Seize the Countryside," which covers up through the 1840s, and for after the Civil War, "The Climax and Decline of the Camp Meeting."[35] The scholarly treatment of Texas Methodists notes that they gathered in camp meetings as early as 1819, devoted an 1839 series to celebration of the Methodist centennial, continued them after the Civil War but had them wane around the turn of the century.[36] Similarly, Michigan Methodists held a camp meeting as early as 1822. The conference historian noted that James Gilruth, as P. E., held four of his eight 1833 summer quarterly conferences at camp meetings, a pattern that apparently continued. After the Civil War, the Detroit and Michigan Annual Conferences established the Bay View Methodist State Camp.[37] The Minnesota Annual Conference also continued camp meetings from its organization in 1856 through the century, putting them as did many conferences to the various other uses to which we give attention below.[38] Similarly, commentators on Indiana Methodism noted that "During the seventies camp meetings were still commonly held and each of the districts had their own camps.... and even circuits conducted their own camp and grove meetings. The old time camp meeting, however, seemed to be on the decline, for articles in their defense begin to frequently appear in the columns of the church papers."[39]

Sounding the same note earlier, four retrospective *Methodist Magazine* articles from the second half of the nineteenth century signaled to its educated (and one suspects largely town-and-city readership) that camp meetings were affairs of the past.[40] And Peter Cartwright, who devoted four whole chapters to camp meetings and alluded to them throughout his 1856 *Autobiography*, ended with a call to Methodism to revive the camp meeting. He lived, after being appointed a presiding elder, "in the tented grove from two to three months a year." He was certain "that the most successful part of my ministry has been on camp-ground." He desired greatly "to see a revival of camp-meetings in the Methodist Episcopal Church." And then he "prayed," "May the day be eternally distant when camp-meetings, class-meetings, prayer-meetings, and love-feasts shall be laid aside in the Methodist Episcopal Church."[41] Other works defending camp meetings can be and have been read, as well, as signs of their weakness.[42]

Important twentieth-century national studies echo the epitaph. The two-volume treatment of *The Methodist Publishing House* devoted a picture and two pages to camp meetings in its treatment of the first decade of the nineteenth century and let that suffice.[43] The most thorough twentieth-century study of camp meetings, Charles Johnson's *The Frontier Camp Meeting: Religion's Harvest Time*,[44] largely concurs with Bangs in seeing the camp meetings as having declined by the 1830s and for the reasons that Bangs assigns. And he construes manuals and other defenses like B. W. Gorham's (to which we turn below) as indices of the camp meeting's decline.[45]

A very different read is that neither Johnson's title nor subtitle do justice to Methodism's camp-meeting experience and to its way of continuing to pursue a forest ministry (albeit wilderness tamed into grove and garden).[46] Long after conquering frontier after frontier, Methodism found camp meetings serviceable. They continue to this very day (actually to these very summers, warm weather remaining a requisite). Several voices sound this very different note. Charles A. Parker, in an important article, pointed persuasively to camp meetings ongoing through the nineteenth century.[47] Most dramatically, my former and now deceased student, Kenneth O. Brown, has documented the continuing vitality of camp meetings in a number of works, most conclusively in *Holy Ground, Too: The Camp Meeting Family Tree*. In roughly a hundred pages, Brown traces both the continuation of primitive camp-meeting patterns and the metamorphosis of camp meetings into fourteen religious impulses (to the first, second, and fourth of which we turn in this volume). His list: the religious resort, holiness camp meetings, the Bible and Prophecy Conference Movement, the Chautauqua Movement, the Keswick Movement, Christian assembly grounds, denominational camp meetings, Pentecostal camp meetings, the family camping movement, tabernacle revivalism, Christian conference centers, Christian retreat centers, models of Christian camping, and Christian rock festivals.[48] Brown's "Working Bibliography," covering over a hundred pages, lists 2,263 items on camp meetings. The U.S. portion of his "Part Three: A Working List of Sites" goes state by state and extends from page 238 to 321 (followed by a couple of pages on Canadian and foreign camp meetings). With each page naming up to forty sites, Brown, of course, lists many camps that have closed and camps of a number of denominations, extending beyond the Methodist/Wesleyan family.

But Brown shows that on camp meetings and forest battles, Bangs gave up for Methodism too soon and that Johnson and a considerable company of other historians trod with Bangs off the frontier. However, Methodists continued to tame wilderness into grove and garden.[49] And camp meetings exercised that office, as observer James Dixon noted. Responding to critics, he observed, "For a great length of time, the evangelists of these western wilds could have no choice between the private dwelling, as a place of worship, and the forest." He continued, "How few must have attended the log-hut service! whereas, by calling the people to the worship of God under His own bright skies, making the wilderness his temple, they found space for the people, whilst their increased numbers would produce a wholesome excitement on the mind of the preacher, and call forth his utmost energies."

Then he reflected at some length on God's gift of the world in all its glory and beauty.

> Why has God made silence impressive, if we are not to be impressed? Why has he put beauty in ten thousand forms, and hues, and tints, if we are not to taste the beautiful? Why has he caused the grove, the forest, the wilderness, to speak in accents of awe or of joy, if we are not to indulge in corresponding feelings?[50]

Let, then, the tribes of our Israel gather annually
to the tented woodland. Let every minister
and every man, whether venerable in years,
or fresh in youth, be at his post
[Primitive]

So B. W. Gorham in his *Camp Meeting Manual* exhorted Methodists to sustain, in some form and for grove and garden, the religious revitalization that wilderness gatherings had featured.[51] Gorham, though writing in the mid-1850s, did not want to let a maturing, increasingly middle class and settled Methodism give up on camp meetings. He sought to offer counsel that would keep its primitive and spirited style and format through more careful ordering and implementation. To be sure, his guidance can be and has been read as an indicator that camp meetings were in decline, as indeed some indicators in the east would have signaled. However, his counsel can and could signal to members how the forests and camp meetings might be sustained and so sustain Methodism's vitalities. Clearly, he had read Methodism's cultural ascendency quite differently than had Bangs. "The decline of Camp Meetings in some parts of the country," he judged, "is, as we fear, a providential indication indeed—an indication painfully distinct, of the growing worldliness of the church." Nor did he think that "the ample supply of church edifices" constituted a reason to give up on camp meetings. Buildings of some sort Methodists, he thought, always had had.[52] And Methodism's urban presence provided no reason to forego "Camp Meetings or some other means of grace of special interest," which he deemed "a permanent want of the church."

[O]ur brethren of the cities, where most ample church room is enjoyed, are reaping large harvests of spiritual profit on the Camp Ground. The Methodists of Boston, Cincinnati, New York, Philadelphia, and Baltimore, and many smaller towns, have their regularly established and furnished Camp Grounds; and the blessed localities of Millennial Grove, Croton, Haverstraw, Sing Sing, Vincent-town, and Black-wood-town, have poured for many years their frequent tides of converts into the churches of those several cities.[53]

Nor would protracted meetings suffice.

1. They do not, like Camp Meetings, call the people away for successive days from their business and cares.
2. They never offer so rich a variety of ministerial talent, as it rarely happens that more than two or three preachers can attend a meeting of that kind simultaneously.
3. Protracted Meetings, as they are called, do not amount to anything like a general convocation of the membership of the church from an extended territory, to labor and pray together for the general good.

Were protracted meetings like camp meetings? Did they reach out to and welcome in the world evangelistically?

On the contrary, they necessarily occupy the church in any particular locality exclusively with its own home interests; and thus, instead of promoting extended acquaintance among the members of the church, and binding in golden bonds of union and fellow feeling the hearts of our people, over large districts of country, they tend to accelerate, or, at best, they do not retard the tendency to isolation, now so rife, and it may be added, so ominous among us.[54]

Here implicitly Gorham stated what he elaborated as a defense to camp meetings—that in them Methodists remained faithful to their own dynamic patterns, to the outdoor public ministry of Jesus and John the Baptist, and especially to the great ingathering covenantal festivals of Israel. The latter he made a type for Methodism's sylvan gatherings. Like Israel in its festivals and feasts, in the camp meeting Methodism needed to be big, dramatic, populous, and so faithful to God and God's covenant with God's people. If Methodism would be God's chosen in America, to the woods they must go. So repeatedly, through his *Manual,* Gorham urged Methodists to keep their camp meetings festival-sized. He offered highly detailed directives as well on site, arrangement, schedule, rules, order.[55]

Keep the faith or at least the practice

So B. W. Gorham exhorted Methodists in his 1854 *Camp Meeting Manual.* A career that had already honored such an exhortation and did so in one of the eastern areas that had concerned Gorham was that of Adam Wallace. Wallace served with distinction on the Delmarva Peninsula beginning in the 1840s, becoming presiding elder for a term.[56] As he wrote of candidacy for ministry and traveling with other preachers, he referred for 1847 to entering "camp meeting season" and attending several. He mentioned attending several the next year—"one of two in new places"—and requiring "hard work to keep order." For 1849, he mentioned the considerable preparations to counter expected "rowdyism" in "a formerly famous grove" for Annamesex. For 1850, then ordained deacon, he participated actively in the area's "camp meeting season," attending ones at Witipquin, Rockawalking, Moores, "two on Princess Anne Circuit," "the original Tangier camp," and Snow Hill. For 1851, Wallace mentioned only two "at Trape, on Princess Anne Circuit" and at Willis' Woods, Dorchester. He succumbed to "a dangerous illness" in 1852 that prevented his assuming responsibility for a camp meeting, but he mentioned later attending two, at Zoar and on Bridgeville Circuit. By mid-decade, with the sectional crisis and slavery dividing Methodists on the Delmarva, "neither the northern or southern people had much heart" for camp meetings, noted Wallace. But he remarked on one that brought MEC and MECS preachers and laity and both whites and blacks together. "White and colored responded grandly....and the closing periods were interrupted by people on their feet in the stand and congregation embracing each other, under a mighty baptism of the Spirit." For 1856 and Sussex County, Wallace remarked again on "partisan activity" but made note nevertheless of camp meetings at "Lamb's School House, Sound, Laurel, Ross' Woods, Three Bridges, Zoar, and the bests of the lot on our own circuit: Morris' Woods."[57]

Wallace's commentary on Methodism's spiritual retreat from forest ministries held generally not just for the MEC. Methodism—in its Methodist Protestant and two Methodist Episcopal churches, all three strongest along the nation's border states—was indeed traumatized by the racial and sectional turmoil leading up to, within, and following the Civil

War and especially in border states. Wilderness, grove, and garden sites came to serve to station troops and unhappily served as battlegrounds. (A camp meeting or so that served as the church prepared for war we will pick up when we turn to the programmatic pattern of camp meetings and the Civil War).

One church that apparently persisted in wilderness ministry during the war was the German-speaking Methodist movement, the Evangelical Association. One published letter from 1861 noted:

Dear Bro. Koch: —

The war is now just 150 miles from our door (referring to Leavenworth, where he resided.—Ed.). Many have gone to the war, others are left behind in great anxiety. Kansas feels the shock. Yet the work of the Lord is moving along better than we feared.

We have held two camp-meetings. One at Holton and the other on Lawrence Mission. Each had four tents, 30 members, 5 preachers, with an attendance of about 100 persons. All the ministers of the district were present except Bro. Kleinsorge, who lives 200 miles away. The meetings were good, and several souls were saved. It was refreshing to see the few friends erect their tents of wagon-covers and poles to hold the first camp-meeting in the great, thinly-settled, wild Kansas.

For 1862:

Two camp-meetings have been held on the district during the summer. The first was held on the Holton work. Ten or twelve seekers came forward, and most of them were converted....

The second camp-meeting was held on Lawrence Mission. At this meeting 8 seekers came forward, and 4 professed conversion. It was a meeting richly blessed of God. There were here also 6 tents, 30 members present, and from 100 to 200 persons in attendance.[58]

These German "Methodists" continued their camp meetings through the war, indeed through the nineteenth century.

For others, forest ministries had to be recovered. So, indeed, did Kentucky Methodists in both its southern (MECS) and northern (MEC) branches. There, in all places, the original home of camp meetings, something of the older, frontier-like primitive camp meeting reappeared.

The old Methodist type of camp-meeting
is that which prevails here

Recovery of forest ministry for Kentucky Methodists, traumatized and split by the war, perhaps proceeded without counsel from a Yankee like Gorham. After all, as preachers in the state that created the camp meeting, they had no need of his counsel. Cane Ridge was theirs. Both the southern (MECS) and northern (MEC) Kentucky Conferences took care after the Civil War to make sure they kept camp meetings true to the primitive template, albeit smoothed over. And both conferences sought to establish permanent sites that would yield the populous, festive Israel-like ingatherings.

The 1874 MECS Kentucky Conference passed a resolution authorizing negotiation for a campground served by the Maysville & Lexington Railroad and another motion setting that as the site for next conference, thus guaranteeing a crowd of members and the best conference preachers.[59] The next year, the conference acknowledged that campground arrangements were "incomplete." Other resolutions pledged cooperation with the Louisville Conference to establish "a permanent camp-meeting ground on the Short Line Railroad, seventeen miles east of Louisville." Another motion proposed that it be named "Kavanaugh Camp-ground," after the southern bishop and son of the Kentucky Conference (H. H. Kavanaugh), the bishop helping to acquire eighty-four acres.[60] The 1876 conference heard details about a "Deering Camp-ground" indicating that "our annual meeting" there had rented "some fifty cottages," gathered five thousand for Sunday, and averaged one thousand daily. The report went on to detail a contract with Washington Manufacturing and Mining Company for the site that guaranteed an event of ten days' duration under the oversight of a specified committee of three. A three-part resolution approved and ratified the agreement, committed to hold the camp meetings, authorized the committee "to enter into agreement on our behalf," and commended the "Deering Camp-meeting Association," its "stock," and clearly the camp meeting "to the attention of the membership of our Church."[61]

The 1877 Kentucky Conference added yet a third camp meeting to its revivalistic menu. A paper on the "Kavanaugh Camp-ground" offered multiple "whereas" findings, including "whereas, lots have recently been sold for the purpose of building tents which will be completed during the Conference year; and whereas, a pavilion has been erected and dedicated, costing about $1,500, one of the largest in its dimensions in the United

States." It then commended the annual event and the lots for purchase. Another "paper"/resolution on campgrounds sought support for the establishment of and patronage of the "Tower Bridge Camp-ground" "on the line of the Cincinnati Southern Railroad," in the center of "a large district, comparatively inaccessible to other Camp-grounds," and proximate to "one of the most wonderful structures of the kind in the world"—the bridge. Another report that the event on the Deering Camp-ground, held August 8-21, had drawn 1,000 daily and 6,000 on Sunday. It had featured forty-three sermons to adults and thirteen sermons to children, as well as daily prayer meetings. "On the last day the sacrament was administered to 283 communicants, and a fine love-feast was held." The event drew twenty-eight Methodist preachers, others from friendly denominations, and Bishop Kavanaugh.[62]

In 1878, the conference focused on the Kavanaugh Camp-ground. Twenty-two lots had been sold "and as many more spoken for, and during the year several cottages will be built, and several will make the place a residence for the summer months of the year. Bishops Kavanaugh, McTyeire, and Wiley, of the M. E. Church, were present, with Drs. McFerrin and Granberry, of Nashville." Weekday attendance had averaged 500–600, the first Sunday had attracted 3,000 and over 5,000 on the second. What the conference affirmed of the Kavanaugh camp meeting doubtless might have been reiterated for the others:

> The old Methodist type of camp-meeting is that which prevails here. This is not a picnic camp-meeting, and never will be, so far as the board can prevent it. We do not wish to sell lots to those who simply wish them as a place of recreation, just as they would go to watering-places to spend a few weeks in the heated term. We wish and intend to keep it as a religious association, where conversion of souls shall be the main object, and the only object which shall attract to this place, dedicated and consecrated to God.[63]

Subsequent annual conferences heard regular accountings of how camp meetings had fared. In 1881, the conference heard about yet a fourth, "The Stevenson Camp-ground in Grant County, near Corinth, was opened this summer with gratifying results. It has many first class improvements and promises great good to the Church."[64] In 1883, a fifth drew the conference's attention and the conference authorized a standard mechanism of overseeing institutions to be kept faithful to their Methodist purposes—namely the appointment of three "visitors."[65] And in 1886, faithfulness yielded directives to keep Kentucky aligned with its covenant. "*Resolved*, That it is the sense of this Conference that its members should not serve on camp-meeting committees where the Sabbath is desecrated by ordinary business and the running of Sunday excursion trains." And another resolution reinforced that on trains: "That we disapprove of any participation by our preachers in the conduct of any camp-meeting whose gates are opened upon the Sabbath."[66]

Northern Methodism's Kentucky Conference, smaller and weaker than the MECS's, also committed itself to camp meetings, albeit on a more modest scale. In 1872, it established a "Committee on Camp Meetings," two members from each district. The Committee on Camp Meetings recommended a conference camp meeting, suggesting that the conference's growth "is such as to make the people feel the need of some method by which they may be brought together in religious exercises" and if that proved impracticable, the committee advised and urged "our people to attend, as far as possible, the national camp meeting at Urbana, Ohio, to be held in August next."[67] The 1879 MEC Kentucky Conference passed a resolution appointing a committee of three preachers and three "laymen" to locate a camp meeting at the junction of Cincinnati Southern and Louisville and Crab Orchard Railroads.[68]

Something of what camp meetings strove for and was achieved earlier in areas not so traumatized by sectionalism and war is captured in a retrospective of Milwaukee camp meetings by a preacher recalling his days as a presiding elder. He explained for 1859:

> The Brookfield Camp-Meeting was held in the latter part of June. The grove on the farm of Robert Curren, Esq., was secured for a term of years, and through the assistance of Brothers Aplin and Bassett, and the brethren on adjacent charges, it was well fitted up for the purposes of a Camp-Meeting. At this meeting we adopted the plan of making our Camp-Meetings self supporting. Instead of relying upon the brethren in the neighborhood to do all the work and keep open doors for the week, we determined to pay our own bills, and thus permit the good people in the vicinity to enjoy the meeting, as well as those who came from abroad. The change was deemed a great improvement. There was a good show of tents, and the attendance was large. The preaching was excellent, as the good brethren were more intent upon saving souls than ventilating their

great sermons. The meeting resulted in the conversion of many souls, while the member-ship was greatly quickened.

Having noted logistic details, this W. G. Miller meditated for several pages on what camp meetings had come to be. "In these latter days the question is sometimes raised," he noted, "Of what advantage are these Camp-Meetings, now that we have good Churches in which to worship God?" He continued, "The question might be answered by another, 'Of what advantage is it to have picnics and other excursions in the open air, and pleasant groves, since we have houses to dwell in and restaurants to supply the cravings of the appetite?'" "The fact is," he concluded, "Camp-Meetings are as thoroughly in harmony with the laws of Philosophy as they are in keeping with the principles of Religion." Then he reflected on this harmony of philosophical and religious law as exemplified in camp meetings.

> Why not go out into the woods, beneath the spreading branches of the trees, or even under the uncurtained canopy of Heaven, and enjoy a grand unbending of the spirit? With the shackles thrown off that have so long fettered the soul, what a Heaven of felicity there is in its conscious freedom.... [T]here are thousands of Christians shut up in the Churches who are dying for a little spiritual freedom. Their poor souls need a holiday. Let them go out to a good thorough going Camp-Meeting, and obtain a new lease of life.... Communing thus with nature in her purest and most lovely moods, the soul is dwelling in the vestibule of God's own sanctuary. No wonder that prayer and song find such grand perfection in the Camp-Meeting. It is there they find their highest inspiration.[69]

Camp meetings, why hold them given the "wilderness" comfort of Methodism's churches? Why? Spiritual freedom! New lease of life! Relocated to "the vestibule of God's own sanctuary"! The New Eden that reclaims human perfection for prayer and song! The heaven in shady grove and garden for Methodism's highest inspiration!

Better than pitting church against grove was the harmony of building and garden achieved in 1850 on the Chesapeake. Having lost the shade for the previous site, Methodists relocated a camp meeting to Park's Grove, erecting the same year "a neat new church...in close proximity to the camp." Nearby as well in time were an academy, a temperance hall, the Post

Office, and a cemetery in which later rested both "Father Thomas" and his youngest son. Camp in 1850 featured a last sermon by Joshua Thomas. The sermon was reproduced and the site described by his biographer and colleague, Adam Wallace (cited liberally above), and, like Thomas, a camp meeting "professional." Wallace nicely captured the harmony of church and camp: "Park's Grove, a charming spot, thickly studded with vigorous oaks, and lying in one of the most beautiful and eligible neighborhoods on the Island, was prepared for the purposes of worship in the woods."[70]

By request of the Conference...a discourse on the leading features of Wesleyanism, on the camp ground[71]
[Programmatic]

Second, camp meetings proved useful as assemblies that might be turned to one or another cause—reform, temperance,[72] Sunday school conventions, relief from hay fever and similar diseases, and even the Confederacy.[73] This programmatic usage, sometimes employed "for the moment" and the cause, has largely escaped scholarly attention. That camp meetings might serve distinct, even divisive purposes doubtless owed something to Methodism's early gathering and ordering of itself by fixing annual conferences in relation to camp meetings. That pattern, as already noted, adopted early for effective gatherings in frontier areas, continued as the church moved west. So a Methodist recollection to be repeated across the continent:

> Our Conference (in 1828) met at the camp-ground, in Salem, Mercer county, Penn., in the same society out of which Bishop Roberts went into the itinerancy, and he presided in the Conference. The sessions were held in the new church near the camp-ground; the gallery of which was filled with beds for lodging the preachers. Most of the preachers boarded in the tents, though some of them went to neighboring houses.
>
> The regular services on the ground were kept up day and night for a week, a portion of the preachers being detailed daily to conduct them; and when not in session, or on committee, all the preachers were present.[74]

Camp meetings did not, however, always further the stated Methodist Episcopal denominational interests. They served, for instance, as a vital forum for the creation of two new Methodist denominations, the Methodist Protestants and Free Methodists. The Wesleyan Methodists used them as well but somewhat less programmatically. And they served, at least in places, for the Evangelical Association as we noted above.

Camp meetings proved immensely important in the late 1820s reform, as the movement that eventuated in the Methodist Protestant Church went from advocacy and agitation to organization. The church's great historian-apologist, Edward Drinkhouse, noted that the first number of the *Mutual Rights and Christian Intelligencer* (successor in 1828 to *Mutual Rights*) carried "notices of camp-meetings, held under the auspices of the Reformers, which were very successful in conversions." Still writing for 1828 he noted, "The Agents, and other leaders, made a specialty of camp-meetings, often with great success, and gathering the first fruits of evangelistic labors." Several pages later he added, "A summary of camp-meetings, held under Reform auspices during the summer and autumn of 1828, will preserve important historical dates and indicate the zeal of the brethren." After naming several important ones, he noted that those were "prior to the provisional organization under the Conventional Articles of November, 1828." For 1830, he reported "Camp-meetings were frequent both North and South. Six were held in Maryland during the summer of 1830, and all of them eminently successful." And he estimated that of the 5,000 adherents to the movement estimated for that year, "2000 were probably conversions under evangelistic labors at camp and revival meetings under Reform auspices."[75]

Reformers more isolated from what would be Methodist Protestant population centers found forest settings useful in sorting through concerns. The Arkansas "Reformers," for instance, too small and isolated to organize on their own, sought alliance with Methodist Protestants in the Tennessee Conference. They did so meeting in 1831 in a camp meeting. Apparently, they continued relying on such a meeting site at least into the mid-1840s.[76]

Unlike the Methodist Episcopal Church, the Methodist Protestants, at least initially made place for camp meetings in their 1830 provisional constitution. Its Article XI covering "Officers of the Church" dealt with the highest officer of the new denomination, a president (not a bishop), under two rubrics. The second specified:

It shall be the duty of the President of an Annual Conference to preside in all meetings of that body; to travel through the district, and visit all the circuits and stations, and to be present, as far as practicable, at all the Quarterly Meetings and Camp Meetings of his district.[77]

Covering 1832 with the aid of the church's magazine, Drinkhouse observed (in passing), "Camp-meetings through the summer months were everywhere held, and a harvest of souls gathered into the new Church." He reported for two years later "Numerous camp-meetings were held in the West during the summer of 1834" and further specified, "No less than twelve camp-meetings were announced for Maryland alone under the Conference presidency of Dr. John S. Reese during the summer of 1834." The use of camp meetings as site and event for evangelistic outreach continued into the 1840s. So for the Methodist Protestant citadel state Drinkhouse noted,

> Meantime everywhere those who were more intent upon soul-saving than controversy gave themselves to evangelistic work, and gracious was the result in many places, East, West, and South. In Maryland twenty-one camp-meetings were held in the summer of 1842.[78]

His next chapter dealt with the slavery issue as it troubled the Methodist Protestants and divided the Methodist Episcopal Church. That trouble made camp meetings unviable for Methodist Protestants as such communal events required some political and racial accord. So they became less a Methodist Protestant signature.

Interestingly, the antislavery movement that eventuated in yet another Methodist denomination, the Wesleyan Methodist Church, made some use of camp meetings but less programmatically and continuously than either the Methodist Protestants or Free Methodists. The first or organizational meetings (1845) for the annual conferences in Ohio, Indiana, and Illinois occurred in connection with camp meetings. On the last of these, Orange Scott, one of the new denomination's leaders, commented:

> On the Sabbath, at 11 o'clock, by request of the Conference, I delivered a discourse on the leading features of Wesleyanism, together with the reasons for its existence. I preached three times during the Conference. All the religious exercises were on the camp ground. The Conference was held in a school house near by. The Camp Meeting continued till Monday morning. The congregation was not large, but much good was done.[79]

Scott, earlier a presiding elder in the Methodist Episcopal Church, had resourced Methodism's woodland ministry with his several editions of

The New and Improved Camp Meeting Hymn Book: Being a Choice Selection of Hymns from the Most Approved Authors. Camp meetings, for Scott, served reform as readily as worship. He employed them as a public context in which to champion antislavery and to resist the denomination's commitment to the conservative colonization movement. To that end, in 1834, he elicited resolutions supporting antislavery discussion in the church's Boston-based Methodist paper, *Zion's Herald.*[80]

A recent denominational history suggests that camp meetings became routine—"the holding of camp meetings during the summer season—was such a common and valued agency used by the Church fathers throughout the denomination in those days."[81] Perhaps because they became so common, Luther Lee, one of the leaders of the antislavery reform movement, eight-year editor of the denominational paper, *True Wesleyan*, and professor in the denomination's Adrian College, made no reference to camp meetings in his *Autobiography.*[82]

Forested camp meetings figured as prominently in the emergence of the Free Methodists as for the Methodist Protestants, perhaps even more centrally. Important in the spiritual pilgrimage of the movement's leadership couple Ellen Stowe and B. T. Roberts from the 1840s on—camp meetings kept the two in contact with Phoebe Palmer and immersed the two in holiness doctrine (to both of which we turn in the next major section).[83] Later, the Wesleyan University-trained and energetic B. T. Roberts took leadership in upstate New York Methodism in the Genesee Annual Conference. Camp meetings figured increasingly as site and symbol for his various renewal efforts. They proved useful as well for furthering the causes when a wing of the conference leadership (he termed the "Buffalo Regency") sought to suppress him and his renewal impulses (they called his following the "Nazarites"). The conflict included efforts by both parties to control and make use of a campground. In his recent groundbreaking study of the denomination, Howard Snyder treats one decisive year in the Roberts's tension with conference leadership in a chapter tellingly entitled, "The Bergen Camp Meeting." Expelled from the conference in 1858 for his critique of a political clique dominating Genesee policy and given no redress by the 1860 General Conference, Roberts furthered his several reform causes—including antislavery—in creating a new denomination. Camp meetings, again here, as Snyder demonstrates with numerous references, had played a decisive role in the maturation of a reform cause into the new denomination.[84]

Camp meetings served as well for reform campaigns that did not produce new denominations. The temperance cause would be furthered by
Methodist women's gatherings late in the century. In its early phase, it
apparently made use of the church's more woodsy convocations. Alfred
Brunson, writing as new presiding elder in eastern Pennsylvania in 1833,
seems to have been describing such usage:

> The great Temperance movement was now in full blast, into which
> I entered with all my force. In my quarterly-meetings I usually spent
> four days each. I commenced on Thursday night, holding a temper-
> ance meeting, and preaching or lecturing on the subject, and orga-
> nizing a Temperance Society, if none existed before. Almost invariably,
> if we succeeded in the temperance movement, a revival of religion
> followed; for when the evil spirit was cast out the good spirit usually
> took possession of the heart, and we had from ten to twenty conver-
> sions at every quarterly-meeting.[85]

At various times and for various interests, including denominational com-
plaints and reform efforts, local preachers made use of camp meetings.
One early such was reported by James Finley for 1819 when appointed
presiding elder over the Lebanon district.

> I commenced my work by attending two camp meetings, one of
> which was six miles west of Springfield. This was a local preachers'
> camp meeting, at which there were present, I think, about twenty
> local preachers. As radicalism had begun to show itself, there was a
> considerable of prejudice against the traveling preachers....
>
> On Saturday afternoon brother Joseph Tatman was deputed to take
> me aside and examine me in regard to my views of Church govern-
> ment. He attended to his duty in a very Christian manner, and I
> presume the expositions I gave him of Methodist polity were satis-
> factory, as I was waited upon, and invited to preach on Sabbath at
> eleven o'clock.[86]

The communicative, influencing, and infectious character and atmosphere of camp meetings apparently made them an inspiration for methods
and arrangements in popular politics, electioneering, style, and communication.[87] One, and perhaps more, such political-communicative usages
of camp meetings occurred as Methodism participated in the sectionalism

that led to the Civil War. Adam Wallace reported on late 1850s camp meetings troubled by strong sectional feelings, as already noted. Such shaking continued up until war engulfed the Delmarva.[88] Angered by an action by the 1860 General Conference against slavery, laity in the Baltimore Conference used a camp meeting at Loudoun to begin the call for public meetings. A camp meeting, as it were, yielded a break from the Baltimore Annual Conference (MEC) and an alignment of dissenting preachers and churches with the Methodist Episcopal Church, South.[89]

[O]ur Tuesday meetings have of late been signally blest…much like tent-meetings or camp-meetings[90]
[Perfectionist]

In 1836, Sarah Lankford and her sister, Phoebe Palmer, launched what would be known as the Tuesday Meetings for the Promotion of Holiness, the signature and stimulus of the holiness movement that would both reverberate established Methodism and eventuate in new Methodist movements (beginning with Free Methodists).[91] Methodist male leaders soon found their way into the initially all-female New York City gatherings and helped produce the recovery (and recasting) of the Wesleyan holiness or perfection doctrine across the church. Radiating the spirituality promoted to elicit another discernable work of grace (after conversion) and producing kindred efforts across urban Methodism, the holiness renewal spirit came quickly to "infect" camp meetings. That contagion owed in no small part to the effective teaching and "preaching" of Palmer. Her and kindred preaching, teaching, praying, and scripting for the new holiness Christian life went easily into camp meetings, especially in eastern and urban area Methodism. These summer gatherings had not yet envisioning their vacation-like potential (discussed below) nor were needed as much to serve unchurched populations like those of previous years or as those then scattered on the church's evangelistic frontiers.[92]

Camp meetings proved to be contexts to violate Methodism's strictures against women playing ministerial or quasiministerial roles. And beginning in 1839, Palmer began to teach holiness in camp meetings—one that year, two in 1840, five in 1841, ten in 1844, eleven in 1850, ten in 1851, sixteen in 1857, and seventeen in 1868. She had "taught" holiness between 1839 and 1859 at 118 camp meetings when she and her husband took "her" ministry to the British Isles. Before their trans-Atlantic efforts, the Palmers took their holiness witness to Canadian camp meetings and furthered

Methodism's forestry ministries there.[93] Phoebe Palmer would doubtless have "preached" holiness (exhorting or praying publically or guiding love feasts and leading sanctification meetings), at many, many more camp meetings had not illness in some years curtailed her ministry.[94] In 1847, when she could make only four camp meetings, Palmer alluded to what was doubtless a more significant leadership role.

> Sing Sing, N. Y., Eastham, Mass.—The state of my health considered, you may be surprised, when I inform you, that I have been at two camp-meetings. One at Sing-Sing, N. Y., the other at Eastham. Mass. The first named was good, very good. Several were converted, but the number of those who received the blessing of holiness exceeded, I think, the number of conversions. We were favored with much of the Divine presence. In our tent, more than a dozen, I think, received the witness of sanctification.
>
> The latter, which was held at Eastham, was a season of power. The grove in which it is held is called "The Millennial Grove." Often, while worshiping with God's sacramental hosts, in this place, was I reminded of the latter-day glory.[95]

In a camp meeting account for the following year, Palmer hinted again at her agency, this time implicitly attributing significant holiness-evangelistic success to her presence.

> New York, *August* 13th, 1848.
>
> *To our much loved friends, Bishop and Mrs. Hamline:*
> I returned to my home yesterday, after an absence of three or four days, which was spent at a Camp Meeting, near Philadelphia. Our dear Sister James was present. How sweetly does her life exhibit the beauty of holiness. I think I never saw an individual more fully possessed of that love that thinketh no evil, than our beloved Sister James, yet as she professes the enjoyment of a state of holiness, she has her trials. She feels sadly assured that many ministers of the New Jersey Conference, do not love explicit testimony on this subject.... Brother Atwood preached a sermon on the subject of holiness, remarkable for the clearness of its views, and the power which attended it, may never be forgotten.

There are reasons why I shall remember this meeting with thanksgiving to God. I had been strongly urged to attend one which was held at the same time at Eastham near Boston. Here Wesleyan views of holiness are much appreciated, and last year while with them, I witnessed many enter into the enjoyment of holiness. I was perhaps equally urged to attend the meeting in New Jersey; but here I well knew, that the doctrine was depreciated, yet I dared not refuse. When I inquired of the Lord which of the two I should attend, it was suggested that the Saviour would not have left His throne in heaven had His only object been the enjoyment of congenial society, and if I would take Him as my example, my way was clear. I yielded and went to New Jersey. Most abundantly have I been rewarded in my own soul, for this act of self-denial.[96]

In a way Palmer transformed established outdoors-permissive patterns of camp-meeting dynamics to the holiness cause, a transformation being effected generally by the often congenial "protracted meetings." (These lent themselves to the holiness cause and to Palmer's ministrations as well.) Palmer's modeling, advocacy, and extensive publications served the holiness cause in a threefold manner.[97] She bid the already converted to sanctification with a "holiness altar invitation." Those responding were urged to immediate attendance at a "believing meeting." And third, she pressed the newly sanctified to witness in "altar testimony." So she transformed what had been aspirin for the unconverted into stimulant for the saved. So the holiness cause could bring wilderness, camp-meeting boisterousness into expression suited to an indoor garden.

Others, of course, kept perfectionism outdoors. In his apology for camp meetings, James Porter insisted *"The relation of such meetings to the subject of holiness, furnishes another powerful argument* in favour of their continuance." He continued, "[M]any of the most holy of our people attend these meetings." And for those not already holy, camp meetings taught the doctrine, encouraged belief in it, and aided attendees to achieve entire consecration. "Thus," he insisted, "we hear it reported of almost every such meeting, that so many were sanctified." He concluded "that much of the spirit of holiness in our church at the present day, is attributable, under God, to the influence of camp-meetings," indeed, he estimated "four-fifths."[98]

A minor figure in the holiness cause—indeed critiqued at one point in "a righteous rebuke in a letter from sister Palmer"—like Palmer found holiness in camp meetings.[99] While still in that quest, this G. W. Henry commented on one meeting, "The meeting grew better and better, and the last night I was bathing and swimming in the ocean of love. It was a Pentecost to me and many others. There was little or no sleeping in the camp that night." Licensed to exhort in 1844, he spoke of Maryland camp meetings that year, affirming, A "Holy Ghost camp-meeting…is more like heaven than any other on earth."[100] He described his own experience of "the blessing of perfect love," acknowledged correcting it in a second edition of his autobiography in light of Palmer's critique, and celebrating his wife's holiness conversion as well.[101] He made provision for others to chart their path to holiness or to celebrate by including in his autobiography a collection of songs to encourage or praise that spirit.[102]

Palmer's increasingly public, beyond-the-cabin-and-in-the-forest camp meeting but also Tuesday meeting roles proved important stimuli to the Revival of 1857–58, sometimes referred to as the businessman's revival.[103] But that flashed in and across urban America engaging various Protestant "laymen" and ministries. It took many religious activities indoors and away from our wilderness-grove-garden concern. But the holiness cause in the Palmer style would return to the woods and even more dramatically, nationally, and productively in another decade as we will note in the next chapter. Here it is important to call attention again to another important prewar movement, one decidedly not reaching out to urban wealth and privilege, the Free Methodists, whose founder, B. T. Roberts, had been close to Palmer, whose church-criticizing concerns included holiness and whose early campaign efforts relied heavily upon camp meetings.[104]

Equally drawn from city to camp meeting for holiness were preachers who catered to Methodist wealth, like Alfred Cookman who served prominent churches in Philadelphia, Pittsburgh, Wilmington, New York, and Newark, and in the Union cause through the Christian Commission.[105] He wrote his sister concerning one of four camp meetings in 1866:

> On Wednesday of this week I went up to Halifax camp-meeting, above Harrisburg. It was the last night of the meeting, but oh, what a night! Old Methodists, who had been going to camp-meeting for nearly half a century, say they never saw any thing like it. Brother George Lybrand preached very forcibly at half-past seven o'clock, and invited penitents. The bench was filled. At eleven o'clock I preached to the Church on the subject of "Holiness." Oh, what an appetite the people exhibited! We knelt in consecration before God,

then followed the Sacrament at the mid-night hour. It brought us to Jesus; He saved us from our fears and doubts, and salvation flowed down in floods. The preachers and people were of one mind and heart touching the great subject of Christian purity.

A holiness body count Cookman could not discern:

> I could not tell you how many entered into the rest of perfect love. The preachers' tent, as at Ennall's Springs, was submerged with the incoming tide. Yesterday morning we gathered at the stand, listened to many witnesses of perfect love, expressed some parting counsels, received the blessing of that venerable man, Father Boehm, marched around the ground, and then, amid songs and shoutings, took the parting hand, rejoicing in the conviction that Christians never part for the last time.[106]

Cookman described this one and three other camp meetings in a longish article for Methodism's *Christian Advocate*. "Two leading facts met my observation at all these meetings," he insisted. "First, the interest in the mind of the Church respecting the experience of personal holiness. Every where ministers and people were groaning for full redemption in the blood of the Lamb. I have seen hundreds at the same moment prostrated before God in the spirit of entire consecration, and concerned to appropriate Jesus as their full and perfect Saviour." After praising the doctrine of holiness at some length, Cookman reported, "The second thing which profoundly impressed me in my camp-meeting observations was, that whenever and wherever the work of sanctification revived among professing Christians, the work of God revived in the conversion of sinners."[107]

For Cookman, as for Methodists—frontier and urban—highly popular holiness gatherings and worship would, postwar, return them to the forest and even cuddle them by the beach. Cookman, who died in 1871, had caught all three of the National Camp Meetings for the prior year (Hamilton [MA], Oakington [MD], and Des Plaines[IL]). Fifty-two of the Nationals energized Methodism over the holiness movement's next fifteen years. Initially embraced by Methodism's leadership—ministers of much more prominence and power than Cookman—the holiness camp meetings would contribute, as we shall see in the next chapter, to a yawning division.[108] Grove-and-garden gatherings dedicated to perfect love would ironically yield conflict, repression, and schism. The forest and camp meetings would divide Methodism into evangelical and liberal as we will discover. As early as 1873, a phenomenology or mapping of the church by a New Englander could, as it were, excommunicate holiness meetings and the holiness cause, even while devoting a chapter to camp meetings. In the book as a whole, Newell Culver spoke three times of "scriptural holiness" and frequently employed "holy" adjectively (for the Spirit and Ghost [four and two times respectively] and for Sabbaths, name, writ, zeal, character, Christianity, office [Bishop Beverly Waugh's], living, beautiful house, communings with God, and Christ's cause. No holiness banner for this member of the New Hampshire Conference! Nor implicitly a holiness banner for the book's endorser, Rev. Lorenzo D. Barrows, D. D., church leader, sometime presiding elder, and president over time of several Methodist colleges.[109]

For others, however, indeed a huge swath of Methodism, the National Camp Meeting Association for the Promotion of Holiness, as we shall see in the next chapter, more faithfully exhibited true Wesleyanism and sustained Methodism's grove and garden witness.[110]

[A]s of late they are more permanently established... and as more people of wealth patronize and attend them
[Popular]

We had able and faithful sermons. The subject of entire consecration received a large share of attention from the preachers, and the good results of the efforts made on tills subject were apparent. Mrs. Palmer, who is deeply interested in this subject, was again present with us and spoke upon it, giving a lucid testimony of her own experience, and pointing out the way of faith to others.[111]

So noted a report on the 1855 Martha's Vineyard increasingly **popular** camp meeting. If the island accommodated holiness preaching, it also increasingly served a clientele as intent on Christian relaxation as on perfection. Among the sixty ministers present, from various conferences, was B. W. Gorham on whose meditation on camp meetings, published the prior year, we commented extensively above. His worries over the domestication of camp meetings might well have been a reflection of the trajectory of that on Martha's Vineyard over the prior two decades. The grounds, schedule, and living arrangements there well modeled and illustrated the direction that camp meetings would take presenting the range of Methodist doctrine but also increasingly accommodating the values, lifestyle, routines, and concerns of Methodism's social fabric. On Martha's Vineyard, Methodists perhaps first mapped, erected, ordered, and dramatized camp meeting signaling their standing as a people increasingly middle class. That worried Hebron Vincent, the camp's first serious commentator.

> It may be remarked, however, that as of late they are more permanently established in particular locations, for a series of years, and as more people of wealth patronize and attend them, the outlay for convenient and permanent fixtures has been correspondingly increased. It is thought by many, however, that the great object of such gatherings was formerly more fully attained than it now is; that the preachers and church members then engaged more heartily and devotedly in labor for the glory of God and the salvation of souls than they now do; and that thus, as a consequence, more signal displays of divine power were realized.

Vincent sought to backtrack, "There may be some truth in these views, but there is much less, we imagine, than is often supposed." But, he immediately reverted to "patronize." "Yet it must be confessed," he conceded, "that, considering the great increase of the numbers of professing Christians assembling, our meetings seem to partake more, relatively, of the social character, and less of the spiritual, than they once did. Still, a large portion of both the ministry and laity are as devoted and laborious as ever, and oftentimes great numbers of sinners are saved."[112]

So Hebron Vincent meditated on the trajectory of the important, trendsetting, and "permanent" camp meeting on Martha's Vineyard. In his report for 1855, he quoted from a newspaper account:

> The printed account of the meeting states: —
> The area of the circle has been somewhat enlarged this year by the removal back of some eight or ten of the large tents, and arrangements have been made for a still further extension next year. There are now some thirty-six large tents in the main circle, and application has already been made to the agent for places for three more next year, and also for six family tents in the roar. This last class have increased greatly of late, insomuch that the whole number of tents

on the ground, including these, the boarding tents, &c., amounted this year to one hundred and eighty. Really we look like quite a city in the woods. We think we are already unequalled in this particular, as well as in eligibility of location, by any other encampment in New England.[113]

To this description, Vincent added his own confirmation of the camp's city-like trajectory, by then served daily (except Sundays) by two steam-boats. "Our city of tents now numbered about 200, of all descriptions; some of those newly erected were on a magnificent scale."

The scale and character of this domestication of the camp meeting, populated by anywhere from five to seven thousand, prompted Vincent's further depiction of and reflection of its "urban" and middle-class accommodations. "Formerly, here as at other camp meetings," he recalled, "each company of brethren and friends coming together, lived, lodged, and held their prayer meetings in one large tent, owned by them or by the church they represented."

> But after a few years, some few brethren, wishing to be more do-mestic in their household affairs, and to enjoy an undisturbed re-treat from the crowd, at least a part of the time, conceived the idea of having separate small family tents, near by, for the objects named; while they would still consider themselves as belonging to the large tent's company, and would go in to enjoy the social means of grace with the mass of their brethren. Very soon others adopted the same style of camp meeting life. From year to year the number has since been increasing, till now some of the large tents seem at times half forsaken. Of the two hundred tents on the ground this year, about one hundred and fifty were of this description.

A city in the woods, even if a camp meeting, could come to reflect urban spiritual diversity. So Vincent worried:

> It has been found that although these small tents afford many tem-poral comforts which could not otherwise be enjoyed here, yet they are calculated to keep a great many away from the preaching and prayer meetings on the ground; and, without some wholesome regulations regarding them, such as have been of late adopted, the custom of having them is liable to be abused by irreligious persons,

to the injury of the camp meetings themselves. It was therefore at this meeting voted, "That no one hereafter be allowed to have a family tent on this ground, unless he be approved as a suitable person to do so, by the church in his vicinity, he being a member or not, as the case may be." It was also, on motion, voted, "That each small tent shall hereafter have on it the name of the owner, and the name of the church recommending him; and that every such tent be under the supervision of the tent-master of the society or company approving it."[114]

Vincent returned to his worries over the trajectory of camp meetings on his report of 1858, the last covered. He noted that "Quite a number of persons came and took up their temporary residence in the grove several days before the time announced for commencing." The meeting commanded reduced fare on railroads, was served twice a day by the steamer "Eagle's Wing," and "great numbers came in steam and sail vessels of less size." On the Sabbath he estimated in the camp some twelve thousand, "six or seven thousand of whom were within the sound of the preacher's voice." Among those present "for a longer or shorter portion of the time" were "His Excellency Governor Banks, and his Aid, Mr. Lincoln; Hon. Samuel H. Walley, Hon. Joseph White, and Hon. J. F. Marsh, Bank Commissioners,— all of Massachusetts; Ex-Governor Harris, of Rhode Island; Hon. Mr. Benson, late M. C. from Maine, and Hon. Mr. Barrot of the same State; and Rev. and Hon. Sidney Dean, M. C. from Connecticut, who preached on Sabbath forenoon one of the most able and eloquent sermons ever delivered on this ground, on 'The Elements of Power in the Gospel of Christ.' "[115] Of the "over one hundred ministers of the Gospel" present at one point or another, most were Methodists.

The preachers, Vincent complained, had not kept up the evangelistic spirit.

The sermons of these brethren were all good, some of them of superior excellence. All were sound in theology. Some of them were of the practical, pointed, old Methodistic stamp; but many others, it was thought by some, lacked that directness of aim so important, especially on a camp ground, to arouse the dormant energies of sluggish professors, and to carry conviction and alarm to the hearts of the unconverted. It was probably owing, in part, to this last-named feature of the preaching, but perhaps more especially to the

prevailing inclination, manifest among all classes, to social and do-
mestic enjoyment, that the meeting, although exceedingly pleasant
and harmonious, was considered to be less spiritual than usual.[116]

Following brief comments on the numbers for and quality of the love
feast, communion service, and baptisms at the event, he continued with
the worry that, in brief, well captured the trajectory of this and other vacation-
like camp meeting sites. "On the whole, this camp meeting, although par-
taking relatively rather too much of the social character, and too little of
deep, earnest, and persistent labor for the conversion of sinners and the
consecration of believers, has been profitable, and has had the effect to
strengthen and extend its own previously good reputation. About twenty
persons have been converted."[117] A small body count out of twelve thousand! Noting that the tent count of 320 exceeded the prior year's by seventy, he reported that "sixty sites for new tents, to be erected new year,
have already been selected by persons on the ground at this meeting." The
tent body count drew his comment, "Quite a city, truly, and an exceedingly
pleasant one."[118] By the 1860s, Wesleyan Grove had become a heavenly
home, a resting place, a religious colony.

> Religious work in Wesleyan Grove now began in early July, with
> morning and evening prayer meetings and several Sunday services.
> Life was simple and domestic. Fathers could be with their children
> all day, a novelty for the businessman. Tired mothers would be
> refreshed as well, even with husbands gone during the week, for it
> was safe to let children roam.... Ministers commuted as well as
> businessmen.... The community was said to be so peaceful that it
> was hard to tell which day was Sunday.... There was a softness, a
> languor, and an ease. Only the clicking of croquet mallets or the
> lapping of water against the shore interrupted thought.[119]

Founded in 1835 and moved and improved over time, Martha's Vineyard
heralded what we have termed the **popular** pattern of camp meeting.
Blossoming after the Civil War at a number of "permanent" sites, these
catered to the diverse populace camp meetings had always served but especially to Methodism's growing middle class. The latter gradually found
highly creative ways of transforming the semicircles of tents into comparatively parade-like, worshipful, and tentlike cottages.[120] As a woodland
spiritual retreat/vacation site, Martha's Vineyard modeled and doubtless

encouraged the replications of such camp meetings across Methodism. So acknowledged bishop/editor/college president/Lincoln confidant Matthew Simpson in his 1876 *Cyclopaedia of Methodism. Embracing Sketches of its Rise, Progress, and Present Condition.*

"Martha's Vineyard Camp-Meeting," Simpson noted to begin a long article, "is the oldest of the permanent camp-meetings, which have now become numerous in the United States, its original foundation having preceded that of all other similar meetings by nearly twenty-five years." Commenting on the development of the camp over time, on lease policy, on strictures about cabin style, he observed that "Wesleyan Grove presents the appearance of a regularly laid out and permanently built summer city of elegant cottages, some of which are quite expensive. A gradual change has also come over the character of the place as a resort." A resort or vacation spot, Simpson affirmed, over time it had become. "After a few years, family tents having been introduced, a few persons would come a few days before the meeting to enjoy a short season of quiet in the grove, with a clam-bake; a few years afterwards they began to arrive several weeks beforehand; and now the grove has become a regular place of residence for families during the whole summer." For Simpson the spiritual retreat/vacation site served a new Methodism quite well.

> Stated religious meetings are held regularly during the whole season of the occupancy of the grove. The meeting has illustrated, most pointedly, by the success which has attended it in all of its aspects, during thirty-two years, how religious growth may be blended with the cultivation of physical vigor, wholesome recreation, and rational, innocent amusement, in such a way as to make each object contribute to the attainment of the other, and secure the higher enjoyment of the double blessing of a sound mind in a sound body.[121]

In his *Cyclopaedia of Methodism*, Simpson devoted portions of seventy-nine pages to camp meetings, included one article on the topic itself, and at a point or so acknowledged their hospitality to national and state "camp-meetings for the promotion of holiness" (affirmed for Round Lake). But this camp meeting, founded in 1868, devoted more attention to and welcomed quite different religious activities, including ten "Conference camp meetings." And like Round Lake and except for Martha's Vineyard, the camp meetings that Simpson treated were birthed post–Civil War. Like Martha's Vineyard, however, Simpson's camp meetings were oriented to

transform Methodists less before the holiness altar than through "the promotion of religion and education." Typifying such purposes was the
Thousand Island Camp-Meeting Association, which annually boasted
"a camp-meeting, a scientific and, aesthetic congress, a temperance con-
vention, and a Sunday-school parliament."[122] Rehoboth Beach camp
ground (near Lewes, Delaware) featured a thousand-yard boardwalk "on
Surf Avenue, on the ocean-side, making a fine promenade. Sunday-school
conventions are held as well as camp-meetings, and the place is occupied
as a seaside resort, and is free from many of the vices found at fashionable
watering-places."[123] Simpson explicitly noted dedication to religious education as well for camp meetings at Chester Heights and Ocean Grove.[124]

One hearthstone laid in the hitherto unbroken solitude of the wilderness, proves the nucleus of a splendid city

In 1876, the copyright date on Simpson's *Cyclopaedia of Methodism*, small
delegations of three preachers and two laymen representing northern and
southern Methodisms, began conversations that would eventuate over
half a century later in the reunion of the two churches (and also the
Methodist Protestants). This meeting had little of the relaxing flavor of
"camp" at Martha's Vineyard. Instead of camp-meeting accord, through
this Joint Commission on Fraternal Relations, meeting at Cape May, New
Jersey, reverberated tensions, antagonisms, and recriminations. Such an
"uncamp" spirit had yielded division in 1844. It had invigorated great
investments in the respective war efforts by the two churches. It had elicited northern missionizing of southern blacks and MECS extrusion of remaining black Methodists into the Colored Methodist Church. And it had
fed various other animosities. Cape May in mood was, to repeat, no
Martha's Vineyard. Yet, Cape May, like Martha's Vineyard and the similar
upscale camp meetings to which Simpson devoted attention, represented
Methodism's effort to get its religious life in accord with its by then respectable and variously signaled place in middle-class America. The two
big Methodisms, at least at leadership levels and in their urban settings,
would complete the transforming of various wildernesses into gardens
and groves. Just such transformations were well caught at roughly the
same time as Simpson had mapped out Methodism's social maturity in
his massive *Cyclopaedia*. Entitled *Crowned Victors. The Memoirs of Over
Four Hundred Methodist Preachers,* the volume celebrated the heritage of
the great Baltimore Conference.

It is well to sing the praises of the great and mighty, if truth and love inspire the singer and the song; it is better to tell the story of holy living, of pious zeal, of unselfish toil, of sacrifices ending only in death, offered gladly and lovingly, that others might live. One hearth-stone laid in the hitherto unbroken solitude of the wilderness, proves the nucleus of a splendid city; and the rude cabin of the venture-some frontiersman becomes the centre of palatial residences, as the hidden seed is the life of the beautiful flower. That lonely cabin and deserted hearth-stone ought never to be forgotten, and will not be. He who writes the history of the great city must needs write of its beginning, though he may not venture to predict its end.

In the pages before you, dear reader, you will find such memories as those we have been writing about—memories of the men and deeds that have given us the broad, rich heritage which we to-day enjoy, and which makes us the wonder of the world. The contrast of a hundred years is almost incredible; it is the picture of the cot and castle, the wilderness and the city, the Tabernacle and the Temple, the march through the desert over the sea, and Jerusalem the glory of Israel.[125]

Not all who thought of themselves as Methodist shared the judgment that the MEC (and MECS) were its castle, city, temple, and Jerusalem. Upscale MECs and MECSs looked more wilderness, cot, tabernacle, and desert to the new CMEs as well as to the AMEs and AMEZs; and to the Wesleyans and Free Methodists. Soon such a landscaping of Methodism's evangelistic efforts birthed the Nazarenes and other Holiness and Pentecostal movements that lived not for Martha's Vineyards but for old-style and perfectionist camp meetings. Wilderness could be metaphorical and spiritual as well as descriptive and geographical. So we will note in the chapter that follows.

5

Two Cities in the Woods, Methodism's Gardening Options

A CONCLUDING NOTE

Really we look like quite a city in the woods. *

SO HEBRON VINCENT had claimed for Martha's Vineyard. The affirmation might as readily be applied to 1869-founded Ocean Grove¹ and 1874-founded Chautauqua.² And what kind of enduring cities in the woods were they? Two much more ambitious in their visions for forest ministry and denominational transformation than vacation friendly "Popular" Martha's Vineyard. Indeed, both campaigned for a renewed Methodism, theirs "Programmatic" but in a more sustained, resolute, and effective fashion than the earlier sometimes forested reforms. They effectively and nicely symbolized two very different woodland and swim options for Methodism nationally, structurally, and programmatically.³ Neither looked or felt like the "Primitive" woodland option. Nor did they content themselves with a local clientele, content, and strategy. "Perfectionist" applied strictly and consistently in all particulars to Ocean Grove and kindred holiness gatherings. The label might be pinned, as we will note, in a more metaphorical sense on Chautauqua. By the late 1870s, Methodists had envisioned two very different, well-institutionalized, nationally mounted, widely appealing, forcefully led paths out of human wilderness and into spiritual renewals in shady grove gardens.

---

* *A History of the Wesleyan Grove,* 147–48. Vincent continued with a claim that the holiness movement soon bettered, "We think we are already unequalled in this particular, as well as in eligibility of location, by any other encampment in New England."

Each understood itself and its cause as desperately needed by and renewing of the denomination. Both claimed John Wesley and both thought of their vision and program as THE faithful mounting of his cause, his campaign, his scheme for spiritual renewal. The "Wesleys" of their own day? Each, at least initially, featured the "forested" participation and endorsement of Methodism's leaders. And each functioned effectively for and with the church's laity—women and men. Both expanded aggressively across the U.S. Each birthed structures and programs that furthered, regularized, and placed its campaigns within Methodism initially and then within the growing array of American organization—albeit one eventually in new holiness denominations and the other in Methodism's exploding religious education processes and structures. In each a dynamic churchman took center stage. Pastor John S. Inskip out of New York City, for one, and for the other, John Heyl Vincent, exercising various New York and Chicago leadership training roles, including later that of bishop.

"The groves were God's first temples"

So quoting W. C. Bryan, Vincent began the chapter on "The Beginning" of the Chautauqua venture to transform Methodism.[4] Methodism's identification with ancient Israel and placement in its sylvan setting would have been equally if not more characteristic of the new national holiness campaign. Both movements offered a compelling vision of and program for the maturing of a Christian, the trek from sin to salvation, the pathway from the first couple's extrusion from Eden to the welcome of the saints into the New Jerusalem. The programs for Christianization? Inskip's offered holiness. Vincent's featured nurture. The first "salvation"—though its sites, rhythms, duration, and program might be extensive—could occur in an instant. For the second, maturation as a Christian entailed a lifelong journey from crib to casket.

Each furthered its cause with national structures, prominent leadership, popular following, and well-planned campaigns. The first we have already noted—the extended holiness efforts that led to the 1867 founding of National Camp Meeting Association for the Promotion of Holiness. Vineland, New Jersey was its organizing site and first national event. Thereafter, the Association moved its national gatherings around each year. National they truly were. For a Sunday, Vineland drew "almost double" the town's "10,000 regular inhabitants." The following year, a Sunday for the national event at Manheim (Pennsylvania) gathered twenty-five thousand folk, including more than three hundred preachers. The national camp meeting for the following year (1869) at Round Lake, New York, functioned under organizational rules that required a formal invitation from the sponsoring site to limit the idle onlookers and prohibited Sunday railroad service. It still drew twenty thousand.[5] Beyond those "corporate" meetings, the new organization provided guidance, programming, and publicity to the already extensive but previously more spontaneous holiness witness at camp meetings across the nation. Methodism's holiness efforts played a not-insignificant part in the dramas that led to modern evangelicalism.

The inaugural year of the diverse educational and renewal efforts related to the second, Chautauqua, was 1874. Chautauqua, as its recent scholarly interpreter, notes, "was a middle-class movement that contributed to modern liberalism."[6]

Both camp-meeting-centered-causes, as already noted, exploded across Methodism. Although each continued a woodland siting of its schemes for renewal of individuals and of the church, they differed markedly in strategy. Holiness leaders gathered crowds expecting one-by-one renewals in the forest events or individually, as well as at church back home. Revival continued to yield personal transformation, an individual's walk to the altar, the lonely conversion, and the applauded and staged second blessing. From the soul's renewal that of the denominational would come. By contrast, out of Chautauqua emerged a vast infrastructural set of places, programs, curricular, visions, and other "Chautauquas" that functioned to equip Christian educators and other leaders for teaching large classes of Sunday school students. (Andrew Rieser counted 101 "independent Chautauqua Assemblies" for the years 1874–1899.[7]) Camp Chautauqua armored troops of teachers and other leaders to armor, train, and lead the troops back on their own battlefields. Their troops? God's children of every age!

The one looked back to Francis Asbury and Methodism's one-on-one conversion of sinners. The other, launched by bishop-to-be John Vincent and merchant and Sunday school superintendent Lewis Miller, looked ahead to Christian nurture on a collective, indeed a mass scale, as it were, the church's contributive role in the organizational revolution.[8] Just a couple of years before the latter two men acquired the Chautauqua camp meeting site and began its transformation into the hub of a giant Christian education training program, they had collaborated on the vision for and building of the Akron Sunday School (1870). Its design? An auditorium, adjacent to the church's sanctuary and ringed on several floors by small classrooms, permitted Sunday school superintendents to open and close a mass gathering, send children to age-graded classrooms, and dismiss teachers and children into the sanctuary through sliding doors.

The Akron design, replicated and modified across Methodism, provided the setting for industrialized religious education. Similarly, Chautauqua provided, modeled, and brought into forested display an array of emerging schemes to equip teachers across Methodism for their role in the church's rapidly expanding, indeed exploding, Sunday school apparatus. An Akron-like factory (Sunday school) in every town! National headquarters and training center at Chautauqua! Christian capitalists in Vincent, Miller, and colleagues!

Called by some a "camp-meeting." But...not...except that the most of us lived in tents

So Vincent explained of the first of the Chautauqua events and in a sense of the Christian education program launched in what indeed had earlier served as a conventional camp meeting. He explained:

> THE Chautauqua Assembly opened as a Sunday-school institute,—a two-weeks' session of lectures, normal lessons, sermons, devotional meetings, conferences, and illustrative exercises, with recreative features in concerts, fireworks, and one or two humorous lectures. It was called by some a "camp-meeting." But a "camp-meeting" it was not, in any sense, except that the most of us lived in tents. There were few sermons preached, and no so-called "evangelistic" services held. It was simply a Sunday-school institute, a protracted institute held in the woods. We called it at the first "The Chautauqua Sunday-school Assembly."[9]

Vincent preceded this declaration and headed this chapter on "The Beginning," with a quotation from W. C. Bryan, *"The groves were God's first temples."* So also for Vincent, America's sylvan temples ought to reclaim what God had first ordained and what Israel lived with, indeed prescribed. In the temple, God would be heard by the reading, indeed the studying, of his Word. For Vincent, engagement with God's Word mandated that Methodists understand the world that God had made. The wider vision, of course, could not be more pertinent because God had welcomed Methodism outside the temple building (its churches) and into God's original temple, the groves. And the little grove at Chautauqua, other camp meeting sites onto which Chautauqua programming might light, and the Sunday school teachers whom such centers would equip could and should instruct Americans generally, so Vincent explained:

> Chautauqua stretches over the land a magnificent temple, broad as the continent, lofty as the heavens, into which homes, churches, schools, and shops may build themselves as parts of a splendid university in which people of all ages and conditions may be enrolled as students. It says: Unify such eager and various multitudes. Let them read the same books, think along the same lines, sing the same songs, observe the same sacred days,—days consecrated to the delights of a lofty intellectual and spiritual life. Let the course of prescribed reading be broad and comprehensive; limited in its first general survey of the wide world of knowledge; opening out into special courses, according to the reader's development, taste, and opportunity.[10]

Chautauqua could reshape American society because the church—including of course Methodists but also the several denominations whose educators proved congenial and/or frequented the programming—had awakened to its responsibility to teach young and old.[11] Vincent waxed eloquent:

> Chautauqua has therefore a message and a mission for the times. It exalts education,—the mental, social, moral, and religious culture of all who have mental, social, moral, and religious faculties; of all, everywhere, without exception. It aims to promote a combination of the old domestic, religious, educational, and industrial agencies; to take people on all sides of their natures, and cultivate them symmetrically, making men, women, and children everywhere more affectionate and sympathetic as members of a family; more conscientious and reverent, as worshippers together of the true God; more intelligent and thoughtful as students in a universe of ideas; and more industrious, economical, just, and generous, as members of society in a work-a-day world. The theory of Chautauqua is that life is one, and that religion belongs everywhere. Our people, young and old, should consider educational advantages as so many religious opportunities. Every day should be sacred. The schoolhouse should be God's house. There should be no break between sabbaths. The

cable of divine motive should stretch through seven days, touching with its sanctifying power every hour of every day.

He continued:

> Kitchen work, farm work, shop work, as well as school work, are divine....
>
> We need an alliance and hearty co-operation of Home, Pulpit, School, and Shop,—an alliance consecrated to universal culture for young and old; for all the days and weeks of all the years; for all the varied faculties of the soul, and in all the possible relations of life.[12]

Vincent amplified this vision of Chautauqua as transformative of American society with an eight-point summation of its (his) understanding of what might make the grove God's temple. The first three of these points should be noted. He says:

> The entire Chautauqua movement is based upon the following propositions: —
>
> 1. The whole of life is a school, with educating agencies and influences all the while at work, from the earliest moment to the day of death. These agencies and influences should be wisely and continuously applied by and in behalf of each individual, through life, according to circumstances, capacities, and conditions.
>
> 2. The true basis of education is religious. The fear of the Lord is the beginning of wisdom,—the recognition of the Divine existence, and of his claims upon us as moral beings; the unity and brotherhood of the race, with all that brotherhood involves; harmony with the Divine character as the ideal of life for time and eternity; and the pursuit and use of all science in personal culture, the increase of reverent love for God, and of affectionate self-sacrifice and labor for the well-being of man.
>
> 3. All knowledge, religious or secular, is sacred to him who reverently surrenders himself to God, that he may become like God, according to the divinely appointed processes for building character. And he has a right to all attainments and enjoyments in the realm of knowledge, for the possession of which he has capacity and opportunity. Science, travel, literature, the works of art, the glories of nature,—

all things are his who is one with God. This law applies to the poor and lowly, as well as to the rich and so-called "favored classes" of society. It gives lofty ideals to lowly life, and transforms humble homes into places of aspiration and blessedness.[13]

The Ocean Grove and National Camp Meeting Association folk would have concurred and certainly affirmed that "all things are his who is one with God." They might also have agreed, if exegeting the affirmation themselves, that "Science, travel, literature, the works of art, the glories of nature,—all things are his who is one with God." But for the revivalists, God's transformation of humans turned more on event than through process. They doubtless thought it strange, irreligious, heretical to view religion as education and education as religion.

The whole of life is a school…from the earliest moment to the day of death

In 1872, the MEC elected eight bishops, six of whom were "friendly with the holiness cause" and its school. So judged one of the movement's most eminent recent interpreters, Melvin Dieter. He claimed and described the holiness "friendship" for Randolph S. Foster, Stephen Merrill, Jesse T. Peck, Gilbert Haven, Thomas Bowman, and William L. Harris.[14] Equally demonstrative by then of the MEC's high commitment to the holiness cause was the role of its most powerful and widely known of the bishops, Matthew Simpson. Simpson, one of the few pope-like successors to Francis Asbury in Methodism's whole history, took a prominent role in the holiness movement's national, structured, programmatic camp meetings. Simpson was the preeminent preacher at the first of the National's[15] holiness camp meetings, that in Vineland. In 1868, he opened the second, that at Mannheim (Pennsylvania) with a sermon. For the third National in 1869 at Round Lake (New York), a gathering of twenty thousand, Simpson celebrated the Lord's Supper on the event's first Sunday. Concluding by calling the preachers present to dedicate themselves to exercising the "apostolic power" conferred to his servants by Christ, he prayed "Help us to preach Christ as we never preached before…His blood cleanseth, cleanseth, CLEANSETH…The blood of Jesus cleanseth from all sin."[16] Simpson, the champion of the holiness cause!

By the late 1870s, when he put together his *Cyclopaedia of Methodism*, Simpson had *been to school* and like much of middle-class Methodism had changed his mind about holiness camp meetings. Seemingly he dropped the holiness movement out of Methodist history as well as his own. Or perhaps, limited as he was to a thousand pages in the *Cyclopaedia* did he discern that there was really not enough room to cover the National Camp Meeting Association for the Promotion of Holiness? And why would an entry on camp meetings effectively skip over the earlier holiness efforts, moving instead from their early days to the vacation friendly "Popular" style? And when treating major Methodist doctrines—holiness, perfection, and sanctification—need one get into American specifics and cover the persons, events, and concerns that dramatized their import for earlier Methodism? Not for Simpson. Treat such doctrines as dealt with Mr. Wesley's and leave it there. The holiness cause was not to be the bishops' thing.

Nor was it a cause or topic for the MEC's chief publicist, James M. Buckley, editor for two decades of the *Christian Advocate*. At the turn of the century, he toured through Methodist history for the denominational volume in the American Church History series (an important, indeed groundbreaking, multivolume church history series). In 700 pages the MEC's chief spokesperson dealt briefly with camp meetings twice. Buckley did so once for their beginning in the early 1800s and the second in a chapter devoted to non-MEC movements and specifically Lorenzo Dow's Primitive Methodists. Neither Phoebe Palmer nor the early holiness imprint on camp meetings movement generally merited attention. He did attend in several chapters to Methodism's denominational divisions. Twice he examined the Free Methodists but without mentioning their holiness commitments. Noting that the *Discipline* of the Wesleyan Methodists included among their Articles of Religion one on entire sanctification, he conceded that it was a subject "which has been much debated in Methodism." That debate he must have deemed quite settled. So sanctification? perfection? holiness?— not even worthy of an entry in the index. Nor did the holiness movement and the National Camp Meeting Association for the Promotion of Holiness deserve attention. But Chautauqua, the colleges, and Methodism's various educational renewal efforts certainly did.[17] If all of life proved not to be a school, certainly for Buckley Methodism did.

An alliance and hearty co-operation of Home, Pulpit, School, and Shop[18]

Methodism proved not disposed to let go of its woodland venture. In gravitating toward these late, widely available and highly orchestrated forested schools, Methodism had ample opportunity to consolidate their occasional theologizing about wilderness, grove, and garden. They might have stepped back, reflected, and developed their regular and substantial sylvan experiences into either a formal, denominational soteriology or a doctrine of creation. But the several older camp-meeting trajectories and especially those two in late-century—seemingly mounted for denominational reinvention and control—militated against a common theological vision. Each of these religious expressions construed forest in its own theological fashion, accenting distinctive construals of garden, grove, and wilderness in so doing. America's forests had once brought Methodists together. They gathered confident that offering spiritual exhortations in a shady grove would in conversions overcome their separation from one another as well as the conquest of sin. And they would be made new in unity through and with the Spirit in God's own garden. "The narrative pattern was the way of the cross." It led, continues Gregory Schneider, "into a particular location." He then insisted,

> The pious Methodist resided in a sacred place set over against a threatening environment. Virtue, peace, resignation, love, and joy all pervaded that place and elevated the believer above the stormy passions of this world. Sometimes, in class meeting, love feast, or camp meeting, this spatial image would be incarnate in the physical arrangement of people and buildings. At other times the image would be conveyed through the language of believers about their inner lives. In either case, the reciprocal tie of the narrative pattern to the spatial image was implied: the way of the cross led to a sacred place that was identified with heaven and homeland, family and friends.[19]

Such unity perhaps prevailed, place to place and within each of the several camp-meeting impulses. But across Methodism? Hardly. Instead of producing a shared vision—within a camp, from one shady grove to another, and across the whole denomination—by the end of the century, the several woodland impulses of prior decades increasingly yielded to two dramatically different, indeed increasingly conflictive, understandings of and strategies for living under the Spirit and into God's garden.

Recent studies of late-century camp meetings suggest that Methodists had some capacity for conceptual exploration of wilderness, grove, and garden. Roger Robins observed, "The Methodist campground...was a self-portraying and self-fulfilling organization of space and time, and so it constitutes a vital record of Methodists' evolving self-image."[20] And, he noted, it offered intellectual resources for denominational self-understanding.

Would the camp meeting be a weapon/implement, subduing the spiritual and moral wilderness? Or would it be a refuge, a garden of spiritual and cultural renaissance to replenish depleted souls and refit them for modern society? Would it reflect a pilgrim people, yearning for "a city whose builder and maker is God," or a landed people acting out ritual landlessness?[21]

So, too, Steven Cooley called attention to the doctrinal possibilities within the camp-meeting initiatives for denominational self-understanding and even unity:

> The sacramentally constructed Victorian Methodist camp meeting sought a solution for living religiously in the modern world.... Within the sacramentally constructed camp-meeting event, the physical world became sacrally significant, the sacral realities became immediately present, and the work of ritual became possible. While official ecclesiology failed to grasp conceptually this sacramental practice of camp meeting, Methodism's vernacular language constructed the camp meeting as a compelling presentation of the sacred. This ideal ritual reality encountered resistance and occasionally disintegrated before the stubborn challenge of its historical realities, but the persistent tension between the ideal and the historical indicates the occasion of the camp meeting's ritual activity. To the extent that the Temple/Eden/camp meeting/Pentecost/Heaven/Canaan/New Jerusalem symbol system embued a place with the sacred, these Methodists pronounced their religious labor successful before moving back into the landscape of the urban industrial North.[22]

And finally in my own earlier assessment I called attention to features of the camp meeting on which Methodism might have pondered:

> The camp meeting, as a self-image, as an intricate and highly stylized recapitulation of the American experience, allowed Methodism to change while seeming to remain the same....

> Sufficiently a novelty to require promotion, it quickly spread over Methodism to become a national institution. Frontier weapon perhaps it was. But some of the camp meeting's power to create frontier community derived from its ritual reenactment of earlier Methodist

community. It was a new way of reliving the old and an old way for living in the new.[23]

By the twentieth century was Methodism still wilderness, grove, garden? Or Home, Pulpit, School, and Shop? Perhaps nostalgically and on some experiential levels the two represented stages of Methodist initiative and to that extent related. But conceptually, theologically? For mainline Methodism, New York City and Chicago were no longer frontiers. Cities were home, the latter in particular. There, in Evanston, Methodism bragged of its great university and seminary (Northwestern and Garrett). Named the streets for Methodist worthies. Spread churches around. And mounted through the WCTU the campaign that would determine what Americans could and could not drink. Wilderness—slums, political bosses, and rum? Grove—tree-lined residential streets? Garden—parks for reading and play? In a sense, mainline Methodism's woodland-like adventures continued. But could editor Buckley grasp the relation of his urban Methodism to the forested of Asbury? And might Buckley's seminary faculty friends at Drew, Boston, and Garrett have rethought, updated, and given doctrinal meaning to wilderness, grove, and garden? Might mainline Methodism have conceptualized theologically the connection between its wilderness and its park ministries?

So also continuing camp meetings dedicated to holiness represented theological as well as organizational possibilities. Some of those engineered the explosive growth of holiness and Pentecostal causes and many Methodists transferred their membership accordingly. These renewal movements, diversely motivated and led, camped in slums, old theaters, and other urban spots as well as in forested settings. And they birthed the array of vibrant Pentecostal movements that spread worldwide, there too camping in city or on landscape as opportunity permitted. Here, as well as in mainline Methodism, old and new wildernesses offered opportunities for doctrinal reconceptualization of the entire Christian enterprise.

MEC/MECS camp meetings across the Bible Belt continued, year-in, year-out as Brown's *Holy Ground, Too* so lavishly documents. These annual, always forested gatherings no longer commanded the denomination's most illustrious leadership or received more than passing notice in a conference's paper. Forested religious renewal, however, continued to sustain family togetherness and religious commitment.[24]

Neither mainline episcopal Methodism nor the Holiness-Pentecostal movements undertook sustained and serious reflection about their highly stylized annual woodland renewals and about their new urban frontier programming. What of wilderness, grove, and garden events as dramas of redemptive activity, as activity that required serious theological claims, as activity occasioning fresh insights about the world that God had made? Methodism's century and a half of forested sacred gatherings might have, by the early twentieth, occasioned on either mainline or renewal side, some biblically informed self-reflection. From its annual experiences of God in God's own creation what did Methodism have to offer the rest of Christianity about experiencing and understanding God's salvific acts? What new insights about the seven days in God's creation, of Eden, of wandering in the wilderness, of the land flowing with milk and honey, of Jesus in the wilderness, of his outdoor preaching, of garden betrayal and resurrection appearance, and of a promised new Eden? For neither mainline nor holiness Methodisms did the forest setting become a text for understanding and conveying the Wesleyan way of being in the world. American Methodism, from its independence in 1784, boasted a purpose statement that might have, with great elaboration and exegesis, become text for a theology of nature.

> *Quest.* 3. What may we reasonably believe to be God's Design, in raising up the Preachers called Methodists?
>
> *Answ.* To reform the Continent, and spread scripture Holiness over these Lands. As a Proof hereof, we have seen in the Course of fifteen Years a great a glorious Work of God, from New-York through the Jersies, Pennsylvania, Maryland, Virginia, North and South Carolina, even to Georgia.[25]

From their own experience already in the forest and from Wesley's injunction for field preaching, American Methodists had ample resources with which to begin to reflect on context. Over the course of the nineteenth century, the American wildernesses, groves, and gardens might have become text as well as context. Toward such denominational theological self-reflection, Methodism's camp-meeting hymns perhaps gestured. But as noted in chapter 3, doctrines of God have to be teased out of the occasional statement or stray verse. And the fracturing of Methodism and of the denomination's forest ministries did not facilitate sustained leisurely theologizing about God, church, and nature (chapter 4). Context did not become text for Methodism.

Or perhaps one should say that when context did become text for Methodism new ministries drove reflection to focus on city rather than forest. In the twentieth century, church leadership pressed the two Methodist Episcopal churches and their successor denomination into Home, Pulpit, School, and Shop. And while the Holiness-Pentecostal movements were initially less visible in Vincent's "Home, Pulpit, School, and Shop," they too discovered that radio ministries, schools and colleges, and urban ministries reached those neglected by the churches. Camping programs, wars, pollution, food and commodity challenges, and scientific probes of the miniscule and the universal would, later in the twentieth century, spur more serious reflection in the church about nature, the globe, the universe. For such reflection would Methodism revisit Asbury and ministry in the creation's wilds? The new studies typically found resources for thinking elsewhere than in Methodism's century and a half of wilderness, grove, and garden experience.

John Wesley Preaching under Trees and in Groves

The Works of the Reverend John Wesley, A.M., ed. John Emory, 7 volumes (New York: Published by B. Waugh and T. Mason for the Methodist Episcopal Church, 1835).

The Works of John Wesley; begun as "The Oxford Edition of The Works of John Wesley" (Oxford: Clarendon Press, 1975–1983); continued as "The Bicentennial Edition of The Works of John Wesley" (Nashville: Abingdon Press, 1984–) 34 vols. Projected. *Journals and Diaries*, I-VII, *Works* 18-24. Abbreviated *Works* x, *Journals and Diaries*, x, pp.

June 1741

Sat. 13.—In the morning I preached on those words, "To him that worketh not, but believeth on Him that justifieth the ungodly, his faith is counted to him for righteousness." We then set out for Melbourn, where, finding the house too small to contain those who were come together, I stood under a large tree, and declared Him whom God hath exalted to be a Prince and a Saviour, to give repentance unto Israel, and remission of sins." Thence I went to Hemmington, where also, the house not being large enough to contain the people, they stood about the door, and at both the windows, while I showed "what" we " must do to be saved." *The Works of the Reverend John Wesley*, 3: 213; *Works* 19, *Journals and Diaries*, II, 199–200.

June 1745

Sun. 23.—I preached in Gwennap at five, and about eight at Stithians, to a large and quiet congregation. Thence we went to Wendron church. At two I preached a mile and a half from the church, under a large shady tree, on part of the epistle for the day, "Marvel not, if the world hate you." *The Works of the Reverend John Wesley*, 3: 339; *Works* 20, *Journals and Diaries*, III, 72.

Aug. 1747

Sat. 29.—About noon we came to Builth. At three I preached in the main street, and at Garth in the evening; where I met my brother going to Ireland. Sun. 30.—He preached at Builth about nine. Thence we went to Maesmennys church. But it would not near contain the congregation; so that I was constrained to preach in the church yard. Thence I rode to Lanzunfried. Here also the church not being able to hold the people, I came out to a large tombstone, under a shady tree, and proclaimed "the grace of our Lord Jesus Christ." *The Works of the Reverend John Wesley*, 3: 407; *Works* 20, *Journals and Diaries*, III, 192.

May 1748

Whit Sunday, May 29.—Our first service began about four, at the Weaver's Hall. At seven I preached in the Old Orchard. At ten I began in Kingswood; where, at two (the house being too small for the congregation) I preached under the sycamore tree. At five I preached in the Old Orchard, and then rode to Kingswood; where we concluded the day with a love-feast. *The Works of the Reverend John Wesley*, 3: 427; *Works* 20, *Journals and Diaries*, III, 227.

August 26, 1748

The place in which I preached was an oval spot of ground, surrounded with spreading trees, scooped out, as it were, in the side of the hill, which rose round like a theatre. The congregation was equal to that at Leeds; but such serious and earnest attention! It lifted up my hands, so that I preached as I scarce ever did in my life. *The Works of the Reverend John Wesley*, 3: 436; *Works* 20, *Journals and Diaries*, III, 436.

June 1753

Wed. 6.—It being still sultry hot, I preached under a shady tree at Barley Hall; and in an open place at Rotherham in the evening. *The Works of the Reverend John Wesley*, 3: 556; *Works* 20, *Journals and Diaries*, III, 556.

April 1759

April 30.—We had a numerous congregation at Acton Bridge, two or three miles from Northwich. Some large trees screened us both from the sun and wind. *The Works of the Reverend John Wesley*, 4: 22; *Works* 21, *Journals and Diaries*, IV, 189.

Aug. 1764

Sun. 5.—I preached in Prince's-street at eight; at two, under the sycamore tree at Kingswood; and at five, near King's Square, in Bristol. How many thousands in this city do see in this "their day, the things that belong to their peace!" *The Works of the Reverend John Wesley*, 4: 190; *Works* 21, *Journals and Diaries*, IV, 485.

July 1765

Mon. 15.—I had the pleasure of meeting many of my friends from various parts at Coolylough. I preached at twelve under the shade of some spreading trees, and again at six in the evening. Tuesday, 16.—I preached at Tyrrel's Pass, with a peculiar blessing from God, though many persons of fortune were in the congregation. But the poor and the rich are his. Wed. 17.—I preached in the Grove at Edinderry. *The Works of the Reverend John Wesley*, 4: 215; *Works* 22, *Journals and Diaries*, V, 12.

Sept. 1765

Tues. 10.—They filled the house at five. I preached in Breage at twelve, under a lovely shade of trees. About six I began at St. John's, near Helstone, once as furious a town as Redruth. Now almost all the gentry of the town were present, and heard with the deepest attention. *The Works of the Reverend John Wesley*, 4: 219; *Works* 22, *Journals and Diaries*, V, 20.

Sept. 1765

Wed. 25.—About one I preached at Paulton, under a large, shady tree. *The Works of the Reverend John Wesley*, 4: 220; *Works 22, Journals and Diaries*, V, 22.

April 1766

Mon. 28.—I preached at Thorne. Although a great part of the congregation had never heard one preach under a tree before, yet they behaved extremely well. Before we came to York, I was thoroughly tired; but my strength quickly returned; so that, after preaching to a large congregation, and meeting the society, I was fresher than when I began. *The Works of the Reverend John Wesley*, 4: 228; *Works 22, Journals and Diaries*, V, 39.

July 1767

Thur. 16.—About ten I reached Donard, seven or eight-and-twenty English miles from Dublin. Standing under some shady tree, I enforced upon a serious congregation, "All things are ready; come unto the marriage." *The Works of the Reverend John Wesley*, 4: 255; *Works 22, Journals and Diaries*, V, 90.

April 9, 1767

About noon I preached near Dawson's Grove, to a large and serious congregation; but to a far larger in the evening at Kilmararty. *The Works of the Reverend John Wesley*, 4: 247; *Works 22, Journals and Diaries*, V, 76.

Sept. 1767

Sunday, 20, (as the Sunday before,) I preached in Princes-street at eight; about two under the sycamore tree at Kingswood; and at five in the new square, to a larger congregation than, I think, was ever there before. *The Works of the Reverend John Wesley*, 4: 262; *Works 22, Journals and Diaries*, V, 103.

May 1768

Sat. 21.—About noon I preached at Morpeth, and in the evening at Newcastle, in the old custom house, a large commodious room near the quayside, the grand resort of publicans and sinners. Sunday, 22.—I preached in the morning under the trees in Gateshead, to a large and serious multitude; and at two, on the Fell, to a much larger. But the largest of all attended at the Garth Heads in the evening; and great part of them were not curious hearers, but well acquainted with the things of the kingdom of God. *The Works of the Reverend John Wesley*, 4: 279; *Works 22, Journals and Diaries*, V, 134–35.

June 1768

Thur. 2.—I preached, at noon, at a farmer's house, near Brough, in Westmoreland. The sun was hot enough, but some shady trees covered both me and most of the congregation. *The Works of the Reverend John Wesley*, 4: 286; *Works 22, Journals and Diaries*, V, 146.

April 1769

Tues. 11.—I preached in the market house in Tanderagee to one of the liveliest congregations in the kingdom. Thursday and Friday I preached at Dawson's Grove and Kilmararty;... *The Works of the Reverend John Wesley*, 4: 301; *Works 22, Journals and Diaries*, V, 178.

Aug. 1770

Mon. 20.—I rode to Charlton. The violent heat continuing, I preached in the evening under a tree, to a congregation who were all attention. *The Works of the Reverend John Wesley*, 4: 335–36; *Works* 22, *Journals and Diaries*, V, 244.

Sept. 1770

Sun. 9.—My voice was weak when I preached at Princes-street in the morning. It was stronger at two in the afternoon, while I was preaching under the sycamore tree in Kingswood; and strongest of all at five in the evening, when we assembled near King's Square in Bristol. *The Works of the Reverend John Wesley*, 4: 338; *Works* 22, *Journals and Diaries*, V, 249.

June 1772

Tues. 23.—About eleven I preached at Driffield. The sun was extremely hot; but I was tolerably screened by a shady tree. In the evening I preached at Beverley, and on Wednesday, 24, in the new house at Hull, extremely well finished, and, upon the whole, one of the prettiest preaching houses in England. *The Works of the Reverend John Wesley*, 4: 380; *Works* 22, *Journals and Diaries*, V, 339.

July 1772

Thur. 23.—I preached at Barrow, and at five on Friday; about nine, at Awkborough; and at two, for the first time, in Messingham, under a wide-spread tree. *The Works of the Reverend John Wesley*, 4: 382; *Works* 22, *Journals and Diaries*, V, 343.

June 11-12, 1773

On Friday and Saturday I preached at Portadown, Kilmararty, Dawson's Grove, and Tanderagee. *The Works of the Reverend John Wesley*, 4: 397; *Works* 22, *Journals and Diaries*, V, 375.

July 1774

Sat. 30.—I went on to Madeley; and in the evening preached under a sycamore tree, in Madeley Wood, to a large congregation, good part of them colliers, who drank in every word. Surely never were places more alike, than Madeley Wood, Gateshead Fell, and Kingswood. *The Works of the Reverend John Wesley*, 4: 419; *Works* 22, *Journals and Diaries*, V, 422–23.

Sept. 1776

Sun. 22.—After reading prayers, preaching, and administering the sacrament, at Bristol, I hastened away to Kingswood, and preached under the trees to such a multitude as had not been lately seen there. *The Works of the Reverend John Wesley*, 4: 463; *Works* 23, *Journals and Diaries*, VI, 35.

June 1778

Sat. 13.—I took my stand in the middle of the Grove; the people standing before me on the gradually rising ground, which formed a beautiful theatre: the sun just glimmered through the trees, but did not hinder me at all. It was a glorious opportunity: the whole congregation seemed to drink into one spirit. Sun. 14.—I preached at Dunsford in the morning. In the evening the congregation in the Grove exceeded even that at Belfast; and I verily believe all of them were almost persuaded to be

Christians. *The Works of the Reverend John Wesley,* 4: 491; *Works 23, Journals and Diaries,* VI, 94.

June, 19, 1778.

I preached here at the bottom of the garden; the table was placed under a tree, and most of the people sat on the grass before it; and every thing seemed to concur with the exhortation, "Acquaint thyself now with him, and be at peace."

Tues. 23.—I went on to Tanderagee, one of the pleasantest towns in Ireland. As it was a fair, calm evening, I had designed to preach in the avenue to the castle; but being desired to preach in the court yard, I took my place under a tall spreading tree, in the midst of a numerous congregation, who were still as night. There could not be devised a more pleasing scene: the clear sky, the setting sun, the surrounding woods, the plain, unaffected people, were just suitable to the subject, "My yoke is easy, and my burden is light." *The Works of the Reverend John Wesley,* 4: 492; *Works 23, Journals and Diaries,* VI, 95–97.

Sept. 1778

Sunday, 6.—At eight I preached near the Drawbridge; at two, near Kingswood school, under the tree which I planted for the use of the next generation; and at five, near King's Square, to a very numerous and exceeding serious congregation. *The Works of the Reverend John Wesley,* 4: 496; *Works 23, Journals and Diaries,* VI, 106.

Sept. 1784

Sun. 12.—Dr. Coke read prayers, and I preached, in the new room. Afterward I hastened to Kingswood, and preached under the shade of that double row of trees which I planted about forty years ago. How little did any one then think that they would answer such an intention! The sun shone as hot as it used to do even in Georgia; but his rays could not pierce our canopy; and our Lord, meantime, shone upon many souls, and refreshed them that were weary. *The Works of the Reverend John Wesley,* 4: 602; *Works 23, Journals and Diaries,* VI, 331.

June 1785

Fri. 10.—We came to Downpatrick; where, the preaching house being too small, we repaired, as usual, to the Grove; a most lovely plain, very near the venerable ruins of the cathedral. The congregation was as large as that at Belfast, but abundantly more awakened. *The Works of the Reverend John Wesley,* 4: 620; *Works 23, Journals and Diaries,* VI, 366–67.

June 1785

Sun. 12.—We had a solemn opportunity in the morning. In the afternoon, as no building could contain the people, I stood abroad and proclaimed, "There is joy in heaven over one sinner that repenteth, more than over ninety and nine just persons who need no repentance." The hearers (allowing five persons to a square yard) were seven or eight thousand. At eleven I preached in the church yard at Lurgan. The sun shone extremely hot; but we were sheltered from it, partly by the church, and partly by the spreading trees....

At six I stood in the grove, where the tall elms shaded both me and the numerous congregation. Several gentlemen and several clergymen were among them; and all behaved with serious attention. *The Works of the Reverend John Wesley*, 4: 620–21; *Works* 23, *Journals and Diaries*, VI, 367–68.

June 19, 1786

We reached Swinfleet between six and seven, having gone, in all, seventy-six miles. A numerous congregation was assembled under the shade of tall trees. Sufficient for this day was the labour thereof; but still I was no more tired than when I rose in the morning. *The Works of the Reverend John Wesley*, 4: 634; *Works* 23, *Journals and Diaries*, VI, 398.

June 1786

Sun. 25.—I preached at Misterton. I was grieved to see so small a congregation at Haxey church. It was not so when Mr. Harle lived here. O what a curse in this poor land are pluralities and non-residence! But these are evils that God alone can cure. About one I preached at Overthorpe, where the spreading trees sheltered both me and the congregation. But we had a far larger at Epworth, between four and five in the afternoon. *The Works of the Reverend John Wesley*, 4: 635; *Works* 23, *Journals and Diaries*, VI, 400.

July 1786

Wed. 5.—Notice was given, without my knowledge, of my preaching at Belper, seven miles short of Derby. I was nothing glad of this, as it obliged me to quit the turnpike road, to hobble over a miserable common. The people, gathered from all parts, were waiting. So I went immediately to the market place; and, standing under a large tree, testified, "This is life eternal, to know thee, the only true God, and Jesus Christ whom thou has sent." The house at Derby was throughly filled in the evening. As many of the better sort (so called) were there, I explained, (what seemed to be more adapted to their circumstances and experience,) "This only have I found, that God made man upright; but they have found out many inventions." *The Works of the Reverend John Wesley*, 4: 638; *Works* 23, *Journals and Diaries*, VI, 406.

Aug. 17, 1787

In the evening I did not attempt to go into the house, but stood near it, in the yard surrounded with tall, shady trees, and proclaimed to a large congregation, "God is a spirit; and they that worship him must worship him in spirit and in truth." I believe many were cut to the heart this hour, and some not a little comforted. *The Works of the Reverend John Wesley*, 4: 675; *Works* 24, *Journals and Diaries*, VII, 51.

June 10, 1789

A multitude of people were waiting; (twice as many as were in the Green at Downpatrick;) when, finding no want of strength, I earnestly proclaimed, "God was in Christ reconciling the world unto himself." Such a congregation I have not seen since I came into the kingdom; neither such a pleasing place, shaded with tall, spreading trees, near which ran a clear river: and all the people listened with quiet and deep attention, to "drink of the water of life freely."

Fri. 12.—I had a day of rest in the same delightful grove; and preached on, "Thou shalt love the Lord thy God with all thy heart, and with all thy soul." Sat. 13.—I had another quiet day to answer my letters and revise my papers. I think the evening congregation was the largest we have seen in the kingdom; and they all seemed to feel the application of these words, which God applied with uncommon power, "Thou shalt love thy neighbour as thyself." *The Works of the Reverend John Wesley,* 4: 724; *Works 24, Journals and Diaries,* VII, 51, 142–43.

July 1790: JW

Sun. 4.—I went over to Misterton, where likewise the work of God was exceedingly decayed. The house being far too small to contain the multitude of people, I stood under a spreading tree; and strongly exhorted them to "strengthen the things that remained," which were "ready to die." *The Works of the Reverend John Wesley,* 4: 774; *Works 24, Journals and Diaries,* VII, 51, 183.

Oct. 1790

Thur. 7.—I went over to that poor skeleton of ancient Winchelsea. It is beautifully situated on the top of a steep hill, and was regularly built in broad streets, crossing each other, and encompassing a very large square; in the midst of which was a large church, now in ruins. I stood under a large tree, on the side of it, and called to most of the inhabitants of the town, "The kingdom of heaven is at hand; repent, and believe the Gospel." It seemed as if all that heard were, for the present, almost persuaded to be Christians. *The Works of the Reverend John Wesley,* 4: 748; *Works 24, Journals and Diaries,* VII, 191.

Notes

INTRODUCTION

1. Bishop Thomas Coke in November 1784 on a tour across the eastern seaboard prior to the Christmas Conference that organized the Methodist Episcopal Church. The omitted sentences in Rankin's sighting of land: "None can conceive, but those who have experienced it, the sensations that arise in the breast on seeing the land, after some weeks of viewing nothing but the sea and open firmament. I believe we all felt grateful to the God of all our mercies, and most earnestly prayed that he would go with us to a strange land and among a strange people." For a scholarly redo of the journals, see John A. Vickers, ed., *The Journals of Dr. Thomas Coke* (Nashville: Kingswood Books/Abingdon, 2005). See also John A. Vickers, ed., *The Letters of Dr. Thomas Coke* (Nashville: Kingswood Books/Abingdon Press, 2013) and Peter Forsaith and Martin Wellings, eds., *Methodism and History: Essays in Honour of John Vickers* (Oxford: Applied Theology Press, 2010).

2. On Pietism as a trans-Atlantic movement, see Ted A. Campbell, *The Religion of the Heart: A Study of European Religious Life in the Seventeenth and Eighteenth Centuries* (Columbia: University of South Carolina Press, 1991); W. Reginald Ward, *The Protestant Evangelical Awakening* (Cambridge: Cambridge University Press, 1992) and *Early Evangelicalism: A Global Intellectual History, 1670–1789* (Cambridge, UK; New York: Cambridge University Press, 2006); Peter C. Erb, ed., *Pietists: Selected Writings* (New York, Ramsey, Toronto: Paulist Press, 1983); the several writings by F. Ernest Stoeffler, *The Rise of Evangelical Pietism* (Leiden: Brill, 1965), *German Pietism during the Eighteenth Century* (Leiden: Brill, 1973), and *Continental Pietism and Early American Christianity* (Grand Rapids: Eerdmans, 1976). On John Wesley's relation to Pietism, see Martin Schmidt, *John Wesley: A Theological Biography*, trans. Norman P. Goldhawk, 2 volumes in 3 (Nashville: Abingdon Press, 1963–1973).

3. Harry S. Stout, *The Divine Dramatist: George Whitefield and the Rise of Modern Evangelicalism* Grand Rapids: W. B. Eerdmans, 1991); Jerome Dean Mahaffey. *The Accidental Revolutionary: George Whitefield and the Creation of America* (Waco: Baylor University Press, 2011); Frank Lambert, *Pedlar in Divinity: George Whitefield and the Transatlantic Revivals, 1737–1770* (Princeton: Princeton University Press, 1994); Dee E. Andrews, *The Methodists and Revolutionary America, 1760–1800: The Shaping of an Evangelical Culture* (Princeton: Princeton University Press, 2000), 19–31; and Frank Baker, *From Wesley to Asbury: Studies in Early American Methodism* (Durham: Duke University Press, 1976), 23–27.

4. On the Wesley program, see Richard P. Heitzenrater, *Wesley and the People Called Methodists* (Nashville: Abingdon Press, 1995), 99–100, 113–14, 144–45, 149–51, 153, 161–63, 165, 172, 176–77, 179, 185, 194, 225, 231.

5. *The Works of John Wesley;* begun as "The Oxford Edition of The Works of John Wesley" (Oxford: Clarendon Press, 1975–1983); continued as "The Bicentennial Edition of The Works of John Wesley" (Nashville: Abingdon Press, 1984–) 34 vols. Projected. *Works* 21: *Journals and Diaries*, IV (1755–1765), 230.

6. See the appendix for the forty-some times that John Wesley reported preaching under trees or in a grove and the few instances for which heat drove him there. The sylvan occasions, while worth noting, represent a very, very small percentage of the thousands of times that Wesley preached outdoors.

7. Francis Asbury, *Journal of Rev. Francis Asbury: Bishop of the Methodist Episcopal Church*, 3 vols. (New York and Cincinnati: Eaton & Mains; Jennings & Pye, 1821) 1: 425; cf. *The Journal and Letters of Francis Asbury*, ed. Elmer T. Clark, 3 vols. (London: Epworth, and Nashville: Abingdon, 1958), 1: 405. Hereinafter noted as "Asbury, *Journal*" and "JLFA" respectively. In July 1776, Asbury had dwelt on the twofold character of the forest—confessional and challenge, the latter in this case not from the forest but from its Native American inhabitants:

> *Wednesday,* 31. Spent some time in the **woods** alone with God, and found it a peculiar time of love and joy. O delightful employment! All my soul was centred in God! The next day I unexpectedly met with brother W.; and while preaching at three o'clock to an increased company, the word produced great seriousness and attention. And we had a happy, powerful meeting in the evening at Mr. G.'s. But my mind is in some degree disturbed by the reports of battles and slaughters. It seems the Cherokee Indians have also begun to break out, and the English ships have been coasting to and fro, watching for some advantages: but what can they expect to accomplish without an army of two or three hundred thousand men? And even then, there would be but little prospect of their success. O that this dispensation might answer its proper end! that the people would fear the Lord, and sincerely devote themselves to his service! Then, no doubt, wars and bloodshed would cease. Asbury, *Journal* 1:193 and JLFA 1:195.

8. Asbury, *Journal* 2: 14, 16–17; cf. JLFA 1: 544–46, 548–49.

9. On these developments, see John H. Wigger, *Taking Heaven by Storm: Methodism and the Rise of Popular Christianity in America* (New York & Oxford: Oxford University Press, 1998) and *American Saint: Francis Asbury and the Methodists* (Oxford & New York, 2009).

10. See George H. Williams, *Wilderness and Paradise in Christian Thought* (New York: Harper, 1962); Roderick Nash, *Wilderness and the American Mind*, 3d. ed. (New Haven: Yale University Press, 1982)

11. See Catherine L. Albanese, *Nature Religion in America* (Chicago and London: University of Chicago Press, 1990); Myra Jehlen, *American Incarnation: The Individual, the Nation, and the Continent* (Cambridge: Harvard University Press, 1986); Arthur A. Eklich, *Man and Nature in America* (New York: Columbia University Press, 1963).

12. Conrad Cherry, *Nature and Religious Imagination: From Edwards to Bushnell* (Philadelphia: Fortress Press, 1980); Leo Marx, *The Machine in the Garden: Technology and the Pastoral Ideal in America* (London: Oxford University Press, 1964).

13. See Cherry and Marx, but also, for instance, David R. Williams, *Wilderness Lost: The Religious Origins of the American Mind* (Selinsgrove: Susquehanna University Press; London and Toronto: Associated University Presses, 1987). He begins with the Puritans, treats "The Great Awakening of Fear" then "Revival and Revolution" followed by part III, "The Literary Remains," which deals with "The Transcendentalism Growth," "Hawthorne, Very, and Dickinson: The Wilderness of the Mind," and then chapters on Herman Melville and Oliver Wendell Holmes. Methodists simply do not figure. In an elaborate six-page index, two columns do not even include camp meetings or Methodism. He does have pages devoted to Arminianism scattered through the book (see 47–48 and 52–54 for Arminianism definitions focused on Puritanism).

14. See A. Gregory Schneider, *The Way of the Cross Leads Home: The Domestication of American Methodism* (Bloomington and Indianapolis: Indiana University Press, 1993).

15. See Ellen Weiss, *City in the Woods: The Life and Design of an American Camp Meeting on Martha's Vineyard* (New York and Oxford: Oxford University Press, 1987); Troy Messenger, *Holy Leisure: Recreation and Religion in God's Square Mile* (Minneapolis and London: University of Minnesota Press, 1999); Dickson D. Bruce, Jr., *And They All Sang Hallelujah: Plain-Folk Camp-Meeting Religion, 1800–1845* (Knoxville: University of Tennessee Press, 1974); Charles A. Johnson, *The Frontier Camp Meeting: Religion's Harvest Time* (Dallas: Southern Methodist University Press, 1955, 1985). The latter provides a very full bibliography of items then available and/or published (303–19).

16. See Richey, "Four Languages of Methodist Self-Understanding," *Doctrine in Experience: A Methodist Theology of Church and Ministry* (Nashville: Kingswood

Books/Abingdon Press, 2009), 3–20, the original of which appeared in *Methodist History*, 28 (April 1990), 155–71. See also the essay that initially made the four languages-camp meeting connection: Steven D. Cooley, "Manna and the Manual: Sacramental and Instrumental Constructions of the Victorian Methodist Camp Meeting during the Mid-Nineteenth Century," *Religion and American Culture: A Journal of Interpretation,* 6 (Summer 1996), 131–59 and "Applying the Vagueness of Language: Poetic Strategies and Campmeeting Piety in the Mid-Nineteenth Century," *Church History* 63 (Dec. 1994), 570–86. See also Roger Robins, "Vernacular American Landscape: Methodists, Camp Meetings, and Social Respectability," *Religion and American Culture: A Journal of Interpretation,* 4 (Summer 1994), 165–91.

17. *Episcopacy in the Methodist Tradition: Perspectives and Proposals,* with Thomas Edward Frank, (Nashville: Abingdon Press, 2004); *Marks of Methodism: Practices of Ecclesiology,* with Dennis M. Campbell and William B. Lawrence, United Methodism and American Culture, V, (Nashville: Abingdon Press, 2005); *Mr. Wesley's True Heirs: Extension Ministers* (Nashville: General Board of Higher Education and Ministry, UMC, 2008); *Doctrine in Experience: A Methodist Theology of Church and Ministry* (Nashville: Kingswood Books/Abingdon Press, 2009); and *Methodist Connectionalism: Historical Perspectives* (Nashville: General Board of Higher Education and Ministry, UMC, 2010); *Denominationalism Illustrated and Explained* (Eugene, OR: Cascade Books, 2013). *Formation for Ministry in American Methodism* is currently under consideration by the General Board of Higher Education and Ministry, UMC.

18. But see my "Methodism as New Creation: An Historical-Theological Enquiry," in M. Douglas Meeks, ed., *Wesleyan Perspectives on the New Creation* (Nashville: Kingswood Books/Abingdon Press, 2004), 73–92).

19. William J. Abraham and James E. Kirby, eds., *The Oxford Handbook of Methodist Studies* (Oxford and New York: Oxford University Press, 2009); Charles Yrigoyen Jr., ed., *T & T Clark Companion to Methodism* (London and New York: T & T Clark International, 2010); Jason E. Vickers, ed., *The Cambridge Companion to American Methodism,* (New York: Cambridge University Press, 2013); Rex Matthews, *Timetables of History for Students of Methodism* (Nashville: Abingdon Press, 2007); W. Harrison Daniel, *Historical Atlas of the Methodist Movement* (Nashville: Abingdon Press, 2009); Charles Yrigoyen, Jr. and Susan E. Warrick, eds. *Historical Dictionary of Methodism* (Lanham, MD: Scarecrow Press, 2005); William Gibson, Peter Forsaith, and Martin Wellings, eds., *The Ashgate Research Companion to World Methodism* (Farnham, Eng.: Ashgate Publishing Limited, 2013), and Nolan B. Harmon, et al., *The Encyclopedia of World Methodism,* 2 vols. Sponsored by the World Methodist Council and the Commission on Archives and History, UMC (Nashville: The United Methodist Publishing House, 1974). Various websites, including those of Methodist seminaries and especially that of the UMC's General Commission on Archives and History, offer basic information.

20. *The Methodists*, with James Kirby and Kenneth E. Rowe (Westport, CT: Greenwood, 1996; Praeger (Student Edition), 1998); *The Methodist Experience in America: A History*, with Kenneth E. Rowe and Jean Miller Schmidt, Vol. I, (Nashville: Abingdon Press, 2010); *American Methodism: A Compact History*, also with Rowe and Schmidt (Nashville: Abingdon Press, 2012). Hereinafter, the two volumes, the 2010 *History* and 2000 *Sourcebook* are abbreviated MEA 1 and MEA 2, with a page number or, in some cases for the latter, a **bolded date** indicating the referenced document.

21. *The Experience and Travels of Mr. Freeborn Garrettson, Minister of the Methodist Episcopal Church in North America* (Philadelphia: Printed by Perry Hall, 1791) as reprinted in Robert D. Simpson, ed., *American Methodist Pioneer: The Life and Journals of the Rev. Freeborn Garrettson, 1752–1827* (Rutland, VT: Academy Books for Drew University Library, 1984), 36.

22. See the works cited above (note 17), especially *Doctrine in Experience* and *Methodist Connectionalism*.

CHAPTER I

1. Wesley, *Works 21, Journals and Diaries*, IV (1755–1765), 479, for July 17, 1764. Context for this statement: After preaching on the square in Chester to a gathering that included "many wild, rude people," Wesley noted "they were outnumbered by those who were civil and attentive. And I believe some impression was made on the wildest. What can shake Satan's kingdom like *field preaching*!"

2. Heitzenrater, *Wesley and the People Called Methodists*, 113–16.

3. In "a short state of the case between the clergy and us," dated March 11, 1745, Wesley outlined in some detail the frustrated attempts to preach in church settings that led to the fields, squares, and other outdoor venues. *Works 20, Journals and Diaries*, V (1743–1754), 55–58. There are some thirty references to field preaching in his journals.

4. *Works 9, The Methodist Societies: History, Nature, and Design*, 431. Similarly, *Thoughts upon Methodism* (1786), in describing the Methodist revival and not being allowed to preach in churches, Wesley insisted he "began to preach in the fields." *Works 9, The Methodist Societies: History, Nature, and Design*, 528.

5. *Works 21, Journals and Diaries*, IV (1755–1765), 203, for June 25-26, 1759.

6. *Works 21, Journals and Diaries*, IV (1755–1765), 333, for Sunday, July 5, 1761.

7. *Works 21, Journals and Diaries*, IV (1755–1765), 473, for Sunday June 24, 1764.

8. *Works 22, Journals and Diaries*, V (1765–1775), 8, for June 18, 1765.

9. *Works 22, Journals and Diaries*, V (1765–1775), 106, for September 30, 1767. Compare other statements:

> "Thousands of hearers, rich and poor, received the word near the New Square with the deepest attention. This is the way to shake the trembling gates of hell. Still, I see, nothing can do this so effectually as *field-preaching*."
> *Works 22, Journals and Diaries*, V (1765–1775), 153, for August 21, 1768.

Wesley spoke of one of his congregation as having a little increase: "But there cannot be much without more field-preaching. Wherever this is intermitted, the work of God stands still if it does not go back."

Works 22, *Journals and Diaries*, V (1765–1775), 190, for June 26, 1769.

Preaching in the Royal Square to a gathering including many soldiers, he commented "By what means but field-preaching could we have reached these poor souls?" *Works* 22, *Journals and Diaries*, V (1765–1775), 196, for July 23, 1769.

10. *Works* 10, *The Methodist Societies: The Minutes of Conference*, 845.

11. For comparison of the "Large" Minutes and first *Discipline*, see Jno. J. Tigert, *A Constitutional History of American Episcopal Methodism*, 3rd ed., revised and enlarged (Nashville: Publishing House of the Methodist Episcopal Church, South, 1908), Appendix VII, 532–602, and specifically 535–36. Italics in the Minutes were carried over into the *Discipline*. See *Discipline*/MEC 1785, 4–5. This short form of notation standardizes reference to a book of discipline (variously titled) to the church (in this case the Methodist Episcopal Church or MEC) and to the date. So a reference to the *Discipline* of The United Methodist Church for 2008 would be cited; e.g., *Discipline*/UMC 2008. The *Discipline* here cited actually bears the title, *Minutes of Several Conversations Between The Rev. Thomas Coke, LL.D. The Rev. Francis Asbury and Others at a Conference, . . . in the Year 1784. Composing a Form of Discipline for the Ministers, Preachers and other Members of the Methodist Episcopal Church in America* (Philadelphia, 1785).

12. Thomas Taylor's April 1768 letter asking Wesley to send preachers to America, in Russell E. Richey, Kenneth E. Rowe, Jean Miller Schmidt, *The Methodist Experience in America*, 2 vols. (Nashville: Abingdon Press, 2000, 2010), 2, *A Sourcebook*, 50. Hereinafter, the two volumes, the 2010 *History* and 2000 *Sourcebook* are abbreviated MEA 1 and MEA 2, with a page number or, in some cases for the latter, a **bolded date** indicating the referenced document.

13. MEA 2: 51.

14. Frederick E. Maser and Howard T. Maag, eds., *The Journal of Joseph Pilmore: Methodist Itinerant. For the Years August 1, 1769 to January 2, 1774* (Philadelphia: Message Publishing Co., for the Historical Society of the Philadelphia annual Conference of the United Methodist Church, 1969), 141. Spelling honors the Maser-Maag treatment.

15. See MEA 1, chapters 1–3.

16. *Journal of Joseph Pilmore*, 91, 142. Once, in late 1807 or early 1808, Seth Crowell reported preaching in Connecticut "in a wagon in the street." But he also reported preaching "in the woods to a large congregation of people," "in a barn, in consequence of the number of people being so great that the house could not contain them," and "in a grove of woods, to a numerous assembly of people of

various descriptions." *The Journal of Seth Crowell; Containing an Account of his Travels as a Methodist Preacher, for Twelve Years. Written by Himself* (New York: J. C. Totten, 1813), 82, 51, 79.

17. *Journal of Joseph Pilmore*, 101, 104, 108. The one "sic" will need to stand for the various spellings in this quotation.

18. *Journal of Joseph Pilmore*, 140–42. See entries also for May 17, 1772; June 8, 1772; June 16, 1772; the two instances already cited follow; then also July 26, 1772; September 15, 1772.

19. *The Works of the Reverend John Wesley, A.M.*, ed. John Emory, 7 volumes (New York: Published by B. Waugh and T. Mason for the Methodist Episcopal Church, 1835), 3: 556; 4: 602; *The Works of John Wesley*; begun as "The Oxford Edition of The Works of John Wesley" (Oxford: Clarendon Press, 1975–1983); continued as "The Bicentennial Edition of The Works of John Wesley" (Nashville: Abingdon Press, 1984–; 34 vols. Projected. *Journals and Diaries*, I–VII, *Works* 18–24), *Works* 20, *Journals and Diaries*, III, 556; *Works* 23, *Journals and Diaries*, VI, 331. See the appendix for the forty-some accounts of Wesley's preaching in the shade, out of thousands and thousands of preaching sites. See especially April 30, 1759, June 2, 1768, August 20, 1770, June 23, 1772, Sept, 12, 1784, and June, 12, 1785.

20. *The Experience and Travels of Mr. Freeborn Garrettson, Minister of the Methodist Episcopal Church in North America* (Philadelphia: Printed by Perry Hall, 1791) as reprinted in Robert D. Simpson, ed., *American Methodist Pioneer: The Life and Journals of the Rev. Freeborn Garrettson, 1752–1827* (Rutland, VT: Academy Books for Drew University Library, 1984), 54, 73, 77, 80, 85, 86.

21. *American Methodist Pioneer*, 154, 179, 219, 221, 228, 242, 266.

22. Jesse Lee, *A Short History of the Methodists* (Baltimore, 1810: facsimile ed. Rutland, VT: Academy Books, 1974), 59. Similarly, Francis Asbury reported on a Sept. 5–6, 1801 quarterly meeting:

> "*Saturday* and *Sabbath day* were spent at Rockingham quarterly meeting, held in Harrisonburg: the brethren were lively in the sacramental meeting. Many came from far, although the heat was very great. N. Snethen preached on *Saturday* upon Rom. xii, 17, and *Sabbath day*, Rom. xii, 1. My subject was 1 Pet. iv, 17. The house could not at all contain the people, we therefore took to the woods; but we failed in shade, and felt some inconvenience in the sun."

Francis Asbury, *Journal of Rev. Francis Asbury: Bishop of the Methodist Episcopal Church* 3 vols. (New York and Cincinnati: Eaton & Mains; Jennings & Pye, 1821) 3: 33; cf. *The Journal and Letters of Francis Asbury*, ed. Elmer T. Clark, 3 vols. (London: Epworth, and Nashville: Abingdon Press, 1958), 2: 305. Hereinafter Asbury, *Journal* and JLFA respectively. Cf. accounts by Devereux Jarratt, Thomas Saunders, John Dickens, and Thomas Rankin in JLFA 1: 207–24.

23. *Minutes of the Annual Conferences of the Methodist Episcopal Church, for the years 1773–1828* (New York: T. Mason and G. Lane for the Methodist Episcopal Church, 1840), 12.

24. John Kobler, Journal and Sermons, Lovely Lane, I. Journal 1789–1792: 79, 86.

25. S. M. Merrill, ed., *Recollections of a Superannuate: Or, Sketches of Life, Labor, and Experience in the Methodist Itinerancy by Rev. David Lewis of the Ohio Annual Conference* (Cincinnati: Printed at the Methodist Book Concern for the Author, 1857), 82.

26. Seymour Landon, *Fifty Years in the Itinerant Ministry by S. Landon, of New York East Conference, of the Methodist Episcopal Church. Delivered in Brooklyn in May, 1868, And ordered to be Published by said Conference* (New York, 1868), 21.

27. "To Dr. COKE, Mr. ASBURY, and our Brethren in *NORTH-AMERICA*. BRISTOL, Sept. 10, 1784," John Telford, ed. *The Letters of the Rev. John Wesley.* 8 vols. London: Epworth Press, 1931. 7: 237–38; MEA 2, 1784a.

28. Heitzenrater, *Wesley and the People Called Methodists*, 287–90.

29. Karen B. Westerfield Tucker, *American Methodist Worship* (Oxford and New York: Oxford University Press, 2001), 4–12.

30. For a first-hand account of the 1784 conference and the naming of the new church, see *Sketches of The Life and Travels of Rev. Thomas Ware... Written by Himself* (New York: G. Lane & P. P. Sandford for the Methodist Episcopal Church, 1842), 104–25.

31. *Discipline*/MEC 1787, 3–7.

32. For comparison of the "Large" Minutes and first *Discipline* see Tigert, *Constitutional History*, Appendix VII, 532–602.

33. *Discipline*/MEC 1787, title page and 23.

34. *American Methodist Pioneer*, 282–87, reproduced from Garrettson's manuscript. In the omitted entries, Garrettson did not indicate whether others traveled with him.

35. Thomas Coke and Francis Asbury. *The Doctrines and Disciplines of the Methodist Episcopal Church, in America* (Philadelphia: Henry Tuckniss, 1798), 41–42.

36. James B. Finley, *Sketches of Western Methodism: Biographical, Historical and Miscellaneous, Illustrative of Pioneer Life* (Cincinnati: The Methodist Book Concern, 1854), 17.

37. *Autobiography of Rev. James B. Finley, or Pioneer Life in the West,* W. P. Strickland, ed. (Cincinnati: The Methodist Book Concern, 1856), 158. Finley added, "To be sure one has said, 'A great city is a great desert'; but it is a desert of depraved humanity, where every one is wrapped up in selfishness, and guards himself against his neighbor while his heart rankles with envy at his prosperity, or his wild, unbridled ambition urges him on the reckless course of outstripping all his competitors. Not so in the woods. There pride, envy, selfishness, and ambition have no abode. The only evil spirit that haunts the woods is Melancholy," 158–59.

38. Schneider, *The Way of the Cross Leads Home*, 57.

39. Two classic treatments of the American experience of forest and wilderness with essentially nothing to say about Methodism and camp meetings remain

very useful: Roderick Nash, *Wilderness and the American Mind*, rev. ed. (New Haven and London: Yale University Press, 1973) and Marx, *The Machine in the Garden*. For very different takes on the encounter with the land, see also Cherry, *Nature and Religious Imagination* and Albanese, *Nature Religion in America*.

40. "An Appeal to the Methodists, in Opposition to the Changes Proposed in Their Church Government," (1827) in Thomas E. Bond, *The Economy of Methodism Illustrated and Defended* (New York: Lane & Scott, 1852), 9–56, p. 19.

41. *American Methodist Pioneer*, 79, 81–82.

42. John F. Marlay, *The Life of Rev. Thomas A. Morris, D.D., Late Senior Bishop of the Methodist Episcopal Church* (Cincinnati: Hitchcock and Walden: New York: Nelson and Phillips, 1875), 344–45. This was one of ten such "spirits" by which Morris characterized Methodism.

43. John F. Wright, *Sketches of the Life and Labors of James Quinn* (Cincinnati: The Methodist Book Concern, 1851), 58.

44. Ibid., 100.

45. Thomas Coke, *Extracts of the Journals of the Rev. Dr. Coke's Five visits to America* (London, Printed by G. Paramore; and sold by G. Whitfield, 1793), 27.

46. Minton Thrift, *Memoir of the Rev. Jesse Lee, with Extracts from his Journals* (New York, Published by N. Bangs and T. Mason for the Methodist Episcopal Church, 1823), 65–66.

47. Geo. A. Phoebus, comp., *Beams of Light on Early Methodism in America. Chiefly Drawn from the Diary, Letters, Manuscripts, Documents, and Original Tracts of the Rev. Ezekiel Cooper* (New York; Cincinnati: Phillips & Hunt; Cranston & Stowe, 1887), 80–81.

48. *Journal of the Travels of William Colbert*, Typescript 4: 35. On Colbert, see Warren S. Napier, "Formed for Friendship: Revisioning Early American Circuit Riders Through the Journal of William Colbert, 1790–1833," Ph.D. dissertation. Iliff School of Theology/University of Denver, 1996.

49. *Journal of the Travels of William Colbert, Methodist Preacher*, Typescript 4: 97–98. The woman wept, then went motionless, rose up testifying, and was knocked over by another who though opposed to shouting went stiff and fell on the first.

50. Typescript 4: 111–13.

51. On their Kentucky origins and early denominational diversity, see especially Ellen Eslinger, *Citizens of Zion: The Social Origins of Camp Meeting Revivalism* (Knoxville: University of Tennessee Press, 1999).

52. Charles Giles, *Pioneer: A Narrative of the Nativity, Experience, Travels, and Ministerial Labours of Rev. Charles Giles* (New York: G. Lane & P. P. Sandford for the Methodist Episcopal Church, 1844), 83.

53. Typescript 1: 10.

54. Typescript 4: 25. Colbert then commented on the power of the devil in that place, seemingly referencing to racial tensions.

55. Typescript 4: 37.

56. For the early 1770s and before his conversion, he reported, "As I lived a retired life, I frequently read, prayed, and wept till after midnight: and often withdrew to the woods, and other private places for prayer." Garrettson, "Experience and Travels, in *American Methodist Pioneer*, 79, 40.

57. Garrettson, "Experience and Travels, in *American Methodist Pioneer*, 40 and *American Methodist Pioneer*, 153 and 165 for manuscript entries.

58. Garrettson, "Experience and Travels, in *American Methodist Pioneer*, 96.

59. John Ffirth, *The Experience and Gospel Labours of the Rev. Benjamin Abbott* (New York: Published by Ezekiel Cooper and John Wilson, for the Methodist Connection in the United States, 1805), 79. At another point of adversity, after announcing he would "preach from the words of the devil," and following a restless night, Abbott had reported retiring "into the woods" and beseeching "the Lord to discover way to me, that I might deliver his word, if consistent to his will, from the text I proposed" (58). He recorded several instances of sylvan preaching, once noting, "Sometimes we used to assemble in the woods, and under the trees; there not being room in the house for the people that attended" (47).

60. Asbury, *Journal* 1: 385; cf. JLFA 1: 367.

61. J. B. Wakeley, *The Patriarch of One Hundred Years: Being Reminiscences, Historical and Biographical, of Rev. Henry Boehm* (New York: Nelson & Phillips; Cincinnati: Hitchcock & Walden, 1875), 120.

62. Asbury, *Journal* 1: 428–29; cf. JLFA 1: 408—June-July 1781.

63. *The Journal of The Reverend Jacob Lanius. An Itinerant Preacher of the Missouri Conference of the Methodist Episcopal Church from 1831 AD to 1851 AD* (Typescript edited by Elmer T. Clark. 1918), 143, entry for Mar. 31, 1835.

64. "Wrestling Jacob," a popular title for Charles Wesley's "Come, O Thou Traveller Unknown."

65. Phoebus, *Beams of Light*, 17–18. These excerpts come from "A Short Account of the Life and Experience of Ezekiel Cooper," *Beams of Light*, 12–21.

66. Stith Mead, *A Short Account of the Experience and Labors of the Rev. Stith Mead: Preacher of the Gospel, and an Elder in the Methodist Episcopal Church: to which are added, extracts of letters from himself and others in a religious correspondence/written by himself, in a plain style.* (Lynchburg [VA]: Published for, and sold by, the author, 1829), 36, 37, 45.

67. Giles, *Pioneer*, 68, 74, 84. Giles glossed the tree's death soteriologically:

> "After enduring the storms of a hundred years it fell a sacrifice to the crushing powers of time, and is gone down to sleep in ashes, to rise no more to leafy honours, despoiled of a successor, without a kindred branch to tell where it stood. Not so with mortal, immortal man, the holy Christian man; he dies, and yet lives. He not only lives in a perpetual kindred succession, but he truly lives while he lives; lives when he dies, lives after he is dead, and will live forever. But the impenitent sinner is dead while he lives; dies hopeless when he dies; and dies continually after he is dead."

68. Kobler, Journal and Sermons, 56, 93, 133, 103.
69. David L. Steele, ed., "The Autobiography of the Reverend John Young, 1747–1837," *Methodist History* 13 (Oct. 1974), 17–40, 31.
70. *A Journal of the Travels of William Colbert*, Typescript 3: 75.
71. Abner Chase, *Recollections of the Past* (New York: Published for the Author at the Conference Office, 1843), 28.
72. George Brown, *Recollections of Itinerant Life: Including Early Reminiscences. By George Brown, D.D., of the Methodist Protestant Church* (Cincinnati: B. W. Carroll & Co.; Springfield: Methodist Protestant Publishing House, 1866), 41, 61–62.
73. Merrill, ed., *Recollections of a Superannuate*, 39–40
74. *Life and Observations of Rev. E. F. Newell, Who has been More than Forty years an Itinerant Minister in the Methodist Episcopal Church, Compiled from his own Manuscripts* (Worcester: C. W. Ainsworth, 1847), 78.
75. Marlay, *Life of Rev. Thomas A. Morris*, 1875), 22–23.
76. M. M. Henkle, *The Life of Henry Bidleman Bascom, D. D., LL.D., Late Bishop of the Methodist Episcopal Church, South* (Louisville: Published by Morton & Griswold and sold by the Southern Methodist Book Concern, 1854), 46, 47, 48–49, 49–50.
77. Of Bascom's recourse to the forest for spiritual uplift, his biography comments:

> "It was always his custom to walk and study. It would seem that his mind became so surcharged with thought, that his body was impelled to action. He generally betook himself to the woods for mental preparation. I remember an amusing incident in this connection. In 1816, he had gone into a skirt of woods near to where an Irishman was laboring, and it so happened that he discovered Bascom in his retired promenade. He came running to the house under excitement, and declared there was a 'crazy man in the woods.' How do you know he is crazy? I asked, 'Why sir,' he replied, 'he is quite in a *doldrum*, he has been walking for an hour between two trees, and seems to be wonderfully taken with a deep study; do you think he is quite right in his mind?' Go to church to-morrow, said I, and you may judge whether he is crazy."

Henkle, The Life of Henry Bidleman Bascom, 351–52n
78. Asbury, *Journal* 1: 428–29; cf. JLFA 1: 408–09.

CHAPTER 2

1. See the bolded terms throughout Heitzenrater's *Wesley and the People Called Methodists*.
2. See Tigert, *Constitutional History*, Appendix VII, 534. The wording of "Large" *Minutes* and first *Discipline* is essentially the same, save for capitalization, the pluralizing of "Conferences," and the *Discipline*'s omission of the word "this" before "our Labour."

3. JLFA 1: 474–76.

4. My point is that Methodism generally missed a wonderful opportunity for theological self-clarification when it failed to acclaim "conferencing" as its central ecclesiological affirmation. Wesley offered himself and followers hints about such a theological self-understanding but had too much on his plate to work systematically on matters ecclesiological. The Americans, aside from the trans-Atlantic traveling leader Coke, were too weak intellectually in Methodism's first decades to work conceptually on doctrinal clarification. See Richey, *Marks of Methodism: Practices of Ecclesiology, Doctrine in Experience: A Methodist Theology of Church and Ministry*, and *Methodist Connectionalism*.

5. Jno. J. Tigert, *The Making of Methodism: Studies in the Genesis of Institutions* (Nashville: Publishing House of the Methodist Episcopal Church, South), 37.

6. See Lester Ruth, *A Little Heaven Below: Worship at Early Methodist Quarterly Meetings* (Nashville: Kingswood Books/Abingdon Press, 2000), 18–20.

7. Ibid., 103–118.

8. *The Works of the Reverend John Wesley*, 3: 552. See entries also for August 22, 1750, March 31, 1752, June 21, 1760, July 20, 1762, Sept. 15, 1762, Oct. 16 and 17, 1765, July 29, 1767, Sept. 15, 1768, June 23, 1769, July 2, 1769, Sept. 2, 1769, Dec. 13, 1770, July 12, 1774, Sept., 3, 1774, Aug. 30, 1777, June 6, 1780, Aug. 26, 1780, Sept. 4, 1781, July 1, 1782, July 3, 1786, June 11, 1787, June 15, 1787, Feb. 6, 1789, Jan. 29, 1790.

9. Lee, *Short History*, 54–59.

10. Asbury, *Journal* 1: 176; JLFA 1: 178.

11. Ruth, *A Little Heaven Below*, 20–31.

12. Asbury, *Journal* 1: 213, 230, 208–24, 225–30; JLFA 1: 211, 223, 207–19, 219–24.

13. Frank Baker observed: "Quarterly Meeting love-feasts achieved particularly great importance in the United States of America, for in that vast continent greater distances made circuit fellowship so much more difficult to secure. In fact, in American Methodism love-feasts seem at first to have been almost confined to the Quarterly Meetings, which were really minor Conferences, lasting two or three days." The normative structure of love-feast, according to Baker, was "Hymn, Prayer, Grace (sung), Bread distributed by stewards, Collection for the poor, Circulation of loving-cup, Address by the presiding minister, Testimonies and verses of hymns, Spontaneous prayers and verse of hymns, Closing exhortation by the minister, Hymn, Benediction," *Methodism and the Love-Feast* (London: The Epworth Press, 1957) 44, 15. See again, Ruth, *A Little Heaven Below*, 103–118.

14. *Minutes of the Annual Conferences of the Methodist Episcopal Church, for the years 1773–1828* (New York: T. Mason and G. Lane for the Methodist Episcopal Church, 1840), 1780: 12.

15. Ruth, *A Little Heaven Below*, 26–29; Tucker, *American Methodist Worship*, 71–73 and elsewhere.

16. *American Methodist Pioneer*, 173, 177, 178, 182 for April 18–19, Aug. 12–13, Aug. 19–20, Nov. 11–12; JLFA 1: 345.

17. Leigh Eric Schmidt, *Holy Fairs: Scottish Communions and American Revivals in the Early Modern Period* (Princeton: Princeton University Press, 1989).

18. Mr. Allen, "Some Account of the Work of God in America," *Arminian Magazine*, 15 (June 1792), 292. The journal, serialized in June, July, and August issues (288–93, 346–51, 403–08), included several notices of sylvan preaching, 347, 403, and 408.

19. See note 2, Q. 44, instruction (4).

20. See William H. Williams, *The Garden of Methodism* (Wilmington, DE: Scholarly Resources, 1984) and my *Early American Methodism* (Bloomington and Indianapolis: Indiana University Press, 1991), for elaboration of this argument.

21. Tuesday, 27. Yesterday and to-day we held a quarterly meeting near Dover. A great concourse of people attended the ministry of the word; and many serious persons were present at our love-feast. Asbury, *Journal* 1: 309; JLFA 1: 300; Asbury, *Journal* 1: 390–91; JLFA 1: 371–72.

22. Ruth, *A Little Heaven Below*, 30–31.

23. Phoebus, *Beams of Light*, 65. For a quarterly meeting later that year, Cooper said more about the business portion than is typical in preachers' journals. See 79–80.

24. *American Methodist Pioneer*, 221.

25. Phoebus, *Beams of Light*, 27. See 78–81 for several similar crowded quarterly meetings in 1787.

26. See Richey, "Methodist Revivals," in *Encyclopedia of Religious Revivals in America*, ed. Michael J. McClymond, 2 vols. (Westport & London: Greenwood Press) 2007, I, 272–76; and "Revivalism: In Search of a Definition," *Wesleyan Theological Journal*, 28 (Spring-Fall, 1993), 165–75. Revised version "Revivals: An Arminian Definition," in *Theology and Corporate Conscience*, ed. M. Douglas Meeks (Minneapolis: Kirk House, 1999), 302–15.

27. Lee, *Short History*, 130–33.

28. Ibid., 279. On the emergence of the camp meeting and its rootage in Methodist communal life, see Wigger, *American Saint*, 317–28; Tucker, *American Methodist Worship*, 74–81, references scattered throughout and graphics, 155–56; and Schneider, *The Way of the Cross Leads Home*, chaps. 1–4.

29. Merrill, ed., *Recollections of a Superannuate*, 61.

30. On the denominational diversity involved in camp meeting origins, see Eslinger, *Citizens of Zion*; John B. Boles, *The Great Revival, 1797–1805: The Origins of the Southern Evangelical Mind* (Lexington: University Press of Kentucky, 1972); Schmidt, *Holy Fairs*; Paul K. Conkin, *Cane Ridge, America's Pentecost* (Madison: University of Wisconsin Press, 1990); and Bruce, *And They All Sang Hallelujah*.

31. *An Apology for Camp-Meetings, Illustrative or Their Good Effects, and Answering The Principal Objections Urged Against Them* (New York: John C. Totten, 1810), 5–6.

See also MEA 2: **1810b** for liberal excerpts from this defense. The title page lists no author. Totten was Methodist and had a brother who was a Methodist preacher.

32. Among the most recent treatments is that of Michael K. Turner's "Revivalism and Preaching," in *The Cambridge Companion to American Methodism*, 119–37, his title understating the centrality of camp meetings in the essay. For more extended examination of their character, origins, and evolution, see the standard treatments, Kenneth O. Brown, *Holy Ground, Too. The Camp Meeting Family Tree*, enlarged and revised edition (Hazleton, PA: Holiness Archives, 1997); Johnson, *The Frontier Camp Meeting*; Bruce, *And They All Sang Hallelujah;.* Boles, *The Great Revival, 1787–1805*; Conkin, *Cane Ridge, America's Pentecost*; Wigger, *Taking Heaven by Storm*; and Lorin Harris Soderwall, "The Rhetoric of the Methodist Camp Meeting Movement: 1800–1850," Ph.D. dissertation, University of Southern California, 1971. For illustrations of camp meeting emotional religiosity, see Lester Ruth, *Early Methodist Life and Spirituality* (Nashville: Kingswood Books/Abingdon Press, 2005), 135–87. On its origins, as well as character, see also his "Reconsidering the Emergence of the Second Great Awakening and Camp Meetings among Early Methodists," *Worship* 75 (July 2001), 334–55.

33. Lee, *Short History*, 360–61.

34. Ibid., 361.

35. Ibid., 284–362, 362.

36. *Apology for Camp-Meetings*, 43, 42–48.

37. (New York: Printed and Sold by John C. Totten, 1813).

38. *The Methodist Magazine*, 25 (London, 1801; letter dated Aug. 20, 1801), 217; 25 (letter dated Oct. 23, 1801), 262–63; 25 (London, 1801), 422–23 and 523. For discussion of literature on the nature and origins of camp meetings, see Richey, *Early American Methodism* and *Methodist Conference in America*, 59–60.

39. Ezekiel Cooper to Thomas Coke, *Methodist Magazine*, 25 (London, 1802), 424. The letter was dated September 7, 1801.

40. JLFA, 3: 252, dated Dec. 2, 1802; 3: 255, dated, Dec. 30, 1802. *Methodist Magazine* 26 (1803), 285, letter dated Jan. 11, 1803.

41. Richey, *Early American Methodism*, 21–32; Ruth, *A Little Heaven Below*, 209–22; Wigger, *American Saint*, 317–28.

42. Wigger, *American Saint*, 365.

43. [Francis Asbury], *Extracts of Letters Containing Some Account of the Work of God Since the Year 1800* (New York: Cooper & Wilson, 1805), 110, 109–11. A second sentence added to the euphoria: "Our strong lunged men exerted themselves until the whole forest echoed, and all the trees of the woods clapped their hands. God came near, sinners fell in abundance, Christians rejoiced and shouted, and a glorious sacrifice of praise ascended to God."

44. JLFA 3: 197, letter dated January 30, 1801 to Daniel Hitt. Compare JLFA 3: 199.

45. James Penn Pilkington, *The Methodist Publishing House: A History*, 2 vols. (Nashville:

Abingdon Press, 1968, 1989), 1: 83–86,111. The second volume was by Walter Newton Vernon, Jr. and added "United" to the title.

46. *Extracts of Letters*, 53–56, dated Bethel, December 28, 1802.

47. *Extracts of Letters*, 101–03, dated Nov. 8, 1804, Harrisonburg, Rockingham County, Virginia.

48. *Extracts of Letters*, 112–14, dated April 4, 1805, Richmond District.

49. *Extracts of Letters*, 114–18, dated Dec. 4, 1803, Baltimore.

50. MEA 2: 176 **(1811b)**.

51. *Book for Recording Steward of Richmond Circuit, 1851–1879*, edited by Harold Lawrence (Milledgeville: Boyd Publishing Company, 1997).

52. Wakeley, *Patriarch of One Hundred Years*, 282, 290, 302.

53. Asbury, *Journal* 3: 290; cf. JLFA 2: 580. Asbury continued on a matter we take up in the following chapter, "We made a regulation respecting slavery: it was, that no member of society, or preacher, should sell or buy a slave unjustly, inhumanly, or covetously; the case, on complaint, to be examined for a member by the quarterly meeting; and for a preacher an appeal to an annual conference. Where the guilt was proved the offender to be expelled. The families of the Hills, Sewalls, and Cannon, were greatly and affectionately attentive to us." For Missouri Conference camp meetings, 1832 and 1833, see *The Journal of The Reverend Jacob Lanius. An Itinerant Preacher of the Missouri Conference of the Methodist Episcopal Church from 1831 A.D. to 1851 A.D.* Edited by Elmer T. Clark. 1918, 5–7. Beggs reported a conference held on the campground, estimated attendance at services at 4,000, and meeting for conference business in a building some twenty feet square. S. R. Beggs, *Pages from the Early History of the West and Northwest* (Cincinnati: Methodist Book Concern 1868), 311–16.

54. *Autobiography of Rev. James B. Finley, or Pioneer Life in the West*, W. P. Strickland, ed. (Cincinnati: The Methodist Book Concern, 1856), 191; Beggs, *Pages from the Early History of the West and Northwest*, 15. For Finley's camp meeting roles, see Charles C. Cole, Jr., *Lion of the Forest* (Lexington: The University Press of Kentucky, 1994), especially 4–7, 26–37, 49 and 70. On the relation of love feast, quarterly meeting, and camp meeting, see Wigger, *Taking Heaven by Storm*, 87–97.

55. *The Journal of The Reverend Jacob Lanius*, entry for Sept. 29th, 1841, 310–11.

> Six years earlier, Lanius had noted [July 14, 1835] "This day I have finished my regular rounds on Richmond Circuit and I shall spend the remainder of the year in attending popular meetings two days three days quarterly and camp meetings the first of which a three days meeting will commence on the next Friday. I expect one every week until conference by which time I presume I shall be paralyzed and almost superannuated." (187–97). (The conference was scheduled for Sept. 10, 1835.)

For 1839, he reported heading homeward after one series around his circuit, "a distance of 180 miles." He said,

"I have now closed my third round on Springfield district. I held 9 quarterly meetings and preached a number of times between them. Travelled
about 800 miles and had a fair opportunity of 'enduring hardships as a
good soldier.' About 40 joined the Church. Some were converted and the
prospects on most of the circuits is good. We look for a glorious harvest
during the camp meeting (next) round" (282).

56. Entries for July 28 -Sept. 15, 1836. Lanius was <u>effectively two months in camp
    meetings</u> and then began another on Oct. 7. *The Journal of The Reverend Jacob
    Lanius,* 270, 275, 277–80. He left conference "in company with Brother Waugh,
    in order to attend a camp meeting on my circuit at Mud Town the seat of our
    revival."

57. *Autobiography of Peter Cartwright,* ed. Charles L. Wallis (Nashville: Abingdon
    Press, 1956; first published 1856), 225–29, 339–40; Peter Cartwright, *Fifty Years
    as a Presiding Elder,* ed. W. S. Hooper (Cincinnati: Hitchcock and Walden; New
    York: Nelson and Phillips, 1871).

58. See, for instance, the camp meeting scenes and notice of camp meetings
    throughout George Peck, *Early Methodism within the Bounds of the Old Genesee
    Conference from 1788 to 1828; or The First Forty Years of Wesleyan Evangelism in
    Northern Pennsylvania, Central and Western New York, and Canada. Containing
    Sketches of Interesting Localities, Exciting Scenes, and Prominent Actors* (New York:
    Carlton & Porter, 1860).

59. Nathan Bangs, *A History of the Methodist Episcopal Church,* 4 vols.; 3rd ed. (New
    York: T. Mason and G. Lake for the Methodist Episcopal Church, 1840–45), 2: 194.
    See similar declarations by Bangs about their spread east as he took account of
    revivalistic activity in the early decades of the nineteenth century, 141–42, 159,
    165, 172–73, 183–4, 250.

60. Asbury, *Journal* 3: 210–11 December 1805; cf. JLFA 2: 488.

61. Note that treatment of Methodism's efforts with Native Americans follows in
    the next chapter.

62. *Discipline*/MEC 1785, 15–17; MEA 2: 84–85. This first *Discipline* bore the quaint
    title of Minutes of Several Conversations Between the Rev, Thomas Coke, LL.
    D., the Rev. Francis Asbury and others, at a Conference, Begun in Baltimore, in
    the State of Maryland, on Monday, the 27th of December, in the Year 1784
    (Philadelphia: Charles Cist, 1785).

63. See J. Gordon Melton, *A Will to Choose: The Origins of African American Methodism*
    (Lanham: Rowman & Littlefield Publishers, 2007) and Cynthia Lynn Lyerly,
    Methodism and the Southern Mind, 1770–1810 (New York and Oxford: Oxford
    University Press, 1998), 47–72. On Methodist contribution to manumissions
    and consequent appeal to African Americans in Baltimore, see Christopher
    Phillips, *Freedom's Port: The African American Community of Baltimore, 1790–
    1860* (Urbana and Chicago: University of Illinois Press, 1997), especially 58–61
    and 117–44; and Charles G. Steffen, *The Mechanics of Baltimore: Workers and*

Politics in the Age of Revolution, 1763–1812 (Urbana and Chicago: University of Illinois Press, 1984), 255–73. For more general treatment, see Christine Leigh Heyrman, *Southern Cross: The Beginnings of the Bible Belt* (New York: Alfred A. Knopf, 1997); Wigger, *Taking Heaven by Storm*; Andrews, *The Methodists and Revolutionary America.*

64. Lorenzo Dow, *Extracts from Original Letters, to the Methodist Bishops, Mostly from their Preachers and Members in North America: Giving an Account of the Work of God since the Year 1800. Prefaced with a Short History of the Spread and Increase of the Methodists; with a Sketch of Camp Meetings* (Liverpool: H. Forshaw, 1806), 19–20.

65. Ibid., 55.

66. For a vigorous statement of this case and the historians who share in this finding, see William Courtland Johnson, " 'To Dance in the Ring of all Creation': Camp Meeting Revivalism and the Color Line, 1799–1825," Ph.D. Dissertation, University of California, Riverside, 1997.

67. Melton, *A Will to Choose*, 132–26 and on other African American camp meeting spirituality, 142–43, 169, 196, 215–12 and 236–39. See also Albert J. Raboteau, *Slave Religion: The "Invisible Institution" in the Antebellum South* (Oxford and New York: Oxford University Press, 1978), 59–61, 67–69, 131–34 and 223–25.

68. Lyerly, *Methodism and the Southern Mind* 60–61. Note that my version of her points (2) and (3) focus her more general judgments about Methodism and slaves on camp meetings specifically.

69. JGC/MECS 1846 65–68.

70. Johnson, *The Frontier Camp Meeting*, 113–18.

71. James Dixon Long, *Pictures of Slavery in Church and State: Including Personal Reminiscences, Biographical Sketches, Anecdotes, Etc. Etc.: With an Appendix Containing the Views of John Wesley and Richard Watson on Slavery*, 3rd ed. (Philadelphia: Published by the Author, 1857), 157–60. The title page identified the author as "a superannuated minister of the Philadelphia Annual Conference of the Methodist Episcopal Church."

72. The Journal of The Reverend Jacob Lanius. An Itinerant Preacher of the Missouri Conference of the Methodist Episcopal Church from 1831 A.D. to 1851 A.D. Edited by Elmer T. Clark. 1918, 47–50.

73. G. W. Henry, *Trials and Triumphs (For Half a Century) in the Life of G. W. Henry*, 2nd ed. (New York: Published for the Author, 1853), 176–77. Henry insisted that "it would be impossible for a stranger to discover which were free, or which were bonded, either in State or in Church, for they are generally taught to know their place, which is prescribed to them by the white population, whether it be right or wrong."

74. Lee, *Short History*, 284–362.

75. MEA 2: **1803.**

76. MEA 2: **1810b.**

77. See also Bangs, *A History of the Methodist Episcopal Church*, 2: 101–19; 261–80.

78. Finley, *Autobiography*, 315.

79. Andrews, *The Methodists and Revolutionary America*, 226. For an assessment that dates later the role of camp meeting participation in enhancing and defining the status and role of preachers in the south, see Heyrman, *Southern Cross*, 231–43. Heyrman comments extensively on camp meetings in southern religion.

80. Lyerly, *Methodism and the Southern Mind*, 180–81.

CHAPTER 3

1. For a very helpful effort to map camp meeting Methodist (southern Methodist and especially lay participants') expression and dramatization of its theology, see Bruce, *And They All Sang Hallelujah*, chap. IV, "And We'll All Sing Hallelujah: The Religion of the Spiritual Choruses." Bruce focuses (nicely complementary to this chapter's attention to the Godhead) on the camp meeting convert's theological-spiritual pilgrimage—conversion, assurance, sense of new life, viewing heaven as home, and breaking with the old life. Doctrines of God, especially of Christ, and implicitly on the Holy Spirit focus on the camp meeting's accompanying the soul from corrupt world to life amidst the people of the new heavenly Canaan. For a mapping that focuses on the early camp meeting's spiritual impact, see Eslinger, *Citizens of Zion*, 213–41, the final chapter entitled "The Social Significance of Camp Meeting Revivalism." For a study that ranges broadly over Methodism's theology as environmental sensitive, see Frank Everett Johnson, "Constructing the Church Triumphant: Methodism and the Emergence of the Midwest, 1800–1856," Ph.D. Diss., Department of History, Michigan State University, 1996. See especially 32–47 and 186–247, especially 211–28 of the latter.

2. For the list of publications, see John Vickers, *Thomas Coke: Apostle of Methodism* (Nashville and New York: Abingdon Press, 1969), 375–82. See also Vickers, ed., *Journals of Dr. Thomas Coke*.

3. Asbury, *Journal* 2: 433–34; cf. JLFA 2: 214.

4. But see Asbury's statement in chapter 1, note 43 (Asbury, *Journal* 1: 321; cf. JLFA 1: 310) and comments thereon.

5. Asbury, *Journal* 2: 479; cf. JLFA 2: 260. The underscoring is mine.

6. The heading references John Wesley's *A Survey of the Wisdom of God in the Creation: or A Compendium of Natural Philosophy. Containing an Abridgment of that Beautiful Work, "The Contemplation of Nature." By Mr. Bonnet, of Geneva*, 3rd American edition, revised and enlarged; with notes by B. Mayo, 2 vols. (New York: N. Bangs and T. Mason for the Methodist Episcopal Church, 1823).

7. Theodore Runyon, *The New Creation: John Wesley's Theology Today* (Nashville: Abingdon Press, 1998), 8. This section draws on Runyon, on M. Douglas Meeks, ed., *Wesleyan Perspectives on the New Creation* (Nashville: Kingswood

Books/Abingdon Press, 2004) and on Kenneth J. Collins, *The Theology of John Wesley* (Nashville: Abingdon Press, 2007).

8. *A Christian Library: Consisting of Extracts from and Abridgments of the Choicest Pieces of Practical Divinity Which Have Been Published in the English Tongue* 50 vols. (Bristol, 1749–55).

9. Wesley, *Survey*, 1: viii, x.

10. Wesley, "Spiritual Worship," *Sermons, Works* 3:88–114; 91–95. The emphasis was Wesley's.

11. Wesley, "God's Approbation of His Works," *Sermons, Works* 2: 387–99, 387. Toward the end of the sermon, Wesley reiterated the above and added: "It was good in the highest degree whereof it was capable, and without any mixture of evil. Every part was exactly suited to the others, and conducive to the good of the whole. There was 'a golden chain' (to use the expression of *Plato*) 'let down from the throne of God'—an exact connected series of beings, from the highest to the lowest: from dead earth, through fossils, vegetables, animals, to man, created in the image of God, and designed to know, to love, and enjoy his Creator to all eternity," 387, 396–97.

12. Wesley, "The Wilderness State," *Sermons, Works* 2: 205–21, 205.

13. Wesley, "The New Birth," *Sermons, Works* 2: 186–201, 187.

14. Wesley, *Sermons, Works* 2: 97–124; 436–50; 500–20.

15. Wesley, "The General Deliverance," *Sermons, Works* 2: 436–50; 438, 442, 446, 447, 448, 449.

16. Wesley, "On God's Vineyard," *Sermons, Works* 3: 502–17; 503.

17. Coke and Asbury, *Doctrines and Disciplines of the Methodist Episcopal Church*, 34.

18. *Minutes of the Annual Conferences of the Methodist Episcopal Church, for the years 1773–1828* (New York: T. Mason and G. Lane for the Methodist Episcopal Church, 1840), 5 (1773), 21 (1785).

19. Ibid. Emphasis in the original. The bishops continued, "They would necessarily endeavour to obtain the most able and lively preachers for their respective circuits, without entering, perhaps at all, into that enlarged, apostolic spirit, which would endeavour, whatever might be the sacrifice, to make all things *tally*." The bishops continued at some length against such localism.

20. For a contemporary effort to think ecclesiologically in somewhat similar terms, rejecting notions of a church as constituted by a center and periphery, see Hendrik R. Pieterse, "A Worldwide United Methodist Church? Soundings toward a Connectional Theological Imagination," *Methodist Review: A Journal of Wesleyan and Methodist Studies* 5 (2013): 1–23. An earlier version of this essay, along with similar efforts to think creatively about church by Wendy J. Deichmann, W. Stephen Gunter, and Mary Elizabeth Moore appeared in *The Renewal of United Methodism: Mission, Ministry and Connectionalism. Essays in Honor of Russell E. Richey*, ed. Rex D. Matthews (Nashville: General Board of Higher Education and Ministry, 2012).

21. H. Richard Niebuhr, *Christ and Culture* (New York: Harper & Brothers Publishers, 1951).
22. *Early American Methodism*, chapter 3.
23. JLFA 3: 566. Aug. 2, 1806.
24. MEA 2, 1789b for the bishops' letter and President Washington's response.
25. MEA 2, 1800a.
26. Robins, "Vernacular American Landscape." 166, 176.
27. Cooley, "Applying the Vagueness of Language," 571; "Manna and the Manual," 133.
28. This is a reordering of the biblical images in Cooley's "Manna and the Manual," 136, 153. See as well his "Applying the Vagueness of Language," 570–86 and Robins, "Vernacular American Landscape," 165–91.
29. Coke and Asbury, *Doctrines and Disciplines of the Methodist Episcopal Church*, 132–45.
30. Phrasing from the longer Asbury statement cited and given emphasis in the first section of this chapter. Asbury, *Journal* 2: 479; cf. JLFA 2: 260.
31. Johnson, "Constructing the Church Triumphant," 171–72. For theological mining of the landscape, see his chapter, "The Place of Pioneer Worship," especially 139–55, respectively treating rivers, forests, and prairies.
32. *Apology for Camp-Meetings*, 10–11, 42. The first passage referenced Psalm 8:3, 4, 9 and also quoted Romans 11:33–36. From Totten also came *A Collection of the Most Admired Hymns and Spiritual Songs*. By 1826, an eighteenth edition of this had appeared. In this study we give only passing attention to camp meeting hymnody. Another important hymnbook came from Orange Scott, *The New and Improved Camp Meeting Hymn Book: Being a Choice Selection of Hymns from the Most Approved Authors. Designed to Aid in the Public and Private Devotion of Christians* (Brookfield, 1830).
33. Donald G. Mathews, "The Second Great Awakening as an Organizing Process, 1780–1830: An Hypothesis," *American Quarterly*, 21 (Spring, 1969), 23–43.
34. *The Sunday Service of the Methodists in North America. With other Occasional Services.* (London, 1784); Reprinted as *John Wesley's Sunday Service of the Methodists in North America*, with an introduction by James F. White, *Quarterly Review*, 1984: 310.
35. For my efforts to elaborate an ecclesiology centering on connectionalism, see *Marks of Methodism: Practices of Ecclesiology; Doctrine in Experience: A Methodist Theology of Church and Ministry;* and *Methodist Connectionalism: Historical Perspectives*.
36. Asbury, *Journal* 2: 479; cf. JLFA 2: 260. The underscoring is mine.
37. For the Christology as expressed in camp meeting hymnody, see Bruce, *And They All Sang Hallelujah*, 108–14.
38. *Discipline/MEC* 1785: 20.
39. Coke and Asbury, *Doctrines and Disciplines of the Methodist Episcopal Church*, 41–42.
40. Richey, *Marks of Methodism: Practices of Ecclesiology*, 46–52.
41. Coke and Asbury, *Doctrines and Disciplines of the Methodist Episcopal Church*, 54–55, 46, 38–39.

42. Ibid., 5–7. Emphasis in the original.

43. Ibid., 36. Emphasis in the original.

44. Joseph M. Trimble, *Semi-centennial Address...Before the Ohio Conference of the Methodist Episcopal Church* (Columbus: Gazette Steam Printing House, 1878), 11.

45. Peter Cartwright, *Autobiography of Peter Cartwright: The Backwoods Preacher*, ed. W. P. Strickland (New York: Carlton & Porter, 1857), 485–87.

46. S. R. Beggs, *Pages from the Early History of the West and Northwest* (Cincinnati: Methodist Book Concern 1868), 15.

47. W. P. Strickland, ed., *Autobiography of Dan Young, A New England Preacher of the Olden Time* (New York: Carlton & Porter, 1860), 47–48.

48. For a mapping of Methodist leadership responding to Christ's call in non-Disciplinary vocational tasks, see Johnson, "Constructing the Church Triumphant," 46–72. His ministerial types are sojourner, patriarch, persistent pioneer, mystic, and showman.

49. MEA 2: 1800b, 137, 139 (2), 140 (2), 142 (4) and (2), 143 (2).

50. Coke, *Extracts of the Journals of the Rev. Dr. Coke's Five visits to America*, 151. Coke's preceding comments warrant inclusion. He noted, "April 2. We began our Conference for *North-Carolina* at the house of Brother *M'Knight* on the River *Yeadkin*, There were in all about thirty Preachers, several of whom came from the other side of the *Appalachian* Mountains.

> "At this Conference, a remarkable spirit of prayer was poured forth on the Preachers. Every night, before we concluded, Heaven itself seemed to be opened to our believing souls. One of the Preachers was so blessed in the course of our prayers, that he was constrained to cry, 'O I never was so happy in all my life before! O what a heaven of heavens I feel.'"

51. *Discipline*/MEC 1785: 3; cf. Coke and Asbury, *Doctrines and Disciplines of the Methodist Episcopal Church*, 31–32.

52. *Apology for Camp-Meetings*, 12–13. An asterisk identified the hymn as written at a June 1810 camp meeting. For a list of published camp meeting hymnals, see Johnson, *The Frontier Camp Meeting*, 310–11.

53. On the process of adoption, see chapter 8 of my *Methodist Connectionalism: Historical Perspectives*.

54. A. H. Redford, *The History of Methodism in Kentucky*, 3 vols. (Nashville, TN: Southern Methodist publishing house, 1868–1870), 1: 287–88.

55. These can be followed in the successive Journals, but may be most conveniently visualized in Robert Emory, *History of The Discipline of the Methodist Episcopal Church*, rev. W. P. Strickland (New York: Carlton & Porter [1857]). His section, "Of the Boundaries of the Annual Conferences," 246–94, details the changes in General Conference legislation, for each successive General Conference, including the specific wording of provisos.

56. The last included "an annual conference on the western coast of Africa, to be denominated The Liberian Mission Annual Conference." See Emory, *History of The Discipline,* 246–60.

57. Coke and Asbury, *Doctrines and Disciplines of the Methodist Episcopal Church,* iii, 59.

58. Kobler. Journal and Sermons, 93 for June 15, 1790. One of several statements quoted from Kobler's journal in chapter 1. The whole entry read: "This morning I feel a great hunger and thirst after righteousness. I retired into a wood where I found the Lord to be very precious to my soul, the very trees of the wood is praising of him, much more reason honor I who am a Brand plucked out of the fire."

59. Finley, *Autobiography,* 398. He specified the gathering as "on the farm of the Rev. John Collins, on the east fork of the Little Miami."

60. For an exploration of layfolk's experience of Methodist forest ministry and of the theological implications thereof, especially with regard to the Holy Spirit, see Cooley, "Manna and the Manual," especially 136–38.

61. Emory, *History of the Discipline,* 191–202. Lee had calculated the number and proportions of local preachers to traveling: in 1799 there were 850 local to 269 traveling, in 1809 1610 local to 589 traveling. Lee, *Short History,* 255, 359, 362. McKendree gave the same proportions for 1812: 2,000 to 700. Mudge noted:

> "The lay or local preachers and exhorters have formed, from the beginning, a very important factor in the work. The great extent of the early circuits would of itself imply this.... We have no way of ascertaining accurately the number of these early local preachers, for the statistics of the Minutes do not recognize them till 1837, when the number in the whole church is given as 4,954 as against 2,933 in the itinerant ranks. Only eighty-five are reported at that time from the New England Conference, or about half the number of those traveling. In 1850 the local preachers of this Conference were eighty as compared with 113 traveling, and in the whole church 5,420 as compared with 3,777. In 1870 there were 10,340 local, and 8,830 traveling. In 1890 the numbers were practically equal, 14,072 local and 14,792 traveling. At present there are 14,743 local and 19,421 traveling."

James Mudge, *History of the New England Conference of the Methodist Episcopal Church, 1796–1910* (Boston: Published by the Conference, 1910), 239–40.

62. See *Minutes of the Methodist Conferences, Annually Held in America; From 1773 to 1813, Inclusive* or minutes for any subsequent year.

63. See Lee, *Short History,* 354 or the year-end tally for any prior year. Bangs took a similar "body" count. See Nathan Bangs, *A History of the Methodist Episcopal Church,* 12th ed., 4 vols. (New York: Carlton & Porter, 1860), III, 183 for the 1820 accounting.

64. JGC/MEC 1816, 148–52. That concern made the conference no more receptive to petitions by local preachers for representation (1816), 166–69.

65. See Richey, *The Methodist Conference in America.*

66. See, for instance, MEA 2: 1841a.

67. MEA 2: 246 (1839) from George G. Cookman, *Speeches Delivered on Various Occasions* (New York: George Lane for the MEC, 1840), 127–37.

68. See Kenneth J. Collins, *The Theology of John Wesley: Holy Love and the Shape of Grace* (Nashville: Abingdon Press, 2007), 307–12; Randy L. Maddox, *Responsible Grace: John Wesley's Practical Theology* (Nashville: Kingswood Books, 1994), 157.

69. The following paragraphs derive, with very slight emendations, from Richey, *Marks of Methodism: Practices of Ecclesiology*, 50–52, and are reproduced here with permission.

70. Coke and Asbury, *Doctrines and Disciplines of the Methodist Episcopal Church*, iii–iv.

71. Asbury reported for February 1804 while in North Carolina: "Saturday, 11. At Rork's, at Town Creek, brother M'Caine preached: I also spoke, enforcing, 'Be thou faithful unto death, and I will give thee a crown of life.' A late camp-meeting upon Town Creek has given a revival to religion amongst both whites and blacks. I thought I perceived intimations of this in my last visits. About the going down of the sun we came into Wilmington, faint and feeble." Asbury, *Journal* 3: 145; cf. JLFA 2: 425.

72. J. G. Bruce "A Semi-Centennial Sermon, delivered before the Kentucky Conference…September 30, 1881" *Minutes of the Fifty-fifth Session of the Kentucky Annual Conference of the Methodist Episcopal Church*, 1881, 57–64, 61–62.

73. James B. Finley, *Life Among the Indians; or Personal Reminiscences and Historical Incidents Illustrative of Indian Life and Character*, ed. Rev. D. W. Clark (Cincinnati: Hitchcock and Walden; New York: Carlton and Lanahan, 1857), 266–69; 308–13, 470. See also Cole, *Lion of the Forest*, 49, 70.

74. William G. McLoughlin, *The Cherokees and Christianity, 1794–1870*, ed. Walter H. Conser, Jr. (Athens and London: University of Georgia Press, 1994), 29. McLoughlin continued, "The Methodist missionaries were also admired for their public attacks on [President Andrew] Jackson's removal policy in 1830." That action was soon rebuked by Methodism's mission board and McLoughlin noted, "Methodism thereafter lost Cherokee support." For other treatment of Methodism in that volume, see especially 40–41, 198–201 and 206–09.

75. William G. McLoughlin, *Cherokees and Missionaries, 1789–1839* (New Haven and London: Yale University Press, 1984), 169. For Methodism's early camp meeting revivalism among Cherokees, see 163–79 and 289–97 for the church's compromising stances when the Cherokee people were removed. See also his *Cherokee Renaissance in the New Republic* (Princeton: Princeton University Press, 1986), 363–64, 380–84,, 440–43, and 381, especially on camp meetings. For the nation's later history, see *After the Trail of Tears: The Cherokees' Struggle for Sovereignty, 1839–1880* (Chapel Hill and London: University of North Carolina Press, 1993).

76. *A Son of the Forest: The Experience of William Apess, Native of the Forest.* Written by Himself. 2nd ed., rev. and corrected. (New York: Published by the Author, G. F. Bunce, Printer, 1831), 83–84.

77. Ibid., 88–89.

78. Douglas M. Strong, "The Nineteenth Century: Expansion and Fragmentation," *The Cambridge Companion to American Methodism,* Jason E. Vickers, ed. (New York: Cambridge University Press, 2013), 63–96: 69. In this same volume, Ted A. Campbell treats Native American William Apess in "Spiritual Biography and Autobiography," 243–60.

79. Donald L. Parman, ed., *Window to a Changed World: The Personal Memoirs of William Graham* (Indianapolis: Indiana Historical Society, 1998), 58, 61–75.

80. Margaret Burnham Macmillan, *The Methodist Church in Michigan: The Nineteenth Century* (Grand Rapids: Michigan Area Methodist Historical Society and William B. Eerdmans Publishing, 1967), 166–68.

81. Henry B. Ridgaway, D. D., *The Life of the Rev. Alfred Cookman; With Some Account of His Father, the Rev. George Grimston Cookman. With a Preface by the Rev. R.S. Foster, LL.D.* (London: Hodder and Stoughton, 1873), 240. In his preceding paragraph Cookman reported to his wife,

> "Arriving on the ground in time for afternoon preaching, heard a sermon from a Brother Littlewood on 'Enduring hardship as a good soldier of Jesus Christ'; in the evening, a Brother Bates on the 'Conversion of St. Paul.' On Wednesday morning Dr. True preached about Moses. In the afternoon an old veteran of the Troy Conference discoursed on the subject of 'Holiness'; in the evening Brother D. Buck on 'Mercy and righteousness have met together,' etc. Thursday, Dr. Wentworth preached in his usual effective camp-meeting style on 'Christ crucified'; in the afternoon Brother Newman on 'Holiness'—an excellent sermon. In the evening Rev. H. Cox, of St. Louis, occupied the time in presenting his cause and taking a collection. Friday, Brother Pegg preached in the morning on 'This treasure in earthen vessels'; in the afternoon Brother Fox, of Forty-third Street, on 'I have a baptism to be baptized with, and I am straitened until it is accomplished'; and in the evening your poor unworthy husband on 'Redeeming the time,' 239–40.

CHAPTER 4

1. Wigger, *American Saint*, 365, 384; JLFA, 3, 380–81; 455.

2. See Brown, *Holy Ground, Too*, 238–321 for his listing of over thirty camp meetings per page. Brown identifies camp meetings by state with indications of whether the camp meeting continued (to the point of his writing) and of its denominational affiliation. The three pages covering my home state, North Carolina, indicate that only a handful explicitly identify themselves as United Methodist but the great preponderance belong within the Methodist family.

3. For different takes on the division in Methodism prefigured, if not begun, in this fifth stage, see Riley B. Case, *Evangelical and Methodist: A Popular History* (Nashville: Abingdon Press, 2004) and Andrew C. Rieser, *The Chautauqua Moment: Protestants, Progressives, and the Culture of Modern Liberalism* (New York: Columbia University Press, 2003). For a more extensive and extended list of camp meeting outcomes, see my former student Kenneth O. Brown's *Holy Ground, Too*, 3 5, 51. The camp meeting family tree includes, according to Brown: the religious resort, holiness camp meetings, the Bible and Prophecy Conference Movement, the Chautauqua Movement, the Keswick Movement, Christian assembly grounds, denominational camp meetings, Pentecostal camp meetings, the family camping movement, tabernacle revivalism, Christian conference centers, Christian retreat centers, models of Christian camping, and Christian rock festivals. He insists, "all of these are camp meeting's children" (5).

4. On temperance, see Tait, *Poisoned Chalice*.

5. Bangs, *History of the Methodist Episcopal Church*, 2: 265–80, 265, 267–68.

6. Ibid., 269.

7. Bangs, *History of the Methodist Episcopal Church*, 4: 52–53. He continued, "As a means of awakening sinners to a sense of their sinfulness, and leading them to Jesus Christ for life and salvation, they have been abundantly blessed and owned of God, and should there be kept up so long as they are productive of these results."

8. Nathan Bangs, *An Original Church of Christ: or A Scriptural Vindication of the Orders and Powers of the Ministry of the Methodist Episcopal Church* (New York: Published by T. Mason and G. Lane, for the Methodist Episcopal Church, 1837).

9. For our effort to credit Bangs with such agency, see MEA 1, chapter VI.

10. In 1818, at General Conference's behest, Joshua Soule launched the *Methodist Magazine*, authorized as *The Methodist Missionary Magazine* and variously titled thereafter (*Methodist Magazine and Quarterly Review, Methodist Quarterly Review, Methodist Review, Religion in Life, Quarterly Review*, now again *Methodist Review* (an online and peer-reviewed venture of which I am an editor).

11. Bangs elaborated all these points with gusto in his *The Present State, Prospects, and Responsibilities of the Methodist Episcopal Church. With an Appendix of Ecclesiastical Statistics* (New York: Lane & Scott, 1850). So, for instance:

> "We have improved temporally. The most of those who embraced Methodism in its early days were among the poorer class of society. In consequence of their embracing the religion of the Lord Jesus—and this is what I understand by their becoming Methodists—they have become sober, industrious, frugal in their manner of living, and thus many have become wealthy; others are in comfortable and thriving circumstances; while comparatively few are suffering from poverty, but most of them are reaping the fruits of honest industry" (29).

Similarly, Methodism's property-holding climbed with its membership:

> "In former days, most of the preaching-places, more particularly in the country villages and settlements, were private houses, school-houses, barns, and groves; even when a church edifice was erected, a site was generally selected in some obscure retreat, remote from the centre of population, as though the Methodists were ashamed to be seen and heard by their neighbours; and even this small edifice was frequently but half finished, and left to fall down under its own rottenness.... Now there are large and commodious houses of worship." (31).

12. *The Errors of Hopkinsianism Detected and Refuted* (New York, 1815); *The Reformer Reformed: or A Second Part of the Errors of Hopkinsianism Detected and Refuted* (New York, 1816); *An Examination of the Doctrine of Predestination* (New York, 1817); *A Vindication of Methodist Episcopacy* (New York, 1820). See Thomas A. Langford, *Practical Divinity: Theology in the Wesleyan Tradition* (Nashville: Abingdon Press, 1983), 78–86.

13. See Bangs, *An Original Church of Christ.*

14. Bangs, *Present State.*

15. Ibid., 205–06.

16. For a well-presented case for such a reading in the life of a preacher, see David L. Kimbrough, *Reverend Joseph Tarkington, Methodist Circuit Rider. From Frontier Evangelism to Refined Religion* (Knoxville: University of Tennessee Press, 1997). See especially 4, 7, 37, 46–47, 103, 109–10.

17. [James Porter], *An Essay on Camp-Meetings by the Author of "The True Evangelist"* (New York: Lane & Scott, 1849), 19. Porter's more extended defense of camp meetings is worth quoting:

> "As Methodists, we need these great occasions for *all* the people. Our general and annual conferences embrace the preachers only, but they exert a salutary influence. Though the meetings of these bodies are principally for business purposes, they subserve mutual friendship, and strengthen the members for their arduous work. But few of the *people* enjoy the privilege of attending them. This loss was formerly recompensed by the quarterly meetings, which convened a large number of preachers and people from different parts of an extended circuit.... How much the union and devotion of Methodism owe to these occasions, we are not authorized to say. It is certain, however, they have been immensely useful in promoting and preserving the vitality of religion among us. And in those sections where they are maintained they are still beneficial. But, as great occasion, quarterly meetings have no existence in a considerable part of our country. Few attend them beyond the limits of the society where they are held, and we see no prospect of restoring them to their former greatness" (18–19).

18. See, for instance, Books III and IV of George Peck, *Early Methodism within the Bounds of the Old Genesee Conference from 1788 to 1828; or The First Forty Years of Wesleyan Evangelism in Northern Pennsylvania, Central and Western New York, and Canada. Containing Sketches of Interesting Localities, Exciting Scenes, and Prominent Actors* (New York: Carlton & Porter, 1860).

19. Andrew Carroll, *Moral and Religious Sketches and Collections, with Incidents of Ten years' Itinerancy in the West* (Cincinnati: Printed at the Methodist Book Concern, for the Author, 1857), 36–38. For other camp meeting accounts, see 23, 25–26, 34, 35–37, 48–49, 71, 72, 134, 137–38, 149, and 150. For another account of Ohio and of Illinois camp meetings from the 1820s to the 1850s, see *Autobiography of a Pioneer: or The Nativity, Experience, Travels, and Ministerial Labors of Rev. Jacob Young, with Incidents, Observations and Reflections* (Cincinnati: Cranston and Curts; New York: Hunt and Eaton, 1860). Note, for instance, 397, 462–64, 476, 496–97. The routinization of the camp meetings he captures by commenting several times in some off-handed fashion judgment, as for instance "We closed our labors on this circuit with a camp meeting—some little good was done" (476).

20. See Chapter XII "Quarterly Conference Records, 1808-52" in William Warren Sweet, *Religion on the American Frontier. 1783–1840,* 4 vols. Vol. IV: *The Methodists: A Collection of Source Materials* (Chicago: University of Chicago Press, 1946), 552–639. The records attest numerous camp meetings, sometimes noted just in a minor heading or otherwise obscure entry but now discoverable when the volume is accessed online. See 562, 566, 567, 569, 571, 576, 577, 580, 581, 583, 584, 587, 590, 593 (2), 594, 596–97 (2), 600, 605, 606, 611, 612, 625, 626, 631, 632 (2), 639. The last section, entitled "Camp Ground Near San Augustine Oct. 25th A.D. 1851," covers 1851 and 1852 for this Texas Circuit. The first of these records included this item:

> "The Conference then proceeded to elect Trustees for the camp-ground near San Augustine and these persons whose names appear in the deed was elected trustees" (no period, 632). The last of the records which Sweet included, the "Report of Stewards," buried the camp meeting as a financial item "Public Collection at Camp Ground" (639).

21. Geo. G. Smith, Jr., *The History of Methodism in Georgia and Florida, From 1785 to 1865* (Macon, GA: Wno. W. Burke & Co., 1877), 255–56. For a recent scholarly confirmation of Smith's judgment, see Christopher H. Owen, *The Sacred Flame of Love: Methodism and Society in Nineteenth-Century Georgia* (Athens and London: University of Georgia Press, 1998). His chapter 2 is subtitled "Camp Meeting Methodism in Georgia, 1801–1820." And he treats the phenomenon elsewhere including its use with Native Americans, 36–38. Chapter 2, like the book generally, studies how class, race, and gender figured into and were treated by Methodists in the camp meetings.

22. For details on Arkansas camp meetings, see Stanley T. Baugh, *Camp Grounds and Camp Meetings in the Little Rock Conference, The Methodist Church* (Little Rock: Epworth Press, [1953]). His list of old campgrounds numbers twenty-six,

a number with dates approximate, but including: Bailey, 1827–38; Liberty, 1856–1880; Pump Spring, 1850s–1900; Bethel (Saline), 1850s–1920; and Red Colony, 1855, burned by soldiers in 1863.

23. Nancy Britton, *Two Centuries of Methodism in Arkansas, 1800–2000* (Little Rock: August House Publishers, 2000), 33–34.

24. W. S. Woodard, *Annals of Methodism in Missouri, Containing an outline of the ministerial life of more than One Thousand Preachers, and sketches of MORE THAN THREE HUNDRED, Also sketches of Charges, Churches and Laymen from the beginning in 1806 to The Centennial Year, 1884, containing Seventy-Eight Years of History,* (Columbia, MO: E. W. Stephens, Publisher, 1893), 65, 135, 139, 275.

25. John L. Smith, *Indiana Methodism: A Series of Sketches and Incidents, Grave AND Humorous Concerning Preachers AND People of the West* (Valpariso: no publisher listed, 1892). See also William Warren Sweet, Circuit-Rider Days in Indiana (W. K. STEWART CO. Indianapolis, 1916) who reported camp meetings as well for the 1830s and 1840s.

26. J. C. Smith, *Reminiscences of Early Methodism in Indiana, Including Sketches of Various Prominent Ministers, Together with Narratives of Women Eminent for Piety, Poetry and Song. Also Descriptions of Remarkable Camp Meetings, Revivals, Incidents and Other Miscellany. With an Appendix Containing Essays on Various Theological Subjects of Practical Interest* (Indianapolis, J. M. Olcott, 1879).

27. J. J. Fleharty, *Glimpses of the Life of Rev. A. E. Phelps and his Co-Laborers: Or, Twenty-five Years in the Methodist Itinerancy* (Cincinnati: Hitchcock & Walden, 1878), 133, 334.

28. The first portion of the first of ten verses in one of three camp meeting hymns in Lorenzo Dow, *Vicissitudes in the Wilderness; Exemplified in the Journal of Peggy "Dow." To Which is Added an Appendix of her Death, and also Reflections on Matrimony* (Norwich, CT: Printed by William Faulkner, 1833). The remainder of that verse? "The lilies grow and thrive, Refreshing streams of grace divine, From Jesus flow, that living vine Which makes the dead revive."

29. Stephen Allen, D. D., *The Life of Rev. John Allen, Better Known as "Camp-Meeting John," to which is added Tributes and Eulogies by Dr. Charles Cullis, Rev. R.B Howard, Rev. Mark Trafton, D. D., Rev. J. W. Hamilton, D. D., Rev. William McDonald, Rev. L. B. Bates, D. D., and others* (Boston: B. B. Russell, 1888), 21–26, 43–44, 74.

30. Alfred Brunson, *A Western Pioneer: or, Incidents of the Life and Times of Rev. Alfred Brunson, A. M, D. D., Embracing a Period of Over Seventy Years. Written by Himself.* 2 vols. (Cincinnati: Hitchcock and Walden, 1872, 1877), 1: 416–8.

"Now the things which I write unto you, behold, before God, I lie not." Galatians i, 20.

"Come and hear, all ye that fear God, and I will declare what he hath done for my soul." Psalm lxvi, 16.

31. Smith, *The History of Methodism in Georgia and Florida*, 347–49. Echoing such sentiments was an editorial in the *St. Louis Advocate:*

It can not be denied but that this particular institution seemed to have been providentially called up to meet the moral and spiritual necessities of a people scattered thinly over a large extent of country, and who, but for the institution of Camp-meetings, must have been deprived of many religious advantages and much spiritual good which through them they derived. But it is now contended that as the country is more thickly inhabited, and the people more settled, their attention, and the attention and efforts of the Church, should be directed more specially to erecting church and school-houses in every neighborhood; organizing societies, and endeavoring to give to our whole system a permanency in its operations corresponding with the increasing permanent character of the population, and in this there is much force. Still, a large portion of our people, and a proportionately larger portion of our preachers, are in favor of camp-meetings.

An excerpt from the longer editorial reprinted in Charles F. Deems, ed., *Annals of Southern Methodism for 1855* (New York: J. A. Gray's, 1856), 370–71.

32. James Penn Pilkington, *The Methodist Publishing House: A History*, vol. 1 (Nashville: Abingdon Press, 1968), 321 (from the *Nashville Christian Advocate*, April 3, 1850, 3). For a meditative account of earlier Tennessee camp meetings, see John Brooks, *The Life and Times of the Rev. John Brooks, in Which are Contained A History of the Great Revival in Tennessee; with Many Incidents of Thrilling Interest. Written by Himself* (Nashville: Published at the Nashville Christian Advocate Office, 1848), especially 39–44. His portrayal is worth citing, even in a note.

> "At the close of these meetings the scene was very affecting; the brethren parting with their preachers and each other, with a hearty shake of the hand, and often a strong hug. I have often seen the whole encampment thus bathed in tears, sisters embracing sisters, brothers embracing brothers, while the loud shouts and hallelujahs were pealing from the mouths of many. They appeared to have to use a kind of violence to separate. They would part and go off shouting and crying. I have frequently gone with and passed such companies, on their way home, laughing, and crying, and shouting, singing the songs of Zion. The whole forest would seem to be sweetened with the glory of God. Oh my God, shall I ever see such times again?" 43.

33. Charles F. Deems, ed., *Annals of Southern Methodism for 1855* (New York: J. A. Gray's, 1856). Chapter is entitled "Reports of Revivals," 104–18.

34. Scott, comp. *The New and Improved Camp Meeting Hymn Book.* Hymn 51 of the 135 hymns in this version of his compilation. There are 166 hymns in 1836 version. These two lines conclude the first of five verses. The verse as a whole: "THOU, in whose presence my soul takes delight, On whom in affliction I call, My comfort by day, and my song in the night, My hope, my salvation, my all;

Where dost thou at noontide resort with thy sheep, To feed on the pasture of love? Oh why in the valley of death shall I weep, Or alone in the wilderness rove?"

35. Frederick E. Maser, *Methodism in Central Pennsylvania, 1771–1969* (N.p.: Central Pennsylvania Annual Conference, 1971), 53, 57, 69, 72, 74, 78–83, 100, 138–43, 146, 228. The opening sentence of the second chapter: "After the organization of the Central Pennsylvania Conference in 1869, the advance of the Methodist Episcopal Church in the area continued through its camp meetings and its revivals."

36. Walter N. Vernon, Robert W. Sledge, Robert C. Monk and Norman W. Spellmann, *The Methodist Excitement in Texas: A History* (Dallas: The Texas United Methodist Historical Society, 1984), 25, 31, 33–42, 57, 62, 72, 82, 87–89, 103, 145, 181–82. For a lively account of Texas revivalism, see "The Texas Camp-Meeting" apparently by Charles Summerfield in J. V. Watson, *Tales and Takings, Sketches and Incidents, from the Itinerant and Editorial Budget of Rev. J. V. Watson, D. D. Editor of the Northwestern Christian Advocate* (New York: Carton & Porter, 1856), 299–310.

37. Margaret Burnham Macmillan, *The Methodist Church in Michigan: The Nineteenth Century* (Grand Rapids: Michigan Area Methodist Historical Society and William B. Eerdmans Publishing, 1967), 54–55, 60, 81, 86–87, 99–102, 114, 150, 166–68 (on Native American camp meetings), 306–14 (on the 1870s), 356 and 365–67 (on Chautauqua).

38. T. Otto Nall, *Forever Beginning: A History of the United Methodist Church and Her Antecendents in Minnesota to 1969* (N.p.: Commission on Archives and History, Minnesota Conference, 1973), 43–47.

39. H. N. Herrick and William Warren Sweet, *A History of the North Indiana Conference of the Methodist Episcopal Church* (Indianapolis: W. K. Stewart Company, 1917), 126. See other references to camp meetings on 21, 25, 29, 38, 47, 65, and 107. For an Indiana contemporary's sense that the church had moved beyond camp meetings and minimal mention of them, see Donald L. Parman, ed., *Window to a Changed World: The Personal Memoirs of William Graham* (Indianapolis: Indiana Historical Society, 1998), especially, xv–xvi, xviii, 28–29, 46–47, 80, 155.

40. See Elmer J. O'Brien, comp. and ed., *Methodist Reviews Index 1818–1985: A retrospective Index of Periodical articles and Book Reviews*, 2 vols. (Nashville: Board of Higher Education and Ministry, The United Methodist Church, 1989), vol. 1: "Periodical Articles," 43–44.

41. Cartwright, *Autobiography*, 340–41. See on Cartwright *Fifty Years as a Presiding Elder*, ed. W. S. Hooper (Cincinnati: Hitchcock and Walden; New York: Nelson and Phillips, 1871).

42. See [Porter], *An Essay on Camp Meetings.* His seven chapter titles as well as his exposition suggest defensiveness:

  1. Camp-Meetings; Their Origin and History
  2. Camp-Meetings Supported by Sound Philosophy
  3. Other Arguments Considered

4. Objections Considered

5. Other Objections Examined

6. The Personal Improvement of Camp-Meetings

The Subject Applied

43. See Pilkington, *The Methodist Publishing House*, 136–38, and Walter Newton Vernon, Jr., *The United Methodist Publishing House: A History*, vol. 2 (Nashville: Abingdon Press, 1989). The former carried the descriptor "Beginnings to 1870," the latter "1870 to 1988."

44. Johnson, *The Frontier Camp Meeting*. Bruce, in *And They All Sang Hallelujah*, largely concurs. The latter's whole volume deals, in a sense, with camp meetings as the music's context, devotes one of its five chapters to explicitly to them (61–95), and treats them explicitly. See also 4–12, 120–24, and 132–33.

45. Johnson, *The Frontier Camp Meeting*, 249–51.

46. For elaboration of that point, see Schneider, *The Way of the Cross Leads Home*, especially chapters 4–9.

47. Charles A. Parker, "The Camp meeting on the Frontier and the Methodist Resort in the East—Before 1900," *Methodist History* 18 (April 1980), 179–92.

48. Brown, *Holy Ground, Too*, 3 5, 51.

49. A wilderness-to-grove-and-garden tribute to a Kentucky-born circuit rider who served in Indiana connected him with the "march westward of a rude civilization, under the reign and auspices of the 'ax, the rifle, and the saddle-bags,' with Methodism leading a camp, log-cabin, and camp-meeting life alongside of it, to imbue it with the holy leaven of heaven." "Rev. J. L. Thompson, of the Northwestern Indiana Conference," J. V. Watson, *Tales and Takings, Sketches and Incidents, from the Itinerant and Editorial Budget of Rev. J. V. Watson, D. D. Editor of the Northwestern Christian Advocate* (New York: Carton & Porter, 1856), 453–58.

50. James Dixon, *Methodism in America: With the Personal Narrative of the Author, During a Tour Through a Part of the United States and Canada* (London: John Mason, 1849), 347–48. Dixon's commentary on camp meetings extends from 335 to 350.

51. B. W. Gorham, *Camp Meeting Manual: A Practical Book for the Camp Ground; In Two Parts* (Boston: H. V. Degen, 1854), 168. Gorham continued:

> Let there be no idlers among us; no preaching or praying for a name; no gossip; no rant; no idle thronging; no beating the air; but a united, well aimed series of efforts in God's name, that shall drive home the gospel steel at every blow.
>
> Thus conducted, there should, by the blessing of God, be no such thing as failure on the Camp ground. The church would be quickened the mourner comforted, and hundreds awakened and converted. And dark-minded, evil men, who would not yield to truth, should yet confess, "God is come into the camp" (168).

52. Ibid., 23.

53. Ibid., 25–26.

54. Ibid., 32–33.

55. At several points in his *Camp Meeting Manual*, Gorham insisted that the presiding elder needed to be in charge. This counsel is especially suggestive as it bears on the several futures that camp meetings took, not just this primitivist one. They were an abnormality in the Methodist system—almost a mandate while Asbury lived but never incorporated into and therefore regulated by Methodism's *Discipline*. Perhaps as a consequence neither as property nor as program were they tightly secured to the denomination and its leadership. By contrast, Methodism protected churches and parsonages, securing to general and annual conferences such properties under trustees by what was variously termed the model deed, trust clause, or deed of settlement. The 1796 General Conference incorporated this Wesleyan device into the *Discipline*, providing a four-page, detailed template for an indenture or deed of settlement to be adapted "as far as the laws of the states will respectively admit of it." (See Coke and Asbury, *Doctrines and Disciplines of the Methodist Episcopal Church*, 173–77.) Methodism secured its church buildings, however big or small, by the trust clause. By various ownership, trusteeship, local and state laws, and Gorham's injunctions to empower presiding elders, Methodists and their friends sought to protect camp meetings but tied to the formal exercise of Methodist authority they were not.

56. *My Business Was to Fight the Devil: Recollections of Rev. Adam Wallace, Peninsula Circuit Rider, 1847–1865*, ed. with notes and biographical sketch by Joseph F. DiPaolo (Action, MA: Tapestry Press, 1998).

57. Ibid., 9, 38, 52–53, 81–83, 98–99, 114, 150, 155–57, 167. Note that the various chapters in this book, crafted to read like a journal and arranged by year, were published by Wallace in a series of letters in *The Peninsula Methodist* from 1885 to 1887. See Forward by Frederick Maser and editor's Preface, xi–xiv.

58. Evangelical Association of North America, Kansas Conference, *Fifty Years in the Kansas Conference 1864–1914: A Record of the Origin and Development of the Work of the Evangelical Association* (Cleveland: Press of the Evangelical Association, n.d.), 36, 41. Pre-1900 references to camp meetings include 14, 16, 36, 41, 59, 69, 80–82, 88, 95, 101, 117, 130, 143–45, 174, 248–49, 255 (see 143–45 for some description of setting and drama of camp meetings in 1881).

59. *Minutes of the Fifty-fourth Session of the Kentucky Annual Conference of the Methodist Episcopal Church, South*, 1874, Mt. Sterling, Sept 16th to 22nd, 11–12.

60. *Minutes of the Fifty-fifth Session of the Kentucky Annual Conference of the Methodist Episcopal Church, South*, 1875, Maysville, Sept 22nd to 29th, 4, 7.

61. *Minutes of the Fifty-sixth Session of the Kentucky Annual Conference of the Methodist Episcopal Church, South*, 1876, Maysville, Sept 22nd to 29th, 19–20, 21.

62. *Minutes of the Fifty-seventh Session of the Kentucky Annual Conference of the Methodist Episcopal Church, South*, 1877, Winchester, Sept 5th to 12th, 7, 9, 12.

63. *Minutes of the Fifty-eighth Session of the Kentucky Annual Conference of the Methodist Episcopal Church, South,* 1878, Shelbyville, Sept 18th to 25th, 4–5.

64. *Minutes of the Sixty-first Session of the Kentucky Annual Conference of the Methodist Episcopal Church, South,* 1881, Danville, Sept 7th to 12th, 19–20.

65. *Minutes of the Sixty-third Session of the Kentucky Annual Conference of the Methodist Episcopal Church, South,* 1883, Cynthiana, Sept 12th to 18th, 4.

66. *Minutes of the Sixty-sixth Session of the Kentucky Annual Conference of the Methodist Episcopal Church, South,* 1886, Winchester, Sept 8th to 14th, 4.

67. *Minutes of the Kentucky Annual Conference of the Methodist Episcopal Church,* 1872 (20th session), Covington Feb. 21st- 26th, 9, 50.

68. *Minutes of the Fifty-second Session of the Kentucky Annual Conference of the Methodist Episcopal Church,* 1879, Somerset, Mar. 13th–18th, 12.

69. W. G. Miller, *Thirty Years in the Itinerancy* (Milwaukee: I. L. Hauser & Co., 1875), 221–23. For accounts of camp meetings that began and characterized Miller's ministry, see 30, 126, 166, 172 and 221–25 for more of the ruminations that are here cited.

70. Adam Wallace, *The Parson of the Islands: A Biography of the Rev. Joshua Thomas, Embracing Sketches of his Contemporaries and Remarkable Camp Meeting Scenes, Revival Incidents, and Reminiscences of the Introduction of Methodism on the Islands of the Chesapeake, and the Eastern Shores of Maryland and Virginia* (Reprinted, Baltimore: Thomas Evans Printing Co., 1906), 380–81. Wallace's Preface is dated 1861.

71. Lucius C. Matlack, *The Life of Rev. Orange Scott: Compiled from his Personal Narrative, Correspondence, and Other Authentic Sources of Information,* in two parts (New York: C. Prindle and L. C. Matlack at the Wesleyan Methodist Book Room, 1847), 231.

72. On temperance, see Tait, *Poisoned Chalice.*

73. For a Sunday school usage, see Daniel P. Kidder, ed. *The Grove Meeting* (New York: Lane & Scott for the Sunday-School Union of the Methodist Episcopal Church, 1852). Chapter 1 begins, "Mother, what is a grove meeting? Said Eliza Jacobs, as she came home from church on Sunday evening" (7).

74. Brunson, *A Western Pioneer,* 1:331–32.

75. Edward J. Drinkhouse, *History of Methodist Reform. Synoptical of General Methodism, 1703 to 1898, with Special and Comprehensive Reference to its Most Salient Exhibition in the History of the Methodist Protestant Church by Edward J. Drinkhouse, M.D., D.D.* 2 vols. (Baltimore: Board of Publication of the Methodist Protestant Church, 1899), 2: 204, 227, 230, 247–249.

76. Nancy Britton, *Two Centuries of Methodism in Arkansas, 1800–2000* (Little Rock: August House Publishers, 2000), 30–31.

77. Drinkhouse, *History of Methodist Reform,* 2: 264. The two provisos read:

> 1. The President of each Annual Conference shall be elected annually by the ballot of a majority of the members of the Conference. He shall not

be eligible more than three years in succession; and shall be amenable to that body for his official conduct.

2. It shall be the duty of the President of an Annual Conference to preside in all meetings of that body; to travel through the district, and visit all the circuits and stations, and to be present, as far as practicable, at all the Quarterly Meetings and Camp Meetings of his district; and, in the recess of Conference, with the assistance of two or more elders, to ordain those persons who may be elected to orders; to employ such ministers, preachers, and missionaries, as are duly recommended; and to make such changes of preachers as may be necessary, provided, the consent of the preachers to be changed, be first obtained; and to perform such other duties as may be required by his Annual Conference.

78. Drinkhouse, *History of Methodist Reform*, 2: 287, 298, 329.

79. Lucius C. Matlack, *The Life of Rev. Orange Scott: Compiled from his Personal Narrative, Correspondence, and Other Authentic Sources of Information,* in two parts (New York: C. Prindle and L. C. Matlack at the Wesleyan Methodist Book Room, 1847), 231.

80. Matlack, *The Life of Rev. Orange Scott*, 33.

81. Ira Ford McLeister and Roy Stephen Nicholson, *Conscience and Commitment: The History of the Wesleyan Methodist Church of America,* 4th rev. ed. Lee M. Haines, Jr. and Melvin E. Dieter, eds. (Marion, Indiana: The Wesley Press, 1976), 540. For other references to camp meetings see 14, 45, 45, 136, 143, 169, 216, 302–03, 361, 377, 540–45, 548, 553, 600, and 639.

82. Luther Lee, *Autobiography of the Rev. Luther Lee, D. D.* (New York: Phillips & Hunt, 1882). Lee returned to membership in the MEC in 1867.

83. Howard A. Snyder, *Populist Saints: B. T. and Ellen Roberts and the First Free Methodists* (Grand Rapids: William B. Eerdmans Publishing, 2006), 22, 75–77, 91, 94, 127, 169, 179–80, 188, 211–12.

84. Ibid., 289–305 for the chapter. Among the many other references to camp meetings in the Roberts's religious efforts, see especially 211–12, 259, 282–85, 321–22, 347–51, 376–81, 419–21, 489–50, 474–75, 489–93, 518, 181, 592–93. There is some evidence as well for one or more camp meetings at roughly the same time having served not the cause of freedom but that of slavery, providing contexts in which preachers and laity then in the northern church (the MEC) could organize for commitment to the Confederate cause and the MECS.

85. Brunson, *A Western Pioneer* 2: 413–14.

86. Finley, *Autobiography*, 346–47.

87. Richard J. Carwardine, *Evangelicals and Politics in Antebellum America* (New Haven & London: Yale University Press, 1993), 50–55.

88. *My Business Was to Fight the Devil*, 155–57, 167, 209–15.

89. See Gordon Pratt Baker, ed., *Those Incredible Methodists: A History of the Baltimore Conference of the United Methodist Church* (Baltimore: Commission on Archives and History, 1972), 218–28.

90. Richard Wheatley, *The Life and Letters of Mrs. Phoebe Palmer* (New York: W. C. Palmer, Jr., 1876), 244 (the statement is dated for April 1835 but is probably a misprint and is actually from 1845).

91. E. Dale Dunlap, "Tuesday Meetings, Camp Meetings, and Cabinet Meetings: A Perspective on the Holiness Movement in the Methodist Church in the United States in the Nineteenth Century," *A.M.E. Zion Quarterly Review, Methodist History, News Bulletin* (April 1975), 85–106.

92. Interestingly, not all overviews of the holiness movement view camp meetings as essential topics. For instance, in Melvin Dieter, ed., *The 19th-Century Holiness Movement* (Kansas City, MO: Beacon Hill Press of Kansas City, 1998) there is a subject index, roughly a page of entries, two columns, not included "camp meetings," a treatment very unlike his camp-meeting dominated *The Holiness Revival of the Nineteenth Century*, 2nd ed., Studies in Evangelicalism No. 1 (Lanham, Md. and London: The Scarecrow Press, 1996).

    The first-mentioned Dieter volume is the fourth of the six-volume Great Holiness Classics, published 1994–1998 is as follows:

    1 Holiness Teaching—New Testament Times to Wesley
    2 The Wesley Century
    3 Leading Wesleyan Thinkers
    4 The 19th-Century Holiness Movement
    5 Holiness Preachers and Preaching
    6 Holiness Teaching Today.

    A similar forest/camp meeting disinterest is found in Paul M. Bassett and William M. Greathouse, *Exploring Christian Holiness: The Historical Development* (Kansas City, MO: Beacon Hill Press, 1985). This volume is the second of the three-volume *Exploring Christian Holiness*, 1983–1985: vol. 1 W. T. Purkiser, *The Biblical Foundations,* vol. 3 Richard S. Taylor, *The Theological Formulation.* The Bassett-Greathouse volume has a subject index, over two pages of entries, two columns each, not included "camp meetings." Topics indexed include Backsliders, Cleansing, Consecration, Crisis, Filled with the Spirit, Holiness, Instantaneousness, New Birth, Purification, Regeneration, "Revival, holiness," Sanctification (5 subtopics), Second Blessing, Spirit of holiness.

93. See J. Draper, *A Tract in Favor of Camp Meetings, Revivals and Methodism…in Two Letters to a Friend* (Fonthill, 1864). The author was a member of the 2nd Niagara Conference, M. E. Church in Canada. Draper defended Methodism against charges that they are unnecessary in a country "where every neighborhood has or may have a convenient place of worship." He listed eight purposes camp meetings served:

    1st "For social and religious animation. 2nd "For enlarged spiritual intercourse. 3rd For temporary relief from worldly care and toil. 4th For protracted spiritual devotion. 5th For the promotion of social union. 6th For serving the attention of the indifferent. 7th For the conversion of sinners. 8th For the promotion of scriptural holiness.

> He elaborated on the first seven on 17–18 and gave the last the longest exposition, 18–19.

94. Charles Edward White, *The Beauty of Holiness: Phoebe Palmer as Theologian, Revivalist, Feminist and Humanitarian* (Grand Rapids: Francis Asbury Press of Zondervan Publishing House, 1986), chart 237–39. White attends to Palmer's camp-meeting activities throughout the book but gives intensive focus on 38–45.

95. Wheatley, *The Life and Letters of Mrs. Phoebe Palmer*, 276.

96. Ibid., 79–80.

97. These summarize the more extended analysis by Harold E. Raser, *Phoebe Palmer: Her Life and Thought*, Studies in Women and Religion, vol. 22 (Lewiston/Queenston: Edwin Mellen Press, 1987), 109–26 and especially 109–13. Raser judges "Mrs. Palmer (1807–1874) was indeed a significant—perhaps the most significant—catalyst in the movement to promote Christian holiness, or entire sanctification, or the 'higher Christian life' which swept through North American Christianity in the nineteenth century, spilling over into Britain and Europe as well" (2).

98. [James Porter], *An Essay on Camp-Meetings*, 30–32.

99. G. W. Henry, *Trials and Triumphs (For Half a Century) in the Life of G. W. Henry*, 2nd ed. (New York: Published for the Author, 1853) 177, 21–13, 215, 221–28, 233–43, 249–54.

100. Ibid., 177, 215.

101. Ibid., 221–28, 232, 233–43, 249–54.

102. *The Golden Harp; or Camp-Meeting Hymns, Old and New. Set to Music.* Selected by G. W. Henry (New York: Published by the Author, 1853).

103. The literature on this, as on the holiness movement generally, is vast but for Palmer's role and the overall character of the impulse, see especially Kathryn Teresa Long, *The Revival of 1857–58: Interpreting an American Religious Awakening* (New York and Oxford: Oxford University Press, 1998). See also Dieter, *Holiness Revival*, 37–42, 50–52 on Palmer, her growing leadership in camp meetings, and the enhanced public role for women in the holiness cause.

104. See camp meeting page references above for Snyder, *Populist Saints*.

105. For an exploration of popular anxieties over growing urban America, see Helen Lefkowitz Horowitz, *Rereading Sex: Battles over Sexual Knowledge and Suppression in Nineteenth-century America* (New York: Alfred A. Knopf, 2002).

106. Henry B. Ridgaway, D. D., *The Life of the Rev. Alfred Cookman; With Some Account of His Father, the Rev. George Grimston Cookman. With a Preface by the Rev. R.S. Foster, LL.D.* (London: Hodder and Stoughton, 1873), 301–02.

107. Ibid., 304, 305. Just before his second point, Cookman proclaimed:

> This revival of the doctrine and experience of holiness is in our view the most encouraging fact which our centenary year has as yet developed.

> Let the friends of this great grace rejoice, for the spotless banner of Christian purity begins again to float in triumph upon the battlements of American Methodism.

There are numerous references to camp meetings throughout this biography and a number of chapters out of the twenty-six devoted explicitly to the topic. Chapter 24 (425–41), was entitled "The Last Camp-Meetings—Failing Health—the Last Sermon."

108. Dunlap, "Tuesday Meetings, Camp meetings, and Cabinet Meetings, 85–106, 94 on the number held.

109. Newell Culver, *Methodism Forty Years Ago and Now, Embracing Many Interesting Reminiscences and Incidents. Also the Responsibilities, Present and Prospective, of the Methodist Episcopal Church.* Member of the New Hampshire Conference. With an Introduction by Rev. Lorenzo D. Barrows, D. D. (New York: Nelson & Phillips; Cincinnati: Hitchcock & Walden, 1873).

110. The literature on the holiness movement and its contributions to later Pentecostalism is immense. See the several volumes by Charles Edwin Jones, *The Holiness-Pentecostal Movement: A Comprehensive Guide,* ATLA Bibliography Series 54 (Lanham, MD: American Theological Library Association, 2008); *The Wesleyan Holiness Movement: A Comprehensive Guide* 2 vols. (Lanham, MD: American Theological Library Association, 2005). The first provides 466 pages of scholarly items, the second 1,723 and builds on several other of his ATLA bibliographies. See also his monograph, *Perfectionist Persuasion: The Holiness Movement and American Methodism, 1867–1936* ATLA Monograph Series (Metuchen, NJ: Scarecrow Press, 1974).

111. Hebron Vincent, *A History of the Wesleyan Grove, Martha's Vineyard, Camp Meeting, From the First Meeting Held There in 1835, to That of 1858, Inclusive* (Boston: Geo. C. Rand & Avery, 1858), 145–46.

112. Ibid., 11. Vincent's further meditation on the impact of camp meetings' changing clientele:

> To such as come merely or mainly for other purposes than those strictly spiritual, it may be said, that although the physical and social benefits of such a gathering of Christian friends—where they can untie themselves from the cares and trials of business, live under nature's arbor, breathe a pure air, acquire and satiate a good appetite, and exchange friendly greetings—that although all these are indeed great benefits, and amply sufficient to compensate for all the expense of the sojourn, yet the chief object should still be the cultivation and strengthening of the moral and religious principle in ourselves and in all believers associated with us, and striving to bring our unconverted fellow-men to the cross of Christ. Would that in this respect, as well as in many other things, the simple-hearted earnestness of the fathers were more fully adopted by all their sons (11–12).

113. Ibid., 147–48.
114. Ibid., 155; 159–61. For 1857, Vincent meditated (168):

> Many of our friends were on the ground this year quite in advance of the time of beginning. About one hundred and fifty tents were covered before the evening of the day preceding, and it was estimated that about three hundred persons lodged in the grove that night. There were about two hundred and fifty tents of all kinds during the meeting. It was delightful merely to behold this city of tents, the white coverings beautifully contrasting with the green foliage so gorgeously overshadowing them. But it was better still to mingle with the population of this sequestered city, to listen to the word of the Lord preached by his faithful heralds for six successive days, and to join in the prayers offered and the praises sung by the assembled multitude of devoted Christians, and here to battle for the right and for the salvation of our fellow-men.

115. Ibid., 182, 184–87.
116. Ibid., 189–90.
117. Ibid., 190–91.
118. Ibid., 191.
119. Weiss, *City in the Woods*, 120 for images, 121–22 for quotation.
120. For ample and wonderful graphics as well as a superb study of this very camp meeting, do see Weiss, *City in the Woods*.
121. Matthew Simpson ed., *Cyclopaedia of Methodism. Embracing Sketches of its Rise, Progress, and Present Condition, with Biographical Notices and Numerous Illustration* (Philadelphia: Everts & Stewart, 1878; Addendum begins on 972), 992–93.
122. Ibid., 862.
123. Ibid., 748.
124. More vague were Simpson's treatment of the camp meetings at Bay View, Michigan; Summit Grove (near New Freedom, Pennsylvania); and Crystal Springs (Michigan).
125. J. W. Hedges, comp., *Crowned Victors. The Memoirs of Over Four Hundred Methodist Preachers, Including the First Two Hundred and Fifty Who Died on This Continent*, "Introduction" by A. E. Gibson (Baltimore: Methodist Episcopal Book Depository, 1878), xviii–xix.

CHAPTER 5

1. "Southern New Jersey boasted six camp meetings that continued through much of the 20th century, dated from after the Civil War and functioned within a holiness framework. Most notable among them, of course, was Ocean Grove. Several others, though persisting into the twentieth century, had closed or been conferred to another denomination." See various camp-meeting references in Robert B. Steelman, *What God Has Wrought: A History of the Southern*

New Jersey Conference of The United Methodist Church (Pennington, NJ: Southern New Jersey Commission on Archives and History, 1986), especially 61, 89 and 11–28, the latter a chapter entitled "Camp Meetings in Southern New Jersey."

2. Brown suggests that Ocean Grove was the first permanent interdenominational holiness camp for the 1867-founded National Camp Meeting Association for the Promotion of Holiness (Brown, *Holy Ground, Too*, 54). The founding at Chautauqua, as we note below, was its new education programming.

3. See Messenger, *Holy Leisure*, especially 12–23. See also George Hughes, *Days of Power in the Forest Temple: A Review of the Wonderful Work of God at Fourteen National Camp-Meetings, From 1867–1872* (Boston: John Bent & Co. 1873). For the earlier patterns, see prior chapters here and also Weiss, *City in the Woods*; Bruce, *And They All Sang Hallelujah*; and Johnson, *The Frontier Camp Meeting*.

4. John H. Vincent, *The Chautauqua Movement*, with an Introduction by President Lewis Miller (Boston: Chautauqua Press, 1886), 16.

5. For statistics and organization, see Melvin Dieter, *The Holiness Revival of the Nineteenth Century*, 2nd ed., Studies in Evangelicalism No. 1 (Lanham, MD and London: The Scarecrow Press, 1996), 88–91.

6. Andrew C. Rieser, *The Chautauqua Moment: Protestants, Progressives, and the Culture of Modern Liberalism* (New York: Columbia University Press, 2003). See also James H. McBath, "The Emergence of Chautauqua as a Religious and Educational Institution, 1874–1900," *Methodist History*, 20 (October, 1981), 3–12; and "Darwinism at Chautauqua," *Methodist History*, 24 (July 1986), 227–37. We have noted in chapter 4 the immense literature on the holiness movements. For a compelling appraisal and engagement with recent literature, see Samuel Avery-Quinn, "In the Wild Dark Pines: Crisis, Legitimacy, and the Origins of the National Camp-Meeting Association for the Promotion of Holiness," *Methodist History* 52 (October 2013), 4–18. For an enduring classic reading, see Dieter, *The Holiness Revival of the Nineteenth Century*, especially 81–7. See also his edited volume, *The 19th-Century Holiness Movement*. For a look at the two religious impulses, see my friend Charles H. Lippy's "The Camp Meeting in Transition: The Character and Legacy of the Late Nineteenth Century," *Methodist History* 34 (October 1995), 3–17.

7. Rieser, *The Chautauqua Moment*, 295–97. The assemblies are listed individually by dates.

8. On the movement's ambivalence about organizational revolution: "On the one hand, Chautauqua helped spread the gospel of organizational efficiency and render it in a language acceptable to rural Americans. On the other hand, liberal thought did not pass through Chautauqua circles and assemblies unmodified. In manifold ways—insisting that public life conform to Protestant moral standards, carving bourgeois aesthetics into the landscape, and forcing municipalities to acknowledge middle-class leisure—Chautauqua's boosters demanded that government be made

responsive to the needs of the middle-class citizens." Rieser, *The Chautauqua Moment*, 10.

9. Vincent, *The Chautauqua Movement*, 16.

10. Ibid., 6.

11. For Chautauqua's catholic instinct, see ibid., 24–7. He says (24–5).

> It will thus be seen that the Chautauqua movement began, as of necessity it must have done, with the Methodist-Episcopal Church; and that at the very outset the denominational lines were almost entirely obliterated, people of all the churches invited to participate, and a course of study selected which had already been virtually agreed upon by the several churches. Later on, with the local incorporation of the Chautauqua Sunday-school Assembly, the unfolding of the various departments of the Chautauqua work, the identification with the movement of representative men from all branches of the Church, it became necessary to lift the entire institution to a pan-denominational and catholic platform.
>
> People coming to Chautauqua are not expected to abandon their church relations. They come, without compromising conviction, to join in a broad movement for the increase of power in every branch of the Church, and throughout our American society. True denominationalism is catholic, and he who loves his own wisely is likely to love others generously. At Chautauqua all churches have opportunity to meet in their several centres for prayer and conference. Every Wednesday evening at seven o'clock, prayer-meetings are held by the several denominations in their respective headquarters: Baptist, Congregational, Disciples, Lutheran, Methodist-Episcopal, Presbyterian, United Brethren, United Presbyterian, Protestant Episcopal, Reformed Episcopal, Cumberland Presbyterian, and many others. On one day every season, a denominational congress is held, to discuss some phase of the question, "How can we make Chautauqua helpful to our branch of the Church?" The utmost good feeling has always prevailed. There have never been manifested uncomfortable rivalries.

12. Ibid., 4–5.

13. Ibid., 12–13.

14. Dieter, *The Holiness Revival of the Nineteenth Century*, 107.

15. National Camp Meeting Association for the Promotion of Holiness.

16. Timothy L. Smith, *Called Unto Holiness: The Story of the Nazarenes: The Formative Years* (Kansas City, MO: Nazarene Publishing House, 1962), 15–16. See also Dieter, *The Holiness Revival*, 86–91 and Vinson Synan, *The Holiness-Pentecostal Movement in the United States* (Grand Rapids: William B. Eerdmans, 1971), 35–42.

17. J. M. Buckley, *A History of Methodists in the United States*, 4th edition, American Church History (New York: Charles Scribner's Sons, 1900), 298, 613, 671–2, 502–5, 614–15.

18. Vincent, *Chautauqua Movement*, 4.

19. Schneider, *The Way of the Cross Leads Home*, 57.

20. Robins, "Vernacular American Landscape," 166.

21. Ibid., 175.

22. Cooley, "Manna and the Manual," 152–53.

23. Richey, *Early American Methodism*, 21.

24. Steelman on such continuing relation to the denomination: "Camp meetings are an enduring legacy of southern New Jersey Methodism. They are an integral part of the life of our Church. Some even carry the name of the Conference in official title or incorporation. Their charters require certain numbers of Methodist clergy and laity on their Boards. Yet, no one of these camp meetings has ever, at any time, had an official relationship to this Conference. They are not Conference Camps, but our Conference, our churches, and our people are enhanced through their ministry. The life of Southern New Jersey Methodism is permanently in their debt." Steelman, *What God Has Wrought*, 128.

25. *Discipline*/MEC 1787, 3–7.

Index